The Psychodynamics of Gender and Gender Role

The Psychodynamics of
Gender and Gender Role

Edited by Robert F. Bornstein and Joseph M. Masling

American Psychological Association • Washington, DC

Published by
American Psychological Association
750 First Street, NE
Washington, DC 20002
www.apa.org

To order	Tel: (800) 374-2721, Direct: (202) 336-5510
APA Order Department	Fax: (202) 336-5502, TDD/TTY: (202) 336-6123
P.O. Box 92984	On-line: www.apa.org/books/
Washington, DC 20090-2984	E-mail: order@apa.org

In the U.K., Europe, Africa, and the Middle East, copies may be ordered from
American Psychological Association
3 Henrietta Street
Covent Garden, London
WC2E 8LU England

Typeset in Palatino by EPS Group Inc., Easton, MD

Printer: Sheridan Books, Ann Arbor, MI
Cover Designer: Berg Design, Albany, NY
Technical/Production Editor: Jennifer L. Macomber

The opinions and statements published are the responsibility of the authors, and such opinions and statements do not necessarily represent the policies of the American Psychological Association.

Library of Congress Cataloging-in-Publication Data

The psychodynamics of gender and gender role / edited by
Robert F. Bornstein, Joseph M. Masling.
     p. cm.—(Empirical studies in psychoanalytic theories ; vol. 10)
   Includes bibliographical references and index.
   ISBN 1-55798-894-3 (alk. paper)
    1. Sex differences (Psychology)   2. Sex role.   3. Psychoanalysis.
  I. Bornstein, Robert F. II. Masling, Joseph M. III. Empirical studies of psychoanalytic theories ; vol. 10.

BF175.5.S49 P79 2002
155.3—dc21   2001055301

British Library Cataloguing-in-Publication Data
A CIP record is available from the British Library.

Printed in the United States of America
First Edition

Contents

Contributors

Robert F. Bornstein received his PhD in clinical psychology from the State University of New York at Buffalo in 1986 and is now a professor of psychology at Gettysburg College. Dr. Bornstein wrote *The Dependent Personality* (1993), coauthored (with Mary Languirand) *When Someone You Love Needs Nursing Home Care* (2001), coedited (with Thane Pittman) *Perception Without Awareness: Cognitive, Clinical, and Social Perspectives* (1992), and coedited (with Joseph Masling) six previous volumes of the *Empirical Studies of Psychoanalytic Theories* book series. Dr. Bornstein's research has been funded by grants from the National Institutes of Mental Health and the National Science Foundation, and he received the Society for Personality Assessment's 1995 and 1999 Walter Klopfer Awards for Distinguished Contributions to the Personality Assessment Literature.

Johanna Brock volunteered as a research assistant at the Austen Riggs Center and is currently in her sophomore year at the University of Pennsylvania.

Leslie R. Brody is an associate professor of psychology at Boston University. She served as director of the Clinical Psychology PhD program from 1991 to 1996 and was the Marion Cabor Putnam Fellow at the Radcliffe Bunting Institute from 1994 to 1995. She has published numerous theoretical reviews and research articles concerning gender differences in emotional functioning and is the author of *Gender, Emotion, and the Family* (1999).

Ben Brunnschweiler is currently a mental health worker and a volunteer research assistant at the Austen Riggs Center. Mr. Brunnschweiler studied psychology and earned his bachelor's degree at Clemson University.

Kathleen M. Cain is an associate professor in the Department of Psychology at Gettysburg College. She received her PhD in psychology from the University of Illinois at Urbana–Champaign. She conducts research on shame and helplessness in young children and on young children's trait perceptions.

Phebe Cramer is a professor of psychology at Williams College and a practicing psychotherapist. She earned her PhD in clinical psychology at New York University, studying with David Rapaport, George Klein, and Robert Holt, among others. She has been an associate editor of the *Journal of Personality* and continues to serve on the editorial board of the *Journal of Personality Assessment*. Her research interests include defense mechanisms, identity, gender differences, and children's attributions. She has published numerous scientific articles, as well as three books: *Word Association* (1968); *The Development of Defense Mechanisms* (1990); and *Storytelling, Narrative, and the Thematic Apperception Test* (1996).

Ronda L. Dearing became involved in the study of shame and guilt during her graduate training, while working as a research assistant with June Price Tangney. Prior to her graduate training in psychology, she worked as a medical technologist. She is currently completing her PhD at George Mason University in Fairfax, Virginia. Her dissertation focuses on correlates of psychotherapy help-seeking behaviors of therapists in training. More recent research interests include help seeking in substance abuse and the influence of shame proneness on substance use.

J. Christopher Fowler is currently a member of the medical staff at the Austen Riggs Center. As a clinical research associate he studies treatment outcome as a member of the Follow-Along Study. Dr. Fowler earned his PhD in clinical psychology from the University of Tennessee.

Billy Jansson received his master's degree in psychology at Uppsala University, Sweden. He is currently studying for a PhD in the Department of Psychology at Stockholm University, with a special interest in unconscious defense.

Joseph M. Masling is an emeritus professor of psychology at the State University of New York at Buffalo. He has written numerous articles on interpersonal and situational variables influencing projective tests and has published widely on the empirical study of psychoanalytic concepts. Dr. Masling edited the first three volumes of the *Empirical Studies of Psychoanalytic Theories* book series (1983, 1986, 1990); coedited (with Robert F. Bornstein) the next five volumes, including *Psychoanalytic Perspectives on Developmental Psychology* (1996), *Empirical Studies of the Therapeutic Hour* (1998), and *Empirical Perspectives on the Psychoanalytic Unconscious* (1998); and coedited (with Paul R. Duberstein) the ninth volume in the series, *Psychodynamic Perspectives on Sickness and Health* (2000). Dr. Masling

received the Society for Personality Assessment's 1997 Bruno Klopfer Award for Lifetime Achievement in Personality Assessment.

Serra Muderrisoglu received her PhD in clinical psychology
from Boston University in 1999. She is currently an assistant professor of psychology at Bogazici University in Istanbul, Turkey. Her
research interests include psychodynamic concepts related to the
psychotherapy process and personality disorders and the role of
unconscious affect and unprocessed identity issues in the progression of chronic physical illnesses. Clinically, she is interested
in conceptualizations of psychodynamic cross-cultural psychotherapy.

Ora Nakash-Eisikovits is a PhD candidate in clinical psychology
at Boston University. She received her master's degree in clinical
psychology from Tel Aviv University, Israel. Her research interests
include gender differences in emotional experiences and self-
construals. Her clinical experiences include work in hospital and
community health care settings, and she was licensed as a psychologist by the Israeli Ministry of Health in 1999.

Sandra W. Russ is a professor of psychology at Case Western
Reserve University. She is president of the American Psychological
Association's Division 10 (Psychology and the Arts) and president
of the Society for Personality Assessment. She has published
widely in the area of play, creativity, and child psychotherapy. She
is the author of *Affect and Creativity: The Role of Affect and Play in
the Creative Process* (1993) and editor of *Affect, Creative Experience,
and Psychological Adjustment* (1999).

Staffan Sohlberg is an associate professor of clinical psychology
in the Department of Psychology, Uppsala University, Sweden. He
is the recipient of the Sasakawa Young Leaders' Fund Award; has
been a visiting research scholar at the University of California, Los
Angeles, Neuropsychiatric Institute; and is on the Steering Com-
mittee of the Psychotherapy Research Group sponsored by the
Swedish Research Council for the Humanities and Social Sciences.
Following a clinical research career studying eating disorders, his
interests turned to basic science-oriented studies of the unconscious.

June Price Tangney is a professor of psychology at George Mason University in Fairfax, Virginia. As an undergraduate student,
she worked with Joseph Masling at the State University of New

York at Buffalo and later completed her PhD in clinical psychology from the University of California, Los Angeles, under the direction of Dr. Seymour Feshbach. Coeditor (with Kurt Fischer) of *Self-Conscious Emotions: Shame, Guilt, Embarrassment, and Pride* (1995), she is currently associate editor for *Self and Identity* and is consulting editor for the *Journal of Personality and Social Psychology, Personality and Social Psychology Bulletin, Psychological Assessment,* and the *Journal of Personality.* Her research has been funded by the National Institute of Child Health and Human Development and the John Templeton Foundation.

Introduction:
The Psychodynamics of Gender and Gender Role

Robert F. Bornstein and Joseph M. Masling

If *compromise* describes Freud's view of the way mental mechanisms work, then *controversy* surely describes the world's response to his writings. From the start, Freud's ideas were seen by many as a sinister attack on the accepted beliefs of the day and a threat against the established order. Accused of being a corrupting influence, his theories were subjected to the most extreme forms of criticism and censorship. In fact, when one of Freud's theories was mentioned at the 1910 meeting of the German Congress of Neurologists and Psychiatrists, the meeting's chairman, Professor Wilhelm Weygandt, shouted, "This is not a topic for discussion at a scientific meeting; this is a matter for the police" (quoted in Jones, 1955, p. 109).

It is not surprising that it was (and in some circles still is) common for those sympathetic to psychoanalysis to suffer professionally. In 1908, Ernest Jones was forced to resign his position as neurologist in London when he attempted to obtain sexual histories from his patients (Jones, 1955). Two years later, in 1910, the *Asylum Bulletin*—a journal that had reprinted some of Jones's publications —was shut down by the Ontario government because these articles were deemed "unfit for publication even in a medical periodical" (Jones, 1955, pp. 109–110). Ninety years later, the situation has become less stark, but the fundamental dynamic has not changed: Academic positions for psychodynamic psychologists are few, and federal funding for psychodynamically inspired research is almost nonexistent (Bornstein, 2001).

The early arguments against psychoanalysis were marked by a paucity of logic, an absence of data, and a vehemence not often seen in intellectual debates. Thus, Jones described an event that occurred at the Berlin Psychiatric Clinic, whose director, Professor Theodor Ziehen, was adamantly opposed to psychoanalytic thought. On examining a patient who suffered from an obsessional impulse to lift women's skirts in public, Ziehen

> said to his pupils: "This is an opportunity to test the supposed sexual nature of such obsessions. I will ask him if it applies to older women as well, in which case it evidently cannot be erotic." The patient's reply was: "Oh yes, to all women, even my mother and sister." On which Ziehen triumphantly ordered the entry in the protocol to describe the case as "definitely nonsexual." (quoted in Jones, 1955, pp. 114–115)

Freud on Women: Misunderstanding and Response

As Freud grappled with his inability to comprehend the psychology of women, he made an uncharacteristic admission to Marie Bonaparte: "The great question that has never been answered and which I have not yet been able to answer, despite my thirty years of research into the feminine soul, is 'What does a woman want'" (quoted in Jones, 1955, p. 241). Freud later remarked that "everything we know about feminine development appears to me to be unsatisfactory and uncertain" (quoted in Gay, 1988, p. 501), and he compared his knowledge of the sexual life of women with that of "a dark continent."

It is not surprising that Freud knew so little about women. His interests in archeology and the classics would have familiarized him with Homer's version of male and female behavior. In Homer's view, men—whether good or evil—are consistent and fixed, their behavior predictable. Women were thought to be known quantities as well—but only as long as they were under the control of fathers or husbands. Once the strong male was absent, the behavior of Homer's women was no longer consistent (and hence, no longer predictable). It is no accident that when Ulysses met his wife Penelope for the first time after 20 years of absence he came disguised as a beggar; he thought he did not know her well enough to predict her response. Also, it should be remembered why Ulysses was so concerned that his crew might hear the Sirens' song he sealed their ears with wax: The Sirens were feared because they emphasized knowledge over other obligations (Peradotto, in press). The belief that women are mysterious and essentially unknowable did not begin with Freud but had a long history.[1]

Freud was not guilty of false modesty when he acknowledged knowing little about women's development. His views regarding women were egregiously flawed, despite his extraordinary insights into other aspects of human behavior. Freud (1923/1961a) argued that the superego in women is inherently inferior because it "is never so inexorable, so impersonal, so independent of its emotional origins as we require it to be in men" (p. 257), and he maintained until the very end that a central trauma for every woman is her perceived loss of a penis and resulting penis envy. He made no attempt to hide his disapproval of a John Stuart Mill essay advocating equal rights for women, and when he translated this essay while on Army duty (under arrest for being AWOL), he took particular aim at Mill's advocacy of the right of women to work outside the home:

> It is really a stillborn thought to send women into the struggle for existence exactly as men. . . . Nature has determined

---

[1] We are indebted to John Peradotto for his insights regarding this issue.

women's destiny through beauty, charm, and sweetness. . . .
Law and custom have much to give women that has been with-
held from them, but the position of women will surely be what
it is: in youth an adored darling, and in mature years a loved
wife. (quoted in Jones, 1961, p. 118)

It is tempting to excuse these statements as the work of a young
man of 23, but as Schafer (1974) observed, even in Freud's later
publications (e.g., 1937/1964a, 1940/1964b) he returned to "his earlier, simpler, and patriarchal viewpoint . . . from which female development appears to be both second best and second-rate" (p.
461).[2] Although contemporary psychoanalytic thought has gone
well beyond Freud's speculations regarding gender and gender
role, Schafer correctly pointed out that Freud's "basic assumptions,
indeed the very mode of his thought, are still very much with us
in modern psychoanalysis" (pp. 460–461).

It is ironic that at the same time as Freud infantilized women
and belittled their abilities he attacked in his writings the prudery
of the day and insisted that women were as sensual as men (a
novel concept at the time). In an era when few women were given
the chance to pursue professional careers, Freud helped train numerous female analysts, including Alice Balint, Therese Benedict,
Dorothy Burlingame, Ruth Mack Brunswick, Marie Bonaparte,
Helene Deutsch, Anna Freud, Phyllis Greenacre, Karen Horney,
Melanie Klein, Margaret Mahler, Joan Riviere, Lou Andreas
Salome, and Clara Thompson. Freud not only trained women, but
he also cited their ideas in his writings, and he respected their
analytic work, declaring that "in momentous aspects of analytic
practice, women might be more competent than men" (quoted in
Gay, 1988, p. 503). In fact, when the Vienna Psychoanalytic Society
debated whether to allow women to become members, Freud
spoke vigorously in favor, and on April 27, 1910, Dr. Margaret
Hilferding was the first woman accepted into the society. Freud
was among the 12 members voting in favor, with 2 opposed (Gay,
1988).

---

[2]The earlier articles to which Schafer (1974) referred are those on infantile genital organization (Freud, 1923/1961a) and on the psychical consequences of the anatomical distinction between the sexes (Freud, 1923/
1961b).

To large segments of the public Freud was a hero, willing to confront prejudices and societal restraints and take on the medical and cultural establishments. He was such an inspiration to leading radicals that

> at the Clark meeting in 1909, seated conspicuously in the front row "chastely garbed in white," and with a rose pinned to her waist ... was Emma Goldman [the noted anarchist] who counted herself among his most ardent admirers. Goldman had been a long time follower of psychoanalysis, having attended one of Freud's lectures in Vienna some years earlier. She advocated psychoanalytic ideas and described Freud as a "giant among pygmies." (Buhle, 1988, pp. 1–2)

In many feminist circles Goldman's metaphor has been reversed, and Freud has become more pygmy than giant. Some years ago Mitchell (1974, p. 297) described meetings of feminist groups in the United States in which darts were thrown at a photograph of Freud, with a "bulls-eye just beneath his left eye" and his photograph labeled "Misogynist III." Naomi Weisstein attacked not only Freud's views on women but also his entire corpus of work, asserting that the theory was "wrong, not just about women, but about humans in general" (quoted in Buhle, 1988, p. 20). Not all female writers have been so negative regarding Freud's ideas (see, e.g., Bucci, 1997; Chodorow, 1978), but contentious statements like that of Weisstein are more the norm than the exception.

The political controversy surrounding Freud's work continues. The Library of Congress's 1998–1999 exhibit exploring Freud's influence was delayed several months by the protests of a number of groups, prominent among them some feminist organizations. The exhibition eventually went forward (in modified form), but in this case the last word goes to Freud: *Homo homini lupus*—Humans are wolflike to other humans.

Empirical Evidence and Clinical Data

The predicament Freud created for his beloved theory could have been avoided had he not preferred speculation to data. He had only to read the daily newspaper to grasp what nearly everyone else knew then and knows now—that many more men than women commit crimes, abuse spouses, start wars, rape, loot, and pillage. With so much information at his fingertips Freud chose to rely instead on his intuition about women's development. If anyone in his circle tried to set Freud straight, the record does not show it. On the contrary, his erroneous conclusions resulted from a stunning collusion among his followers (presumably including the women) to not allow public information to correct theoretical adventurism. An aphorism of Oswald Spengler nicely sums up the situation: The stupidity of an idea has never impeded its influence.

The effects of Freud's neglect of data pervade psychoanalytic theory, but perhaps these effects have been most apparent—and most destructive—in the theory's efforts to describe women's development. From the beginning, psychoanalytic theory's focus has been on men, with discussions of women added almost as an afterthought. This emphasis on the psychology of men is also present in empirical studies of psychoanalytic thought, as shown by a recent meta-analysis of 183 empirical studies based on psychodynamic ideas (Masling, Bornstein, Fishman, & Davila, in press). Of these 183 reports, 54 (29%) used only male participants, 17 (9%) used only female participants, and 85 (46%) used both but did not test for gender differences. The remaining studies in Masling et al.'s sample included both men and women, and the results were analyzed by gender. In these 27 investigations men behaved in accordance with theoretical predictions significantly more often than did women.

As might be expected, the vast majority of the studies in Masling et al.'s sample—72%—had male first authors. Thus, one finds that contemporary research based on psychoanalytic theories is primarily a male activity conducted on male participants, with male participants producing more positive results than female participants. Freud's biased legacy lives on, even in scientific inquiry.[3]

Despite Freud's early career as a medical researcher, his reliance on clinical experience and intuition over systematically collected

---

[3]In fairness, similar difficulties characterize other domains of psychology, which are also dominated by researchers of one gender (usually male), focus primarily on participants of one gender, and often neglect to test for gender effects in their analyses (Bornstein & Bartlett, 2001).

data was evident from the beginning of psychoanalysis. Thus, when Saul Rosenzweig wrote to Freud describing his experiments on repression, Freud's response was not encouraging: "I have examined your experimental studies for the verification of psychoanalytic assertions with interest. I cannot put much value on these confirmations because the wealth of reliable observations on which these assertions rest make them independent of experimental verification" (quoted in MacKinnon & Dukes, 1964, p. 703). When an American analysand told Freud that dream interpretation could be confirmed by experimental evidence, Freud replied, "That is a typical American idea, you can't study psychology with statistics" (quoted in Wortis, 1954, p. 86).

This antiscientific stance led Spence (1994) to observe that psychoanalysis has relied

> on an outmoded method of scientific data collection and a preference for fanciful argument over hard fact.... Argument by authority stands directly in the way of the benefits, zealously guarded since the Renaissance, of an adversarial, critical, and dialectical tradition of investigation. (pp. 1–3)

Cooper (1984) said much the same in his presidential address to the American Psychoanalytic Association, when he warned that

> our exciting debates will become arid if they are not sprinkled with new data. Even if we do not feel impelled by our scientific and theoretical curiosity, we might respond to the demands of a society that will not forever allow us to practice clinical psychoanalysis without evidence of its efficacy. (p. 259)

The inevitable result of psychoanalysts' reluctance to look for validation beyond the consulting room is diminished influence within and outside the discipline. Not too many years ago, psychoanalysis was one of the leading forces in American intellectual life (Torrey, 1992). For a variety of reasons, including the advent of behavioral treatments and increased use of psychotropic drugs, psychoanalysis no longer has such a commanding influence (Bornstein, 2001). In an era when significant advances are being made almost daily in the behavioral, biological, and physical sciences, psychoanalysis has remained alone in trying to establish its validity on nothing more substantial than the endorsements of its practitioners.

As a result, psychoanalysis has changed little during the past 100 years. When one compares the present state of such sciences as astronomy, genetics, chemistry, physics, and biology with what they were like in 1900 (the publication date of *The Interpretation of Dreams*), the gravity of the situation becomes even more clear. A geneticist of 1900 could not begin to comprehend a lecture by a contemporary geneticist, but Freud would have no trouble reading a contemporary psychoanalytic journal. Like Miss Havisham presiding regally over her dusty, decaying mansion, psychoanalysis has been content to dwell in the past and deny the present. Although Freud once compared himself to Columbus, peering fearlessly into the future, it is worth noting that statues of great explorers are often visited by pigeons, producing not only an image with great historical value but also the need for an occasional cleaning.

The Limitations of Clinical Evidence: Unconscious Bias and Conscious Distortion

The source of the intellectual paralysis that has diminished psychoanalysis is undeniable: It is analysts' near-exclusive reliance on case history data to test and refine the theory. The problem, of course, is that case history data are subject to all the distorting effects of selective memory, biased perception, and implicit motivation. No wonder so few case histories report sexual contact between therapist and patient (despite the documented frequency of such acts), while Bettleheim's description of his work with children evidently was sharply at odds with his actual practices. Case history material is limited to what the therapist is capable of noticing and willing to disclose.

The ease with which either therapist or patient can affect the behavior of the other without conscious awareness has been amply demonstrated (Masling, 1965, 1966). Psychoanalysis—like other forms of therapy—is not immune to subtle communication and unintended influence. Consider an analytic event reported by Greenson (1967):

> He had been a lifelong Republican (which I had known) and he had tried in recent months to adopt a more liberal point of view because he knew I was a liberal and anti-Republican. He then told me that whenever he said anything favorable about a Republican politician, I always asked for associations. On the other hand, whenever he had a kind word for Roosevelt, I said nothing. Whenever he attacked Roosevelt, I would ask who did Roosevelt remind him of, as though I was out to prove that Roosevelt hating was infantile. I was taken aback because I had been completely unaware of this pattern. Yet, the moment the patient pointed it out, I had to agree that I had done precisely that, albeit unknowingly. (p. 272)

The only unremarkable feature of this incident is that Greenson had the integrity to publish it. Given the intense attention each party in the therapeutic hour pays to what the other says (or does not say), the interaction Greenson described must occur regularly. Freud was aware of the criticism that analysts have powerful influence over suggestible patients, and it is not surprising that he vigorously denied the problem:

> The danger of our leading a patient astray by suggestions, by persuading him to accept things which we ourselves believe but which he ought not to, has certainly been enormously exaggerated. An analyst would have had to behave very incorrectly before such a misfortune could overtake him; above all, he would have to blame himself with not allowing his patients to have their say. I can assert without boasting that such an abuse of "suggestion" has never occurred in my practice. (1937/1964a, p. 262)

Freud's cavalier dismissal of the dangers of subtle influence is, to say the least, unconvincing. Therapists do not respond at random to their patients' statements but decide on the basis of theory and patient history what content is central and what is peripheral, which themes represent core issues and which are transitory. Patients soon learn which topics bring a response and which topics bring silence. Nearly 50 years ago, Murray (1956) examined the verbatim typescripts of a psychotherapy case Carl Rogers had conducted and found that Rogers had systematically commented on some content categories while ignoring others (i.e., he was rewarding some categories of his client's statements while extinguishing others through silence). By the end of therapy the client had stopped talking about the categories that elicited no response and spoke only about those issues to which Rogers had responded. This selective (albeit unintentional) therapist behavior was documented again in a later case (Truax, 1966).

There is nothing inherently improper about this kind of subtle coaching by the therapist. Indeed, it is inevitable—even desirable —that patients learn something about the personality theory that guides their therapy. This implicit learning process may also explain why each school of therapy can point to clinical material that supports its particular view of the world (see Masling & Cohen, 1987). As Marmor once observed, each "theory tends to be self-validating, Freudians elicit material about the Oedipus Complex and castration anxiety, Rankians about separation anxiety, Adlerians about masculine strivings, etc." (quoted in Grunbaum, 1984, p. 289). Thus, although several psychoanalytic "schools" have developed over the years, not one of these theoretical shifts was primarily data based; rather, each new movement was started by a charismatic leader—Rank, Adler, Reich, Reik, Kohut, Jung, Klein, Lacan, Winnicott, Fairbairn, Sullivan—whose clinical experiences differed from those of predecessors. As with competing religions, the "facts" and experiences so compelling to one school are dismissed as unpersuasive by others, a phenomenon yet to be explained by the hermeneutic approach.

The *Empirical Studies of Psychoanalytic Theories* Series

There have been numerous objections to the controlled empirical study of psychoanalytic concepts: some from within the theory, others from outside it. These objections have little merit. To dismiss the entire enterprise of experimental theory testing is as simple-minded as it is to dismiss in toto the case history method. Most of the studies described in this volume and the nine that preceded it do not twist psychoanalytic ideas into unrecognizable shape. On the contrary, the analytic hour has been usefully studied in situ, with no artificial conditions imposed, as the chapters in Volume 8 (Bornstein & Masling, 2000) of this series attest. Quantitative analysis of the analyst–patient exchange allowed Weiss and Sampson (1986) and Gassner and Bush (1998) to compare the heuristic value of Freud's early version of the unconscious with that of his later version. Experimental studies of perception without awareness (Bornstein & Pittman, 1992) have yielded information about unconscious processing that no amount of case history data would ever have revealed. Frame-by-frame analysis of mother–infant interactions has uncovered aspects of the early caregiving relationship hidden in case history material (Beebe, 1986).[4]

Persuasive though these findings may be, some analysts have argued that empirical research—although valuable in certain limited contexts—is a misapplication of psychoanalytic concepts. They contend that psychoanalysis should be used only for the intensive study of individuals and that any attempt to generalize from a single case to categories of people (e.g., compulsives, obsessives, hysterics) is inappropriate. Here critics disregard Freud's own writings and those of other analysts. Freud frequently used a single case to promulgate general laws of behavior (e.g., in his comment about "Rat Man" that behind every fear is a wish repressed, his observations about paranoia from Schreber's autobiography, or his speculations about female development). The great power of psychoanalytic thought is its potential to clarify universal problems of human existence, not its ability to explain the single case. To confine psychoanalysis to hermeneutics is anachronistic and resembles a Luddite devotion to pencil and paper in the hopes of recapturing a computerless world.

Despite the objections of skeptics (and in stark contrast to the misperceptions of the scientific and lay communities), psychoana-

---

[4] Although the case history method remains a rich source of information about human behavior, the information gleaned from it must be checked against a more objective set of criteria than the selective memories of participants in the therapeutic hour. The same method that yields so many psychoanalytic treasures also produces fool's gold, and clinicians have been known to embrace each with equal fervor and conviction.

lytic ideas have inspired considerable research. There have been more well-designed empirical studies testing and extending psychoanalytic theories in the past 30 years than at any time in the history of the discipline, as this volume, the nine that preceded it (e.g., Bornstein & Masling 2000; Masling & Bornstein, 1994), and similar books (e.g., Barron, Eagle, & Wolitzky, 1992; Fisher & Greenberg, 1996; Shapiro & Emde, 1995) can document. It may well be that psychoanalytic thought has generated more research than any other theory of personality, despite the widely held belief that these theories resist experimental testing. Moreover, psychoanalytic ideas have influenced research programs in clinical, social, developmental, and cognitive psychology (see, e.g., Aronson, 1992; Bornstein, 1992; Bowers & Meichenbaum, 1984; Bucci, 1997; Erdelyi, 1985; Horowitz, 1988; Singer, 1990; Stern, 1985; Tabin, 1985; Uleman & Bargh, 1989). Until recently this fact was ignored by the psychoanalytic establishment, and it is still being denied by critics such as Crews (1994).

There is no need for psychoanalysis to be defensive or apprehensive about scientific studies of its theories and methods. Loss of what is not empirically demonstrable would strengthen the theory, not weaken it. Freud's words should be seen as a place to start, not a place to hide. Neither do well-designed research studies —whatever their results—diminish the value of psychoanalytic treatment. Our comments speak to the wisdom of constructing a theory of personality based on controlled empirical data as well as clinical material: How else to counter the wrongheaded conviction of many therapists that the words, dreams, recollections, and associations of their patients reveal much about the patient but nothing about the listener?[5]

---

[5] We wish to distinguish here between treatment and the theory of personality that supports it, because the behavioral and attitudinal changes that follow from therapy may be independent of the therapist's personality theory. The power of placebo and expectancy effects can scarcely be exaggerated, and the therapeutic success of different therapeutic schools suggests that nonspecific forces (e.g., the uncritical, accepting attitude of the therapist, the empathic therapeutic relationship) may be more directly connected to change than is the therapist's theory. Good therapists, of whatever theoretical persuasion, may in the end be more similar than different.

All contributors to the *Empirical Studies of Psychoanalytic Theories* series seek to keep psychoanalytic theory alive and consistent with modern scientific data. For nearly 20 years our tasks have remained largely unchanged: (a) to investigate the extent to which psycho-dynamic theories of personality have a sound scientific base; (b) to indicate where the theories have been found to be inadequate; and (c) to extend psychodynamic thinking into new areas of inquiry, thereby helping to reinvigorate psychoanalytic scholarship, teaching, and practice.

As the 10 volumes in this series demonstrate, more people are engaged in this effort than is commonly appreciated, and more progress is being achieved than is generally recognized. The work, however, is far from complete. Nowhere are the gaps in this literature more glaring than with respect to the psychodynamics of gender and gender role.

The Psychodynamics of Gender and Gender Role

This volume opens with Kathleen M. Cain's insightful discussion of the inter- and intrapersonal dynamics of helplessness and mastery orientations in children. She uses an innovative social–cognitive framework to examine key features of the parent–child relationship, with important implications for personality, developmental, and social psychology. Cain's chapter provides a compelling example of the way controlled laboratory studies can illuminate real-world psychodynamic issues.

Sandra W. Russ also focuses primarily on children, but from a very different perspective. In her provocative and compelling chapter, Russ describes her extensive (and ongoing) program of research examining the links between primary process thinking and creativity. Although the notion of "regression in service of the ego" has a long psychoanalytic history, it is only recently—and thanks largely to Russ and her colleagues—that we have been able to test empirically the parameters of this hypothesized relation.

Phebe Cramer has been a pioneer in the empirical study of ego defense mechanisms, and her persuasive, meticulous review of research in this area integrates an impressive array of data. Using a variety of assessment techniques and outcome measures, Cramer has explored the myriad effects of defensive style on psychological adjustment. As she synthesizes her findings regarding gender differences in defense mechanism use she provides a wealth of new information regarding the etiology of ego mechanisms of defense and the effects of gender role socialization on defensive style.

Few topics (psychodynamic or otherwise) are as strongly associated with gender and gender role as is the study of eating disorders. Integrating diagnostic, projective, archival, and behavioral data, J. Christopher Fowler, Ben Brunnschweiler, and Johanna Brock illuminate the roles of character type, object relations, and defense style in eating disorder symptoms and dynamics. Their chapter should be required reading for any clinician who believes that psychodynamic models of psychopathology—and eating disorders in particular—have limited heuristic value.

Staffan Sohlberg has been a leading figure in subliminal psychodynamic activation (SPA) research for more than a decade and, as his chapter (coauthored with Billy Jansson) illustrates, gender is an important—albeit frequently neglected—moderator of SPA effects. Few techniques provide such direct access to unconscious dynamics as does SPA and, as Sohlberg and Jansson show, results from this paradigm can illuminate a broad range of psychodynamic issues. Sohlberg and Jansson's chapter not only has noteworthy implications for psychoanalytic theory, but it also helps strengthen the developing connection between psychodynamic and cognitive models of the mind.

Leslie R. Brody, Serra Muderrisoglu, and Ora Nakash-Eisikovits review findings from Brody's innovative program of research assessing the links among emotions, defenses, and gender. Building on the well-established finding that women tend to use internalizing defenses, whereas men favor externalizing defenses, Brody and her colleagues blend clinical and laboratory data to demonstrate that the defense–emotion relation is not only real but also has significant real-world implications. As psychoanalytically inspired research continues to address issues in the study of health and illness, research programs like Brody's will become increasingly central to our work—and a model for investigators who strive to connect psychodynamic thinking with other areas of psychology.

Shame and guilt: It is hard to imagine two emotions more fundamental to psychoanalysis. June Price Tangney has studied these phenomena extensively, using a variety of methods and measurement techniques. Her review (coauthored with Ronda L. Dearing) of the implications of her work for the psychodynamics of gender and gender role clarifies the complex inter- and intrapersonal consequences of these two emotional states. Equally valuable is that they demonstrate that vexing methodological challenges can be overcome as an innovative researcher brings a complex topic from the consulting room to the laboratory.

References

Aronson, E. (1992). *The social animal*. New York: Freeman.

Barron, J. W., Eagle, M., & Wolitzky, D. L. (Eds.). (1992). *Interface of psychoanalysis and psychology*. Washington, DC: American Psychological Association.

Beebe, B. (1986). Mother–infant mutual influence and precursors of self- and-object representation. In J. Masling (Ed.), *Empirical studies of psychoanalytic theories* (Vol. 2, pp. 27–48). Hillsdale, NJ: Erlbaum.

Bornstein, R. F. (1992). The dependent personality: Developmental, social, and clinical perspectives. *Psychological Bulletin, 112*, 3–23.

Bornstein, R. F. (2001). The impending death of psychoanalysis. *Psychoanalytic Psychology, 18*, 3–20.

Bornstein, R. F., & Bartlett, M. R. (2001, Summer). Has psychology become the science of questionnaires? A survey of research outcome measures at the close of the 20th century. *The General Psychologist, 36*(2), 36–40.

Bornstein, R. F., & Masling, J. M. (Eds.). (2000). *Empirical studies of the therapeutic hour*. Washington, DC: American Psychological Association.

Bornstein, R. F., & Pittman, T. S. (1992). *Perception without awareness: Cognitive, clinical and social perspectives*. New York: Guilford Press.

Bowers, K. S., & Meichenbaum, D. M. (1984). *The unconscious reconsidered*. New York: Wiley.

Bucci, W. (1997). *Psychoanalysis and cognitive science*. New York: Guilford Press.

Buhle, M. J. (1988). *Feminism and its discontents: A century of struggle with psychoanalysis*. Cambridge, MA: Harvard University Press.

Chodorow, N. (1978). *The reproduction of mothering*. Berkeley: University of California Press.

Cooper, A. M. (1984). Psychoanalysis at one hundred: Beginnings of maturity. *Journal of the American Psychoanalytic Association, 32*, 245–268.

Crews, F. (1994). The verdict on Freud. *Psychological Science, 7*, 63–68.

Erdelyi, M. H. (1985). *Psychoanalysis: Freud's cognitive psychology*. New York: Freeman.

Fisher, S., & Greenberg, R. P. (1996). *Freud scientifically reappraised: Testing the theories and therapy*. New York: Wiley.

Freud, S. (1961a). The infantile genital organization. In J. Strachey (Ed. & Trans.), *The standard edition of the complete psychological works of Sigmund Freud* (Vol. 19, pp. 140–145). London: Hogarth. (Original work published 1923)

Freud, S. (1961b). Some psychical consequences of the anatomical distinction between the sexes. In J. Strachey (Ed. & Trans.), *The standard edition of the complete psychological works of Sigmund Freud* (Vol. 19, pp. 243–258). London: Hogarth. (Original work published 1923)

Freud, S. (1964a). Analysis terminable and interminable. In J. Strachey (Ed. & Trans.), *The standard edition of the complete psychological works of Sigmund Freud* (Vol. 23, pp. 216–254). London: Hogarth. (Original work published 1937)

Freud, S. (1964b). An outline of psycho-analysis. In J. Strachey (Ed. & Trans.), *The standard edition of the complete psychological works of Sigmund Freud* (Vol. 23, pp. 141–207). London: Hogarth. (Original work published 1940)

Gassner, S., & Bush, M. (1998). Research on unconscious mental functioning in relationship to the therapeutic process. In R. F. Bornstein & J. M. Masling (Eds.), *Empirical studies of the therapeutic hour* (pp. 259–300). Washington, DC: American Psychological Association.

Gay, P. (1988). *Freud: A life for our time*. New York: Norton.

Greenson, R. R. (1967). *The technique and practice of psychoanalysis*. Madison, CT: International Universities Press.

Grunbaum, A. (1984). *The foundations of psychoanalysis*. Berkeley: University of California Press.

Horowitz, M. J. (1988). *Psychodynamics and cognition*. Chicago: University of Chicago Press.

Jones, E. (1955). *The life and work of Sigmund Freud: Vol. 2. Years of maturity 1901–1919*. New York: Basic Books.

Jones, E. (1961). *The life and work of Sigmund Freud* (L. Trilling & S. Marcus, Eds.). New York: Basic Books.

MacKinnon, D. W., & Dukes, W. F. (1964). Repression. In L. Postman (Ed.), *Psychology in the making*. New York: Knopf.

Masling, J. M. (1965). Differential indoctrination of examiners and Rorschach responses. *Journal of Consulting Psychology, 29*, 198–201.

Masling, J. (1966). Role-related behavior of the subject and psychologist and its effects upon psychological data. In D. Levine (Ed.), *Nebraska Symposium on Motivation* (pp. 67–104). Lincoln: University of Nebraska Press.

Masling, J. M., & Bornstein, R. F. (Eds.). (1994). *Empirical perspectives on object relations theory.* Washington, DC: American Psychological Association.

Masling, J., Bornstein, R. F., Fishman, I., & Davila, J. (in press). Can Freud explain women as well as men? A meta-analytic review of gender differences in psychoanalytic research. *Psychoanalytic Psychology.*

Masling, J., & Cohen, I. S. (1987). Psychotherapy, clinical evidence, and the self-fulfilling prophecy. *Psychoanalytic Psychology, 4,* 65–79.

Mitchell, J. (1974). *Psychoanalysis and feminism.* New York: Pantheon.

Murray, E. J. (1956). A content-analysis method for studying psychotherapy. *Psychological Monographs, 70*(13, Whole No. 420).

Peradotto, J. (in press). Prophecy and persons: Reading character in the *Odyssey.* In C. Higbie & M. Malamud (Eds.), *Epos and mythos.* Baltimore: Johns Hopkins University Press.

Schafer, R. (1974). Problems in Freud's psychology of women. *Monographs of the Journal of the American Psychoanalytic Association, 22,* 458–485.

Shapiro, T., & Emde, R. N. (1995). *Research in psychoanalysis: Process, development, outcome.* Madison, CT: International Universities Press.

Singer, J. L. (1990). *Repression and dissociation.* Chicago: University of Chicago Press.

Spence, D. P. (1994). *The rhetorical voice of psychoanalysis: Displacement of evidence by theory.* Cambridge, MA: Harvard University Press.

Stern, D. N. (1985). *The interpersonal world of the infant.* New York: Basic Books.

Tabin, J. K. (1985). *On the way to the self.* New York: Columbia University Press.

Torrey, E. F. (1992). *Freudian fraud.* New York: HarperCollins.

Truax, C. B. (1966). Reinforcement and nonreinforcement in Rogerian psychotherapy. *Journal of Abnormal Psychology, 71,* 1–9.

Uleman, J. S., & Bargh, J. A. (1989). *Unintended thought.* New York: Guilford Press.

Weiss, J., & Sampson, H. (1986). Testing alternative psychoanalytic explanations of the therapeutic process. In J. Masling (Ed.), *Empirical studies of psychoanalytic theories* (Vol. 2, pp. 1–26). Hillsdale, NJ: Erlbaum.

Wortis, J. (1954). *Fragments of an analysis with Freud.* Indianapolis, IN: Charter Press.

The Psychodynamics of Gender and Gender Role

Development of Individual Differences in Helplessness:
Relations to Gender and Psychodynamic Theory

Kathleen M. Cain

In a study a colleague and I conducted several years ago (Cain & Dweck, 1995), I presented a set of four puzzles to a first grader named Tanya. The puzzles portrayed familiar cartoon characters such as Winnie the Pooh and Mickey Mouse and initially appeared simple and age appropriate. The first three puzzles were, however, surprisingly challenging—too difficult for a child of this age to solve in the allotted time. The fourth puzzle, although superficially similar, was much easier to solve. After Tanya had seen the puzzles but before she tried them, she said she hoped they would be easy. When I asked her to point to a picture showing how many of the four puzzles she could solve, she predicted that she would solve them all. As Tanya worked on the first puzzle, though, she quickly exclaimed, "I know I don't have that much time! I know I'm not gonna make it.... I can tell. I can't get these puzzles." As she attempted to solve the second puzzle, she remarked, "I know I'm not gonna get this. I'm just trying to find the girl, but I know I'm not gonna get it. I know I can't get even one of these." She continued to make gloomy predictions for her performance on the third puzzle and then successfully solved the fourth puzzle while claiming, "I know I'm not gonna get this. I don't have enough time." Tanya described her emotions after the task as "unhappy," and her facial expressions slipped quickly from neutral on the first puzzle to negative for the remainder of the task, even during the success puzzle. When I asked Tanya which puzzle she'd be willing to try again, she insisted she would try only the one puzzle she had solved already. She attributed her poor performance to being "not good at puzzles" rather than to having insufficient time, and she predicted that she would not be able to solve any puzzles if given four additional puzzles to complete.

Tanya's debilitation in the face of a modest failure is all the more striking when she is compared with other first graders who attempted the same task in this study. Some children focused entirely on strategies, making comments about where various pieces should go and how many pieces were left. Others pointed out the good parts of their performance (e.g., in reference to the Pooh puzzle that portrayed four characters, "I got three people done!") and even expressed positive reactions to the task (e.g., in response to the third failure puzzle, "This is fun, this is fun"). They often exclaimed happily about their success on the fourth puzzle. Many insisted that they could solve all of the puzzles if they had a little more time and expressed a desire to return to a difficult puzzle that they had not yet solved to try it again. These children tended to attribute their performance to insufficient effort or insufficient time rather than to low ability, and they predicted greater success if given four additional puzzles.

Tanya's reaction is an example of helplessness, described in detail by Diener and Dweck (1978, 1980; see also Abramson, Seligman, & Teasdale, 1978; Cain & Dweck, 1995; Dweck & Leggett, 1988; Dweck & Reppucci, 1973). Helplessness typically occurs in reaction to a challenging task or a task that involves failure and, as shown in Table 1.1, involves behavioral, cognitive, and affective components. The behaviors include giving up or using less effective strategies. The cognitions that are part of helplessness include

Table 1.1

Components of the Helpless and Mastery-Oriented Responses to Failure

Component	Helpless	Mastery oriented
Behavior	Lack of persistence	Persistence
	Strategy deterioration	Strategy maintenance or improvement
Cognition		
Focus while working	Note and explain poor performance	Think about task and analyze strategies
Attributions for failure	Low ability	Low effort or external factors
Expectations for future performance	Low	High
Affect	Negative	Neutral or positive

Note. See Cain and Dweck, 1995; Diener and Dweck, 1978, 1980; Dweck and Leggett, 1988.

focusing on one's failure and attempting to explain that failure, attributing poor performance to low ability, and holding low expectations for future success. The primary affective component is negative emotion about one's performance.

Tanya's response to the puzzle task reflected all of the components of helplessness. She showed nonpersistence in her refusal to give a second try to any puzzle but the one on which she had succeeded. Her spontaneous predictions that she would not be able to solve each puzzle, her attribution to low ability, and her expectation of even poorer performance on four additional puzzles reflect the cognitive components of helplessness. Finally, Tanya reported experiencing negative affect, and her emotional facial expressions were also negative. It is interesting that many studies suggest that girls are more susceptible than boys to helplessness (although, as described later, some studies have reported no gender differences) and that Tanya's response is not unusual for a girl faced with a challenging achievement task (e.g., Licht & Dweck, 1983, 1984; Stipek & Hoffman, 1980).

As shown in Table 1.1, Diener and Dweck (1978, 1980) also have described a contrasting mastery-oriented response pattern. The mastery-oriented pattern includes a behavioral component of persisting in the face of failure and maintaining or improving strategies; cognitive components of evaluating strategies, attributing failure to low effort, and holding high expectations for future success; and an affective component of enjoying the challenge presented by the task. This pattern is reflected in the more task-focused and positive comments made by some of Tanya's classmates. Many studies suggest that boys are more likely than girls to show this mastery-oriented response (e.g., Licht & Dweck, 1983, 1984; Stipek & Hoffman, 1980). It is important to note, however, that gender differences do not appear in every study (e.g., Cain & Dweck, 1995; Diener & Dweck, 1978) and that even in studies that do reveal gender differences in helplessness, the distributions of boys and girls overlap considerably.

Why do some children show helplessness in the face of failure, as Tanya did, while others focus on mastering the task? Why might helplessness be more likely to occur in girls than in boys? In this chapter I attempt to answer these questions from the perspective of a social–cognitive approach and to show how this approach might contribute to and benefit from psychodynamic theory. I consider the social–cognitive factors that mediate helplessness as well as socialization processes that may contribute to individual differences and gender differences. Until about 10 years ago, most research on helplessness focused on children ages 9 or 10 years and older, but more recent evidence suggests that helplessness occurs in younger children as well. In this chapter I pay particular attention to the development of helplessness in early childhood.

I begin with an overview of social–cognitive research describing helplessness in older children and adults, including gender differences in its manifestation. I then discuss several psychodynamic theories relevant for understanding helplessness. Next, I review recent social–cognitive research on the development of individual and gender differences in helplessness in young children, and I suggest a model that attempts to explain how helplessness might be socialized and which cognitive processes mediate it in young children. I conclude the chapter with a discussion of how psychodynamic theory can enrich and be informed by the social–

cognitive approach to understanding individual differences and gender differences in motivation.

Individual Differences in Motivation: The Helpless and Mastery-Oriented Patterns

Social–cognitive research on motivation in older children and young adults has focused on the domain of achievement (see Heckhausen & Dweck, 1998). In recent years, many researchers have examined individual differences in mastery motivation and its inverse, lack of persistence (e.g., A. Bandura, Barbaranelli, Caprara, & Pastorelli, 1996; Pomerantz & Ruble, 1997; Stipek, Recchia, & McClintic, 1992; Weiner, 1986). Dweck (1999; Dweck & Leggett, 1988) believed that certain situations provide such strong motivational cues that most people, regardless of individual differences, behave similarly. However, under more ambiguous circumstances, strikingly different helpless and mastery-oriented patterns emerge. These patterns reflect deep-seated differences in individuals' approaches to achievement tasks. Helpless individuals appear quick to define poor performance as a failure and to blame that failure on their own low ability, whereas mastery-oriented individuals seem intent on mastering the task itself and focus more on evaluating and adjusting their strategies than on explaining their failure (see Cain & Dweck, 1995; Dweck, 1999).

Helplessness has been linked, both conceptually and empirically, to other phenomena, such as shame (Burhans & Dweck, 1995; Cain, Gallagher, Staneck, & Myers, 1997; Kelley, Brownell, & Campbell, 2000; M. Lewis, 1992, 1993) and depression (Nolen-Hoeksema, Larson, & Grayson, 1999; Nolen-Hoeksema & Girgus, 1994; Nolen-Hoeksema, Girgus, & Seligman, 1986). Young helpless and mastery-oriented children have similar general abilities, as measured by overall grades or teacher evaluations (e.g., Cain & Dweck, 1995; Heyman, Dweck, & Cain, 1992), as well as similar task-specific ability prior to failure (e.g., Licht & Dweck, 1984; Smiley & Dweck, 1994). However, the helpless pattern predicts decrements in school achievement over time, especially as school tasks grow more challenging in adolescence (Fincham, Hokoda, & Sanders, 1989; Henderson & Dweck, 1990).

In Dweck's model, these distinctive motivational patterns reflect underlying differences in beliefs about ability and in achievement goals (see Dweck, 1999; Dweck & Leggett, 1988). Helpless individuals tend to hold an implicit theory of intelligence as a fixed, unchangeable entity over which they have no control. They typically view achievement tasks as opportunities to pursue performance goals, such as obtaining positive judgments of their ability or avoiding negative judgments thereof (or both), and they see the products or outcomes of their work as the criteria by which their fixed ability should be judged. The entity theory of intelligence, coupled with the performance goal of obtaining or avoiding a judgment of the level of ability they possess, orients helpless individuals toward interpreting challenges and failures as signs of low ability. If one believes one's fixed ability is low, then there is no purpose to continuing a task that is too difficult, the experience of failure is negative in its implications, and expectations for future success are limited. The helpless motivational pattern thus emerges from a constellation of beliefs and goals that orient the individual toward seeking or avoiding judgments of one's fixed intelligence.

In contrast, mastery-oriented individuals in Dweck's (1999; Dweck & Leggett, 1988) framework tend to view intelligence as a malleable quality that they can increase incrementally with effort. This incremental theory of intelligence orients the individual toward a learning goal of increasing one's ability rather than toward the performance goal of judging that ability. For these individuals, failure presents an opportunity to improve intelligence and learn more, rather than an indictment of their personal qualities. If one fails, one can try harder and use new strategies. This experience may be positive, as in an exciting new challenge, or it may be neutral, but it is rarely overwhelmingly negative. Moreover, if one has the potential to increase one's ability, then the possibility of future success remains high.

In general, in Dweck's framework, achievement goals and implicit theories of intelligence predict motivational behavior in relevant contexts. The model can be applied quite broadly, and the two distinctive belief–goal–response clusters are thought to have far-reaching implications for how individuals process information about achievement. Incremental theorists, for instance, report feeling smartest when they are learning something new and challenging, whereas entity theorists report feeling smart when they reach an easy success (see Dweck, 1999). The model also suggests that patterns of goals and beliefs can affect perceptions and behavior in other domains, such as social interactions (Erdley, Cain, Loomis, Dumas-Hines, & Dweck, 1997) and judgments of others (Erdley & Dweck, 1993; see also Dweck & Leggett, 1988). Dweck's approach also has clear clinical implications. Helplessness can be ameliorated, the model predicts, by teaching individuals to focus on learning rather than on performance goals, to attribute failure to low effort rather than to low ability, and to recognize ways in which sustained effort improves ability (see Dweck, 1975, 1999).

Gender Differences in Helplessness

Gender differences in phenomena related to helplessness are well established. Beginning in elementary school, girls are more likely than are boys to attribute achievement failure to low ability, to have lower expectations for future success, and to rate more poorly their competence in novel or traditionally male tasks (e.g., Deaux, 1976; Eccles, Wigfield, Harold, & Blumenfeld, 1993; Lenney, 1977; Licht & Dweck, 1984b; Maccoby & Jacklin, 1974; Roberts, 1991; Ruble, Greulich, Pomerantz, & Gochberg, 1993; Stipek & Gralinski, 1991). Females are also more vulnerable than males to depression (e.g., Nolen-Hoeksema, 1990; Nolen-Hoeksema et al., 1999; Weissman & Klerman, 1977) and to internalizing disorders in general (see Keenan & Shaw, 1997), although this gender difference does not emerge clearly until middle childhood or adolescence (e.g., Brooks-Gunn & Peterson, 1991; Keenan & Shaw, 1997; Nolen-Hoeksema & Girgus, 1994).

Given these differences, it is not surprising that many students have found that girls are more vulnerable to helplessness than are boys (e.g., Dweck & Bush, 1976; Dweck, Goetz, & Strauss, 1980; Dweck & Reppucci, 1973; Leggett, 1985; Licht & Dweck, 1983, 1984; Licht & Shapiro, 1982; Nicholls, 1975; Stipek & Hoffman, 1980). In some studies, bright girls appear to be especially vulnerable to helplessness (see Dweck, 1999; Licht & Dweck, 1984a). It is certainly the case that many boys also behave helplessly and that many girls are mastery oriented, just as many boys make maladaptive self-evaluations and experience depression and many girls do not. Some studies, indeed, have found gender differences in helplessness or related constructs (e.g., Ames & Archer, 1988; A. Bandura et al., 1996; M. Bandura & Dweck, 1985; Cain & Dweck, 1995; Diener & Dweck, 1978; Mueller & Dweck, 1998). Nonetheless, most evidence for older children suggests that girls are more likely than boys to react helplessly to challenging tasks. One possibility that has not been explored empirically is that gender differences in helplessness may be domain specific, with girls being more vulnerable than boys to helplessness when the material is novel or stereotypically male. In addition, most studies have examined gender differences in achievement tasks, so little is known about whether these differences exist in other areas, such as social relationships.

It is interesting that studies of preschoolers and young school-age children have found little or no evidence of gender differences in helplessness (Burhans & Dweck, 1995; Cain & Dweck, 1995; Heyman et al., 1992; Kamins & Dweck, 1999; Smiley & Dweck, 1994). One study revealed gender differences in achievement-related shame in 3-year-olds (Lewis, Alessandri, & Sullivan, 1992), but several others have not (Barrett, Zahn-Waxler, & Cole, 1993; Kelley et al., 2000; Stipek et al., 1992). Cain, Gallagher, et al. (1997) found gender differences in shame among 3-year-olds, but not among 2-year-olds. Similarly to gender differences in depression, gender differences in helplessness may not emerge clearly until middle or later childhood.

Psychodynamic Theory and Helplessness

Psychodynamic theory began with Freud's work in the late 19th and early 20th centuries (e.g., Freud, 1905/1953). Social–cognitive models of motivation became popular during the last 40 years, in part as alternatives to psychodynamic theory (see Heckhausen & Dweck, 1998). Like psychodynamic theory, social–cognitive models view motivation as central to human functioning. They are similar in that both understand human behavior as motivated and shaped by a dynamic interplay of a variety of factors. Neither sees motivation as reducible to global personality traits or to "cold" stimulus–response sequences. In addition, they both regard the study of individual differences as essential to understanding motivation.

At this point, however, the similarities end. As shown in Table 1.2, psychodynamic and socal–cognitive theories differ on numerous dimensions and in fact show little if any overlap in emphases, assumptions, and key concepts. Psychodynamic models tend to focus on unconscious needs and drives, whereas social–cognitive models focus on individuals' pursuit of conscious or potentially conscious goals (see McClelland, Koestner, & Weinberger, 1989). Many psychodynamic theories do not emphasize achievement motivation over other forms of motivation (although the theories of Adler [e.g., 1930], Horney [e.g., 1937], and Erikson [1963] are notable exceptions), but social–cognitive theories often focus primarily on achievement motivation (e.g., Nicholls & Miller 1984) or build models of motivation in other domains from research on achievement (e.g., Duda, 1992; Erdley et al., 1997; but

Table 1.2

Differences Between Psychodynamic and Social–Cognitive Models of Motivation

Dimension	Psychodynamic	Social–cognitive
Nature of motivational construct	Needs (often unconscious)	Goals (conscious or accessible to consciousness)
Emphasis on achievement domain	Often medium to low	Often high
Key variables	Emotion Subjective experience Fantasy	Cognition, including expectations, self-beliefs, strategies, and interpretation of feedback Task-related affect
Predictions	General, long-term predictions regarding activity selection, success, satisfaction	Specific cognitive and behavioral processes during immediate task

see Wentzel, 1996; and Cantor & Sanderson, 1998, for examples of social–cognitive theories of motivation that are not focused on the achievement domain). Whereas psychodynamic theories explore the role of emotion, subjective experience, and fantasy in guiding behavioral choices, social–cognitive models attempt to delineate cognitive factors that shape behavior and the interpretation of feedback, and they tend to treat emotion simplistically, typically as a response to a failure experience. Social–cognitive models can make fairly precise predictions about behavior and cognition during an on-hand achievement task. Psychodynamic theories, however, tend to be more general and long term in their predictions and to give little attention to the details of the mental and behavioral processes that occur during specific achievement tasks (see McClelland et al., 1989).

Several psychodynamic theories do focus on achievement motivation, and they offer ideas consistent with the social–cognitive approach. For example, Erikson (1963) proposed a series of psychosocial issues or crises addressed in stages during normative development, several of which are related to achievement. In the autonomy versus shame and doubt stage (ages 1–3 years), toddlers learn to act independently, make choices, and regulate their behavior, but those who struggle with this process feel ashamed. In the initiative versus guilt stage (3–6 years), young children learn to persist and to carry out their plans and goals enthusiastically, but difficulties result in feelings of self-doubt and guilt. In the industry versus inferiority stage (6 years to puberty), children are specifically concerned with achievement, whether in the context of school or of work to support the family, but feel inadequate or inferior if they do not perform these functions competently. As I outline later in the chapter, the social–cognitive model similarly reveals evidence that early achievement concerns are related to shame and beliefs about self-worth. As children grow older, helplessness increasingly pertains to beliefs about intellectual qualities. Thus, Erikson's broad outline of development is consistent with evidence about the development of helplessness.

Adler (1927, 1930, 1973) and Horney (1937, 1945) saw achievement issues as playing a central role in human personality and suggested mechanisms by which socialization processes could predispose children to maladaptive motivational styles. Adler (1930;

Ansbacher & Ansbacher, 1956) suggested that mothers who view their children as means of proving their own superiority pressure children to achieve and show off their children's accomplishments to others. Such behaviors lead to resentment, hostility, and feelings of inferiority on the part of children. Horney (1945) suggested that hypercompetitive parents may treat their sons and daughters with domination, coldness, criticism, and hostility, which should in turn create basic anxiety in the children. Such children may feel fearful and helpless. Similarly to Adler and Horney, the social–cognitive approach proposes that parents' criticism and controlling behaviors are associated with helplessness in children and that concerns about performance mediate helpless reactions. Horney (1939, 1967) also has discussed ways in which society prepares women to feel inferior to men, and social–cognitive theories likewise suggest that girls are treated in ways that make them more likely to question their ability.

Although Erikson's, Adler's, and Horney's suggestions have proven congruent with social–cognitive evidence, each theory is vague about specific mechanisms that contribute to individual differences. For example, although achievement and feelings of efficacy are centrally important in Erikson's (1963) model, there is little specific information about the manner in which psychosocial crises are resolved that would guide the formation of detailed research questions. Thus, although they address achievement and are essentially consistent with the evidence, their ideas do not shape current research in this area except in the most general sense.

In contrast, although Freud and, more recently, object-relations theorists (e.g., Klein, 1981; Mahler, Pine, & Bergman, 1975; Osofsky, 1995) did not emphasize academic achievement, their theories offer several interesting ideas about helplessness. Freud (1923/1961a, 1940/1964) suggested that a key part of the superego is the *ego ideal*, which contains parental standards for good behavior. Both children and adults strive to meet these standards and can be punished by the superego if they fail to do so. These standards, however, are often opposed to the more realistic goals of the ego and may be held quite rigidly. This model of a superego containing parental standards of behavior may be applicable to children's achievement goals and cognitions as well. If children perceive their parents as negatively critical and as holding high standards for their behavior, they may internalize these standards and in turn criticize themselves when they fail. They may also be more concerned with the negative meaning of this failure, even when such a failure may be a reasonable part of the learning process, and be more focused on performance than on task mastery. Indeed, for some children achievement failures may have moral overtones; perhaps, for example, some children may feel guilty and deserving of punishment for failing academic tasks. These ideas from Freudian theory are consistent in some respects with the model of development I outline in this chapter, although the social–cognitive approach spells out more fully the processes by which self-criticism affects behavior during failure. In contrast to Freud's theory, the mechanisms proposed by the social–cognitive approach are also accessible to conscious awareness and have specific cognitive components.

Object-relations theorists (e.g., Klein, 1981; Kohut, 1977; Mahler et al., 1975) further developed Freud's ideas about internalization of parental standards. Object-relations theory (as well as closely related attachment theory, e.g., Bowlby, 1980; see also Osofsky, 1995) emphasizes socialization processes and the manner in which these affect concepts of self and other. This approach views the relationship between the parent (usually the mother) and infant as the primary basis for the child's developing sense of self. Object-relations theorists propose that children develop an internalized sense of "the other"—typically a parent—who may be accepting or rejecting and that they relate to this "other" throughout their lives. Like the concept of the ego ideal, this idea suggests a means by which helpless children come to be highly concerned with performance goals and to interpret poor performance as evidence of their low ability. Children who internalize images of their parents as harsh judges of their work may be especially vulnerable to helplessness. Although described in different terms, both the object-relations and social–cognitive approaches highlight the centrality of concern of others' judgments among some young children.

Within object-relations theory, the concept of dependency shows some similarity to helplessness. Dependent individuals often behave helplessly to elicit nurturing behaviors from important others such as parents and teachers. Bornstein (1996) suggested that the central goal of dependent individuals is to obtain and maintain nurturant, supportive relationships. Although the outward behaviors of helplessness and dependency are similar in some cases, helplessness as studied by social–cognitive theorists focuses on concerns about achievement tasks and their implications for the value of the self or for one's abilities; the motivational issues do not concern relationships per se (although beliefs about those relationships may play a role). Object-relations theorists propose that a belief that the self is weak and ineffectual underlies dependent behavior (Blatt, 1974, 1991) and that this belief has cognitive, affective, and behavioral consequences (Bornstein, 1996). Self-beliefs are likewise thought to play a pivotal role in helplessness, although the beliefs concern one's ability and worth rather than one's power. Just as helplessness is more common among females than males, more women than men rate themselves as dependent (Bornstein, Manning, Krukonis, Rossner, & Mastrosimone, 1993). As with helplessness and depression, clear gender differences in dependency do not appear until middle childhood (Bornstein, 1992). Although dependency and helplessness are by no means identical, the parallels between them suggest that contemporary research on dependency may also illuminate the processes by which helplessness develops.

Development of Individual Differences in Achievement Motivation: Social–Cognitive Research

Most of the research supporting Dweck's theory was conducted with older children, adolescents, and college students. These age groups are capable of reasonably accurate self-assessment and social comparison and have a relatively rich understanding of intelligence (see Dweck & Elliot, 1983; Nicholls, 1978; Rholes, Newman, & Ruble, 1990; Ruble, Boggiano, Feldman, & Loebl, 1980; Stipek, 1984; Stipek & Hoffman, 1980). In contrast, research on social–cognitive development suggests that young children do not fully understand the concept of ability (Miller, 1985; Nicholls, 1978; Rholes, Jones, & Wade, 1988), may not recognize failure (Rholes,

Blackwell, Jordan, & Walters, 1980) and, as a group, are highly optimistic after failure (Parsons & Ruble, 1977; Stipek, 1984). Until 10 or 15 years ago, many psychologists (e.g., Dweck & Elliot, 1983; Miller, 1985; Nicholls, 1978; Nicholls & Miller, 1984; Stipek, 1984) argued that young children therefore should not be susceptible to helplessness, because the unique properties of their social–cognitive understanding should prevent them from blaming their ability for failure and holding low expectations for future success.

These assumptions have been challenged by recent evidence suggesting that young children's understanding of psychological traits is more sophisticated than previously believed (e.g., Cain, Heyman, & Walker, 1997; Heyman & Dweck, 1998; Heyman & Gelman, 1998, 1999). Consistent with these findings, several studies suggest that some young children, like some older children, are indeed vulnerable to helplessness (Cain & Dweck, 1995; Heyman et al., 1992; Smiley & Dweck, 1994). These studies have used tasks that are highly familiar to children and have clearly recognizable failures (e.g., wooden puzzles depicting popular cartoon characters). To accommodate young children's more limited verbal and cognitive skills, the studies have also used simpler measures of helplessness and beliefs about the self than those used in earlier research. In these studies, few if any gender differences emerged, so gender was not a primary focus of the analyses.

As mentioned earlier, Cain and Dweck (1995) administered a set of four puzzles (three of which were unsolvable in the specified time)[1] to a total of 139 children in first, third, and fifth grade. Children's persistence was assessed by asking them which puzzle they would like to try again if they had more time and their reason for the choice. Children who chose to repeat the puzzle they had previously solved and whose reason for this choice showed signs of challenge avoidance (e.g., "it's not hard") were placed in the *nonpersistent* group. In each grade, some children (37% in first grade) were classified as nonpersistent. These nonpersistent children, even

---

[1]The typical procedure in helplessness studies, including Cain and Dweck's study and others cited in this chapter, involves giving children an extensive mastery experience after they complete the failure task and follow-up questions. In addition, the failure procedure is always terminated early for any child who becomes unduly distressed.

the first-graders, showed other signs of helplessness, such as negative affect, low expectations for future success, and little belief that they could solve the puzzles with effort. It is interesting that although a subset of first graders showed clear signs of helplessness (with responses just as strong as those of helpless older children), first graders as a group continued to appear more optimistic than children in older grades. In earlier studies, the general optimism of younger children apparently masked a lack of optimism in some children of this age group. By focusing on individual differences rather than age differences, more recent research provides evidence of helplessness in younger as well as older children.

In a study with kindergarteners (Heyman et al., 1992), children enacted pretend scenarios with dolls as the experimenter read the scenarios out loud. The pretend format was used to provide negative feedback about children's work in a vivid and realistic way, without actually criticizing participants directly for their own accomplishments. In each scenario, the child doll, who represented the child participant, completed a pretend task for the teacher, such as writing the numbers 1–10. Shortly before giving the finished product to the teacher doll, the child doll noticed a small mistake, such as having left out the number 8. The child doll decided to give the work to the teacher doll anyway. Some scenarios ended there, but in others the teacher doll then criticized the child doll for the mistake. After each scenario, follow-up questions measured children's assessment of the flawed work, self-judgments, persistence, and emotions. When children had never been exposed to the critical-feedback condition, their ratings of the flawed work were universally high (5 or 6 on a 6-point scale showing various numbers of stars). However, after criticism, some children gave their work low ratings (4 or less on the same 6-point scale). Those participants were categorized as *low product raters* and compared with the remaining children who rated the work highly despite the teacher doll's criticism. The low product raters exhibited many characteristics similar to helplessness in older children. For example, in comparison to high product raters, they reported less intention to persist, were more likely to say they were experiencing sadness and anger, and rated more poorly their task-specific ability. Although the procedures differed from those used by Cain and Dweck (1995), the results similarly suggest that some young children react maladaptively to failure, showing behavioral, cognitive, and affective components of helplessness.

If young children can respond helplessly during challenging achievement tasks, what are the social–cognitive mechanisms governing such responses? Research addressing this question is still under way, but several studies provide clues. Cain and Dweck (1995) found that helpless first graders were no more likely than mastery-oriented first graders to endorse a theory of intelligence as a fixed entity, although this difference was replicated for the third and fifth graders in the study. This finding suggests that something other than the view of intelligence as a fixed entity affects young children's helplessness, an outcome that is not surprising given their partial understanding of the nature of intelligence. Other studies suggest that young helpless children, like older helpless children, tend to emphasize performance over learning and to evaluate the self in a global manner that is contingent on performance. These factors may play a critical role in achievement motivation in early childhood.

Evidence for the importance of performance goals comes from research by Smiley and Dweck (1994), Cain and Dweck (1995), and Heyman et al. (1992). Using a set of three failure puzzles and one success puzzle, Smiley and Dweck identified a group of nonpersistent 4- and 5-year-old preschoolers. These children favored performance goals over learning goals in their choices of simple statements of each goal. An additional measure of performance goals included a block-building task administered after the puzzle procedure. In this second task participants were asked to state how many blocks they thought they could stack in a tower and then to try to build the tower. Children classified as nonpersistent on the puzzle task made lower predictions for themselves on the block task. As they built the towers, nonpersisters stopped once they had reached their predicted height, even if the tower was still standing. Persisters, on the other hand, tended to continue to build past the height they had predicted until the tower fell down. Smiley and Dweck concluded that nonpersisters were more concerned with making and meeting easy goals, whereas persisters were more interested in the experience of building the highest tower possible. This finding implies that young helpless children are more concerned with performance goals than are young mastery-oriented children, as is also the case in later childhood.

Cain and Dweck (1995), in a separate interview from the four-puzzle helplessness assessment, asked participants to explain the causes of the good and poor grades that might be received by some children in school. First graders who persisted on the puzzle task tended to explain grades by mentioning specific strategies that children engaged or failed to engage in, such as practicing at home, listening to the teacher, and doing homework. In contrast, nonpersistent first graders tended to refer to the children's products rather than to their strategies. For example, they said that some of their classmates might receive high grades because they got lots of stars and good marks on their homework but that other children might receive low grades because they never got stars or never had work good enough to put on the bulletin boards at school. In other words, mastery-oriented first graders seemed focused on specific steps that enhance learning, but helpless first graders seemed more concerned about products or outcomes, one's ultimate performance at school. Similarly, in Heyman et al.'s (1992) study, when asked to act out what might happen next in each pretend scenario, low product raters were less likely than high product raters to generate constructive solutions. High product raters tended to say they would fix the flawed work, but low product raters said they would throw the flawed work away or go to their room. These findings are consistent with the idea that young helpless children are more concerned with performance goals than are their mastery-oriented counterparts. Mastery-oriented children, in contrast, seem more aware of or interested in the processes that contribute to learning.

Two studies also suggest that young helpless children may be better able to identify others' perspectives, a finding congruent with the idea that they are highly concerned with the manner in which others will judge them. In these studies a false-belief task was used (Bartsch & Wellman, 1989) that assesses children's ability to identify others' beliefs even when these conflict with participants' own knowledge. This task is usually solved successfully by many 4-year-olds but is quite difficult for 3-year-olds. Slomkowski (1993) reported that young preschoolers who solved the false-belief task were more likely than those who could not solve this task to respond helplessly on Heyman et al.'s (1992) pretend teacher procedure 9 months later. Using concurrent data, Cain and Staneck (1999) found that 4- and 5-year-old helpless children performed better on a series of false-belief tasks than did their mastery-oriented counterparts. This finding held even when analyses controlled for general verbal ability, suggesting that helplessness is not a byproduct of higher general ability. Rather, helplessness in young children may be specifically linked to a greater awareness of or concern for others' opinions.

In addition to concern with performance, some evidence suggests that young helpless children may be more likely than their more mastery-oriented peers to question their global self-worth when they fail or are criticized. Heyman et al. (1992) found that low product raters—who, as reported previously, rated their task-specific ability more poorly after criticism—also rated various aspects of their global self more negatively. Although the pretend teacher had criticized only a small mistake in an achievement task, low product raters were more likely than the other children to say that they were not smart, not nice, and not a good person. These extreme ratings suggest that young children's helplessness may involve global conceptions of the self rather than beliefs about intellectual ability in particular. A few low product raters even acted out imaginary endings to the scenarios in which their teacher or parents punished them for their poor performance. These responses suggest a belief that academic achievement reflects on the whole self rather than on task-specific ability or effort. Consistent with this idea, low product raters were more likely than high product raters to answer "yes" when asked if a child who makes mistakes on school work is "bad." Heyman and Dweck (1998) found related patterns of linkages between children's perceptions of the self's goodness and their achievement beliefs among slightly older children. Specifically, 7- and 8-year-old children who viewed sociomoral goodness as stable, in comparison to those who regarded goodness as malleable, were also more likely to emphasize the evaluative meaning of achievement outcomes rather than the processes that shape those outcomes. This finding suggests that children's beliefs about nonintellectual parts of the self may mediate helplessness in achievement tasks as well as other tasks before implicit theories of intelligence predict motivational patterns.

Burhans and Dweck (1995) suggested that young children who have a sense of contingent self-worth—rather than a view of intelligence as a fixed entity—may be especially vulnerable to helplessness; that is, children who believe that the self's worth can be judged from performance or from others' criticisms may be vulnerable to helplessness at an early age, long before they have well-articulated conceptions of ability. Consistent with this proposal, Coulson (2001) reported direct associations between 4- and 5-year-old children's contingent self-worth and the degree of helplessness they showed when working on difficult tasks with their mothers. Indeed, even 2- and 3-year-olds show signs of individual differences in their shame proneness after achievement failure (e.g., Cain, Gallagher, et al., 1997; Kelley et al., 2000; M. Lewis et al., 1992). Shame is thought to involve a global assessment that the self is worthless or bad, and achievement-related shame may be a form of helplessness that appears when children question their self-worth (see Cain, Gallagher, et al., 1997; M. Lewis, 1993). These findings suggest that children's tendency to make global, negative judgments about the self during failure may play an important role in helplessness.

In summary, helplessness does occur in young children. Children who judge the self globally, question its worth during failure or criticism, and are concerned with outward performance or others' judgments rather than with constructive strategies that contribute to learning may be especially vulnerable to helplessness. These characteristics resemble but are not identical to older helpless children's belief that intelligence is a fixed entity and their preference for performance goals.

Socialization of Individual Differences in Achievement Motivation

How do these individual differences in orientation toward achievement arise? Surprisingly few studies have addressed this question. One possibility is that these differences are rooted in biological differences in temperament. Evidence for this hypothesis is mixed, however. Belsky, Domitrovich, and Crnic (1997) examined the contribution of temperament (emotional negativity) at age 12 months to achievement shame at 3 years but found no relation between them. Their study included only boys and did not include measures of temperament at ages 2 or 3, so more research is needed before firm conclusions about the role of temperament can be reached. A study by Smiley and Tan (2001) suggests that a tendency toward anger combined with low interest in 4- to 5-year-olds predicts helplessness 1 year later. By this age, though, it is likely that environmental experiences have modified temperament (Rothbart & Bates, 1998).

Another possibility is that socialization processes help to shape differences in helplessness and mastery orientation. Only a few studies have examined directly relations between parent–child interaction and helplessness. A few additional studies have identified patterns of experimenter-originated feedback that bring about helplessness in the laboratory as well as parent–child interaction processes that predict responses related to helplessness, such as shame or low self-evaluation. The results of these studies suggest that helplessness in children is associated with affectively negative parental criticism, especially of the child's person, and with parental controlling behavior. Overall patterns of results for both girls and boys are described first, and then gender differences in socialization are reviewed.

In the first study of socialization of helplessness, Nolen-Hoeksema, Wolfson, Mumme, and Guskin (1995) asked mothers and their 5- to 7-year-old children to work together on solvable and unsolvable puzzles. Children's helplessness was measured on the unsolvable puzzles as well as through teacher ratings and children's responses to hypothetical scenarios. Helplessness in children was associated with several dimensions of mothers' behavior during the puzzle task. Mothers' negative affect—based on a composite measure that included hostility, irritability, and negative content (such as criticism, frustration, and pointing out the child's mistakes)—correlated positively with helplessness. Mothers' intrusiveness was also associated with helplessness, but only marginally. In addition, mothers' encouragement of mastery when their children became frustrated was associated with greater mastery on the part of the children. Maternal depression was also correlated with some aspects of helplessness in children. Overall, the results provide clear evidence that mothers' negative, critical affect is associated with helplessness in children, with some evidence that maternal intrusiveness and depression also predict children's helplessness.

Using a similar procedure in which mothers and their 4- and 5-year-old children worked on easy and difficult block design problems, Smiley and Tan (2001) found that mothers of helpless children behaved much less warmly toward their children than other mothers during this task. Coulson (2001), using a related procedure, found that contingent maternal warmth (the difference between warmth during a solvable puzzle and warmth during an unsolvable puzzle) predicted helplessness in 4- and 5-year-old children of average IQ. Moreover, for this subsample of children, regression analyses suggested that children's contingent self-worth (measured on separate questions) mediated the relationship between maternal contingent warmth and children's helplessness. In other words, maternal contingent warmth appears to influence children's sense of contingent self-worth, which in turn predicts helplessness.

Other research has yielded consistent findings. First, several studies have examined the association between maternal evaluations of children's work and achievement-related shame (note that these focused on maternal negative evaluation in particular rather than on negative affective tone). Using a procedure in which parents and 3-year-olds worked together on easy and difficult tasks, Alessandri and Lewis (1993) found a positive correlation between parental negative evaluation during these tasks and children's display of shame. Kelley et al. (2000) found that negative maternal evaluation during a challenging task when children were 24 months old predicted children's shame on an achievement task at age 36 months. Also, children whose mothers gave them more positive feedback about their work or corrected their work in a neutral, non-negative tone at age 2 were more likely to display mastery-related behaviors at age 3. These studies suggest that mothers' negative criticism of their children's work predicts achievement-related shame.

Phillips (1987) examined the achievement-related beliefs of parents and their bright third-grade sons and daughters. Some of these children had low perceived academic competence despite high performance in school. The children with low perceived competence resembled helpless individuals in that they preferred less challenging tasks and had lower expectations for their school success. Compared to parents of other children, parents of participants with low perceived competence, especially fathers, estimated their childrens' ability as lower. Fathers of children with low perceived competence also held more stringent standards than other parents for their children's school performance. This finding is consistent with the idea that parents of helpless children tend to evaluate their children's ability more negatively. In fact, path analysis suggested that children's perceived competence was affected more directly by their parents' beliefs about them than by their actual performance in school.

Experimental studies by Dweck and her colleagues support these findings, although they did not actually examine parents' behavior. Using a variant of Heyman et al.'s (1992) pretend teacher task, Kamins and Dweck (1999) exposed 4- and 5-year-old preschoolers to one consistent form of feedback from a pretend teacher during four scenarios in which the child doll made small mistakes in the classroom. In one condition, the teacher doll gave process-related feedback criticizing the child doll's strategies ("Maybe you could think of *another* way to do it"). In another condition, the teacher doll criticized the child doll's person ("I'm very disappointed in you"). Next, all participants responded to an identical scenario in which the child doll made another small mistake (forgetting windows in a Lego house). The teacher doll pointed out the mistake (saying "There are no windows on that house") but did not provide any further feedback. Children's persistence, affect, and self-evaluation were then assessed for this story. Consistent with research cited earlier, participants who had previously received person-oriented feedback showed more helplessness than children in the process-oriented feedback condition. The study thus suggests that negative feedback that criticizes the child's person may cause helplessness.

It is interesting that *praise* that focuses on the child's person or traits may also bring about helplessness. In a second study, Kamins and Dweck (1999) gave preschoolers pretend success scenarios followed by a teacher doll's praise of their effort/process ("You must have tried very hard"), product/outcome ("That's the right way to do it"), or personal ability ("I'm very proud of you" or "You're a good girl/boy"). In a subsequent failure scenario, children who had received person-focused praise were the most vulnerable to helplessness, and children who had received process-focussed praise showed the least helplessness. Mueller and Dweck (1998), using older participants, found similarly that children whom the experimenter praised for being smart differed from children whom the experimenter praised for trying hard in their responses to several subsequent tasks. The participants who received trait praise showed greater interest in performance over learning goals, less persistence during failure, more negative ability attributions, and even a greater tendency to endorse the view of intelligence as a fixed entity. These studies suggest that praise of children's personal traits can bring about helplessness just as criticism can. The key variable in these studies may well be the implicit message that a measurable trait is on display as children work on achievement tasks.

In Nolen-Hoeksema et al.'s (1995) study, maternal intrusiveness as well as negative affect predicted some components of helplessness. Intrusiveness can be seen as a form of control in which the mother imposes her demands on the child regardless of the child's apparent needs. Several studies have examined the association between maternal control and phenomena related to helplessness and have found evidence to support a connection between high maternal control and helplessness. Cain, Gallagher, et al. (1997) asked mothers and their 2- or 3-year-old children to work together on a highly structured task (constructing several predetermined shapes from bristle builders) as well as a less structured task (reading and working on a book with eight activities, such as matching colors, identifying textures, and tying laces). Children later worked by themselves on a nesting-cups task that included a failure component. Participants were classified into shame and no-shame groups on the basis of whether they showed a distinct episode of shame (measured from behavioral criteria) as they worked alone on the nesting-cup task task. During the structured task, mothers of girls in the shame group made 60% more comparisons between their children's constructions and the target models than did mothers of the no-shame girls. On the less structured task, mothers of children (both girls and boys) in the shame group spontaneously set almost 50% more standards, rules, and goals for their children and were rated as being more directive or "bossy." This study suggested that mothers of children who show shame during challenging achievement tasks exercise more control, in part by setting more standards and rules for the task at hand—especially when there are no clear directions as to how the task should be completed. Kelley et al. (2000) found similarly that children whose parents used more autonomy-supporting control ("gentle guidance" as opposed to "intrusive control") at 24 months were less likely to avoid achievement tasks at age 3. Coulson (2001) found that when 4- to 5-year-old children of average IQ scored high on a measure of contingent self-worth, and when their mothers increased control during failure tasks relative to success tasks, children were especially likely to show helplessness.

The evidence thus suggests that socialization practices that involve criticism of children's persons and emotional negativity when children fail predict helplessness (as does praise of children's persons during success). High parental control also predicts helplessness in children. In contrast, socialization practices that encourage mastery and support autonomy may bring about mastery orientation.

How might parental evaluation and parental control strategies shape children's vulnerability to helplessness? Parents' ability-related feedback or hostile criticism may directly influence helpless children's tendency to interpret achievement outcomes as reflecting qualities of the self (see Coulson, 2001). When parents criticize children's work in a negative tone or even praise their ability, children may believe that their ability is being judged from performance and that global qualities of the self are reflected in achievement tasks. At the same time, parents' intrusive control and high standards may heighten a child's focus on performance goals by demonstrating that parents care about such performance. Parental controlling behaviors may also undermine children's efforts to devise their own strategies for completing the task or repairing errors. Deci and Ryan (1987; see also Flink, Boggiano, & Barrett, 1990) proposed that tactics that undermine children's autonomy do not allow the children to gain a sense of personal control over outcomes, an idea consistent with the finding that young helpless children to not focus on constructive strategies for fixing mistakes and that older helpless children downplay the value of effort. The combination of hostile evaluative feedback and high parental control may thus lead children to emphasize performance outcomes, to question their ability or self-worth during failure, and at the same time to find it difficult to identify or focus on the processes and strategies that may help them to perform more successfully during challenges.

It is important to voice several cautions about interpreting such studies. Three of these pertain to shortcomings in research to date. First, these studies (except for Kamins and Dweck [1999] and Mueller and Dweck [1998], which did not include parents) used a correlational design. Parents' differential treatment of helpless children could conceivably arise as a response to their behavior rather than be the cause of it, or children's helplessness and parents' behavior may influence each other in a complex cycle. Second, most studies have not included fathers, but Phillips's (1987) data suggest that fathers' evaluations may be more strongly related to children's self-perceptions than mothers' evaluations are. Third, although some studies do suggest that helplessness is a stable individual difference over several years among elementary school children (Fincham et al., 1989; Nolen-Hoeksema et al., 1986; Nolen-Hoeksema, Girgus, & Seligman, 1992), there is little or no evidence about the stability of helplessness in very young children. Without such evidence one must be cautious in interpreting findings from studies with young children as reflecting on the same processes as those in later childhood.

It is also important to recognize that parents of helpless children do not appear to be obviously and overbearingly negative toward their children in every interaction. Belsky et al. (1997) measured general parenting style during the toddler years as opposed to interaction during achievement tasks. General parenting style was then related to the child's shame and pride during achievement failure and success at age 3. More negative general parenting predicted *less* shame at age 3 and more positive general parenting predicted *less* pride. Belsky et al. suggested that interactions outside the achievement domain may be quite different than those in this domain and that parents of children who show achievement shame may be very positive in other areas.

Gender and the Development of Helplessness

What do socialization studies reveal about processes that may contribute to gender differences in helplessness? In general, parents emphasize both academic and nonacademic achievement more with sons than with daughters and, beginning in adolescence, they expect their sons to perform better than their daughters in academic work, especially in traditionally male subjects such as mathematics (see Eccles, Adler, et al., 1983). In Phillips's (1987) study of bright children with low perceived competence, parents' beliefs that their children were less competent predicted children's self-beliefs. In general, parents' differential expectations for boys and girls may convey subtle or not-so-subtle messages about their beliefs in children's competence.

Few studies have specifically examined socialization of gender differences in helplessness. As noted previously, the studies of young children cited in the preceding sections rarely reported gender differences in children's behavior. Alessandri and Lewis (1993) did find that parents made more spontaneous negative evaluations of girls' than boys' performance when their children worked on easy and difficult achievement tasks, even though girls and boys did not differ in their objective success on these tasks. Nolen-Hoeksema et al. (1995) reported that parents encouraged mastery less for their daughters than for their sons. Cain, Gallagher, et al. (1997), as mentioned earlier, found that mothers of girls who showed shame appeared more concerned than other mothers about meeting task standards on the highly structured task, although this gender difference disappeared in favor of an overall shame-group difference in maternal standard setting on the less structured task. (Except for Cain, Gallagher, et al., none of these studies reported gender differences in children's shame or helplessness.) These findings concern negative criticism and parental control, dimensions that have been associated with individual differences in helplessness in children of both sexes. Perhaps parents' greater tendency to criticize and lesser emphasis on mastery with girls contribute to girls' greater vulnerability to helplessness in later childhood.

The same two themes show up in the few studies that have addressed socialization of gender differences in helplessness more directly. Dweck, Davidson, Nelson, and Enna (1978) observed teachers' spontaneous feedback to older elementary school students in the classroom. Teachers criticized boys more often than girls, and their criticisms of boys were directed toward a wide variety of errors, including conduct, neatness, effort, and ability. When teachers did criticize girls, however, they tended to criticize their ability or poor performance. In a second, experimental study, Dweck et al. (1978) found that when an experimenter used the style of feedback teachers typically directed to girls—that is, giving few criticisms, but concentrating these in the area of ability—children were likely to respond helplessly, whether they were boys or girls. The style used by teachers with boys, however, did not bring about helplessness in children of either gender. Dweck et al. interpreted these findings as suggesting that boys, because they receive criticism for a variety of factors, may learn not to interpret such criticism as reflecting on the self. Girls, however, may learn that criticism of their performance does indeed reflect on qualities of the self. Although related to teachers rather than parents, these findings are consistent with the idea that comments about ability can cause helpless responses to failure and that feedback directed to girls emphasizes these comments.

Pomerantz and Ruble (1998) addressed the variable of control among children aged 6–11 years and their mothers. In this study the dependent measure was children's tendency to attribute failure to low ability, measured both during an interview about the causes of school failures and during a laboratory failure task. For several weeks, mothers kept diaries of their behavior with their children in several domains pertaining to academic achievement, such as helping with homework, and in the domain of general discipline. In this study girls attributed failure to low ability more often than did boys. Interesting differences also emerged in the ways in which mothers reported using control with daughters and sons. Mothers of boys were more likely than mothers of girls to use control in combination with autonomy granting (e.g., helping with homework only when asked to do so). Although mothers did not report using different amounts of control per se with girls versus boys, mothers of daughters were much less likely to use this control in combination with autonomy granting (e.g., mothers of daughters reported helping with homework regardless of whether their daughters requested help). These differences occurred only in the context of achievement; there were no differences between mothers of boys and girls in the nonachievement domain of discipline. Mothers' use of control in combination with low autonomy granting partially mediated girls' greater tendency to attribute failure to poor ability.

Earlier studies provided inconsistent evidence that parents are more controlling with girls than with boys (see Lytton & Romney, 1991). Pomerantz and Ruble (1998) suggested that such differences may show up only in certain domains, such as achievement. They also suggested that the examination of control alone may provide only partial data. Rather, the combination of control with autonomy granting may be the critical difference, with boys receiving control in a context that also allows them some independence. This finding is similar to Kelley et al.'s (2000) finding, reported earlier, in which "gentle guidance" was associated with mastery, but "intrusive control" was associated with avoidance of achievement tasks, although Pomerantz and Ruble's (1998) study specifically relates the use of control to gender differences.

Keenan and Shaw (1997) suggested an alternative possibility as well. They reviewed evidence suggesting that girls' more rapid cognitive development in early life gives them an advantage in perspective taking, an advantage heightened by differential socialization that emphasizes others' feelings more to girls than to boys. This cognitive difference, although useful in many respects, may also make girls more vulnerable to internalizing disorders because they may feel more responsible for others or more guilty about the effects of their actions on others (see also Zahn-Waxler, Cole, & Barrett, 1991). In the present case girls' early perspective-taking skills could conceivably increase their awareness of others' judgments and their concern with performance goals. This possibility has not been explored in relation to helplessness but suggests a plausible mechanism by which girls' unique cognitive qualities may combine with differential socialization to make them more vulnerable to helplessness when they fail to meet performance goals. This finding is also consistent with the findings reviewed earlier that helplessness in young children is associated with superior performance on the false-belief perspective-taking task (Cain & Staneck, 1999; Slomkowski, 1993). If girls recognize others' perspectives more accurately, find their ability criticized more frequently, and encounter controlling interactions that do not permit them to find their own solutions to achievement failures, then it is easy to imagine how achievement challenges could become arenas in which girls experience anxiety about others' judgments, blame their ability, do not persist, and have low expectations for the future.

Overall, research to date suggests that parental criticism and control are related to helplessness in children. However, criticism that doesn't focus on the child's person—and control that is administered with some sensitivity to children's own efforts—do not predict helplessness. Rather, these may teach children to find strategies for fixing errors and thereby help them to learn that performance does not always reflect ability perfectly and that effort can bring about success. The available evidence, however, suggests that girls are less likely than boys to receive these useful forms of feedback and more likely to receive feedback that may engender helplessness.

It is important to note that other factors besides social cognition may also shape gender differences in helplessness or interact with the variables already reviewed. Nolen-Hoeksema et al. (1999) argued that women and girls are exposed to societal factors and life circumstances that produce chronic strain, such as lower job status, lower wages, and more work hours both in the place of employment and at home. Also, women are more likely than men to have a ruminative coping style in which they repetitively reflect on their distress and its causes without actively taking steps to change these. These factors, which are theoretically distinct from those reviewed here, may exacerbate helplessness in females.

The absence of fathers from most of these studies is a serious drawback. In general, fathers' attitudes and behaviors are thought to influence gender differentiation in important ways. For example, fathers are more likely than mothers to encourage masculinity in sons (Jacklin, DiPietro, & Maccoby, 1984), and fathers' tendency to emphasize achievement with sons more than with daughters is greater than mothers' tendency to do so (Eccles et al., 1983). When fathers take on a nontraditional role by participating equally with mothers in child care at home, girls are especially likely to benefit by showing increased independence during elementary school (Hoffman & Kloska, 1995) and increased achievement in mathematics and science during adolescence (Updegraff, McHale, & Crouter, 1996). These general findings suggest that fathers' behavior could be quite important for understanding differences in motivation between girls and boys. Fathers, however, have rarely been included in studies of children's helplessness.

Proposed Model for the Development of Helplessness

The evidence about individual differences and gender differences reviewed here suggests a general model for the development of helplessness in young children. This model is outlined in Figure 1.1. The model is consistent with social–cognitive research on the development and socialization of helplessness, but it has not been tested directly.

In this model parents' tendency to evaluate children's ability, whether positively or negatively, leads children to believe that achievement outcomes reflect their global worth or competence (see also H. B. Lewis, 1971; M. Lewis, 1992). In addition, children whose parents frequently evaluate their ability and show negative affect when they fail may become increasingly concerned with their parents' and teachers' opinions of their worth or competence. These factors can contribute to any individual differences, but they may be especially important for gender differences, given findings that parents and teachers evaluate girls more negatively (Alessandri & Lewis, 1993; Dweck et al., 1978) and have lower expectations for their success (Eccles et al., 1983).

At the same time, when parents are controlling and intrusive while their children complete achievement tasks, children may be less aware of specific steps they can take to master challenges, as well as less likely to believe in the efficacy of such steps, or both. Although its effects are apt to be similar for either gender, parents may be especially likely to use intrusive control with girls (Pomerantz & Ruble, 1998). Parents' controlling behavior may be influenced by their beliefs about their children's ability, especially when they think ability is low. Yet the more they control children's achievement work, the less opportunity parents have to find out that children may be capable of doing this work on their own, and

Parent Behaviors

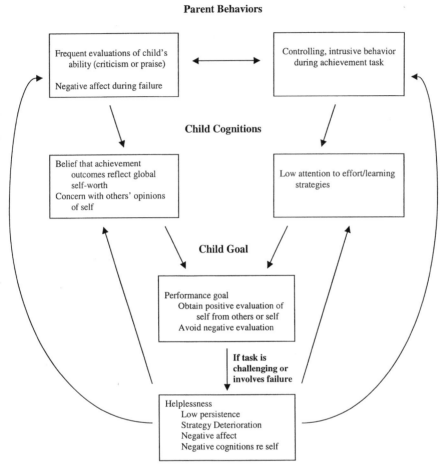

Figure 1.1. Proposed model for development of helplessness in young children.

the more they may think their children's abilities are low. Thus, the evaluation and control components of parents' behavior may feed each other in a continuous cycle.

Children who believe that achievement outcomes reflect their worth, who are concerned with how others judge them, and who have little awareness of or belief in the value of effort should be especially likely to pursue performance goals in the face of achievement challenges (regardless of gender). Rather than taking an interest in learning about the task itself and striving to master it for its own sake, these children may view their performance on the task as centrally important. They hope to obtain a positive judgment of their competence, to avoid receiving a negative evaluation, or both.

Because they focus on their performance and its implications, such children may be quick to look for signs of failure and to interpret these as reflections of their ability or self-worth. When these signs arise, rather than increasing effort to master the task, they debilitate quickly, feel negative about themselves, and judge harshly their ability or self-worth—in other words, they show helplessness. Because they may face more parental criticism and control, girls may be more vulnerable than boys to helplessness.

Helpless reactions in turn can cycle back to other components of the model. Debilitation in the face of failure may increase children's belief that achievement tasks reflect their worth and continue to steer their attention away from constructive solutions to challenges. Parents who see their children react helplessly may evaluate their children's ability even more harshly or may compensate by trying hard to convince their children that they are smart (which still carries the message that performance reflects stable underlying qualities of the self). Concerns about children's helpless behavior may also lead parents to be more intrusive and controlling during achievement tasks, even when they are trying to bring their children success.[2]

Although this model primarily accounts for the development of helplessness in young children, it is consistent with Dweck's model

---

[2]A parallel model for the development of mastery orientation can be proposed as well, although the evidence for many of the components is less direct (in part because some of the key studies focused on predicting helplessness rather than mastery behavior). Parents who praise or constructively criticize their children's effort or objective performance rather than their global qualities, and who offer support without being overly controlling, may lead their children to feel relatively unconcerned with the meaning of achievement outcomes for self-worth and with others' opinions of that worth. The children may also be more aware of how effort and learning strategies lead to task mastery. During achievement tasks they may be more concerned with mastering the task itself than with the manner in which others may judge their performance. If they then fail or meet a challenge, they may persist and experience positive affect.

of helplessness in older children and adults (Dweck & Leggett, 1988). The two models are especially similar in the concepts of performance goals and the important role they play. Moreover, in the present model, children who believe that their self-worth is reflected in achievement tasks and who do not attend to strategies for mastering such tasks can come to believe that their ability is fixed and stable, as in the implicit theory of intelligence as a fixed entity held by older helpless children (see also Burhans & Dweck, 1995). The present model extends Dweck's model, though, by explaining how socialization processes, especially parental criticism and control, can contribute to helplessness. This model also is consistent with evidence about the development and manifestation of helplessness in young children and suggests mechanisms by which socialization processes are related to helplessness in early childhood. The present model also particularly emphasizes the role of others' beliefs about the child and the importance of children's concerns about these beliefs.

It is here, in the realm of parental judgments and children's concerns about these, that psychodynamic theory—specifically, object-relations theory and attachment theory—can contribute to our understanding of the development of helplessness. In the next section I return to the psychodynamic perspective and ask where it is consistent with the social–cognitive approach and how it can inform research on helplessness.

Psychodynamic Theory and Individual Differences in Motivation

The many studies of the development of helplessness reviewed here were conducted independently of psychodynamic theory. Nonetheless, they suggest that parental behaviors may contribute to helplessness and that children's beliefs about how their parents and others judge them may mediate helpless reactions. These ideas —that parent–child interactions shape development and that individuals' beliefs and feelings about parents influence behavior— are the stock in trade of most psychodynamic theories.

Freud (e.g., 1918/1955, 1940/1964) called attention to the important role that family socialization practices play in motivational development, and he emphasized the idea that beliefs, emotions, and fantasies about family members influence behavior. As mentioned earlier, he conceptualized the ego ideal as the part of the irrationally punitive superego that contains parental standards for behavior (Freud, 1923/1961a). Freud's theory suggests that individuals may believe, consciously or unconsciously, that they must meet unreasonably high parental standards and may experience considerable anxiety when they cannot do so. This idea is consistent with Heyman et al.'s (1992) findings that 5-year-old low product raters gave themselves globally low ratings after criticism from a pretend teacher and that some even suggested that the parents and teachers would punish them for mistakes on achievement tasks. In fact, the evidence reviewed here suggests that concerns about global self-worth may play a key role in young children's helplessness, which further implies that their beliefs about achievement may have a moral component to them. Moreover, the notion of the ego ideal is similar in some ways to Dweck's (1999) theory that performance goals—that is, concerns with evaluation by others—mediate helpless reactions.

Freud (1923/1961a, 1925/1961b) proposed that the primary mechanism that shapes the formation of the ego ideal is parental identification, which results from resolution of the Oedipal crisis. He predicted that children who experience greater castration anxiety during the phallic period (ages 4–5) ultimately should identify more strongly with the same-sex parent and internalize higher or stronger standards. Freud argued that, because of anatomical differences between the sexes, boys should experience more intense castration anxiety than girls. Therefore, girls should be less likely than boys to identify fully with either parent and to internalize strong standards. Although Freud was attempting to explain moral development, it is conceivable that standards for achievement could be governed by the same process. There is little empirical evidence, however, that castration anxiety influences later development or that children who identify more strongly with their same-sex parent will adopt stronger standards or experience more guilt for violating those standards (e.g., Sears, Maccoby, & Levin, 1957; Sears, Rau, & Alpert, 1965). Freud's proposal is especially problematic for gender differences in achievement motivation. Not only does his hypothesis about this mechanism make chauvinistic assumptions about females, but it is also contradicted by evidence suggesting that girls may have stronger standards and judge themselves more harshly than boys (e.g., Eccles et al., 1993; Licht & Dweck, 1983).

Interpreted broadly, Freud's idea that beliefs about parental standards influence behavior is consistent with the limited social–cognitive evidence available. However, his suggestion of a developmental mechanism by which these standards are internalized appears to be mistaken. Contemporary theorists from both the social–cognitive and psychodynamic perspectives also disagree with Freud about more general issues, such as the importance of sexuality in children's motivation, basing their objections on the fuller picture of children's development that has emerged from a century of research in developmental psychology (see Dweck, 1999; Westen, 1998).

Object-relations theorists have refined, altered, and expanded Freud's ideas and have cast them in more contemporary, as well as more empirically testable, terms (Westen, 1998). According to both object-relations theory and attachment theory, children's relationships with their parents play a vital and often healthy role in personality development, but troubled relationships with parents can lead children to have maladaptive perceptions of the self and others. For example, evidence from object-relations theory suggests that authoritarian, overprotective parenting predicts dependency in young children, and that dependent behavior is associated with representations of parents as powerful and demanding and the self as weak and needy (Bornstein, 1996). Traditional sex role socialization practices exacerbate these effects for girls.

The object-relations proposal that concepts of self and other are learned in early relationships may help researchers understand how helplessness develops. Specifically, this idea is consistent with my suggestion that parental criticism and hostility contribute to some children's tendency to believe that achievement outcomes reflect self-worth. Both object-relations theory and the model proposed here predict that helpless children should believe that others are harshly judgmental of their work. This hypothesis can be evaluated empirically and indeed has received some support from Phillips's (1987) research. She reported that bright children with low perceived competence accurately believe that their parents are dissatisfied with their performance. The hypothesis is also consistent with evidence that parental criticism of children's personal qualities is associated with helplessness and shame (e.g., Alessandri & Lewis, 1993; Kelley et al., 2000; Nolen-Hoeksema et al., 1995) and the helpless children may be more attuned than mastery-oriented children to others' beliefs (e.g., Cain & Staneck, 1999). Future research questions can readily be identified, many of which test the hypothesis more directly: Do helpless children actually think about their parents' judgments during challenging achievement tasks? Do even young helpless children believe their parents will judge them harshly? Are young children's beliefs about their parents' judgments more crucial for predicting helplessness than their parents' actual judgments? Are parents' evaluations of their children directly related to young children's tendency to question global self-worth during failure? Do girls, who appear better able to identify others' perspectives (Keenan & Shaw, 1997), differ from boys in their beliefs about or concern for parental judgments?

Object-relations theorists, unlike social–cognitive theorists, assign central importance to affect (see Westen, 1998). They see the concepts of self and other learned in early relationships as having strong emotional components. In this respect, object-relations theory provides a fuller model of the manner in which concerns about parental judgments may affect children during their development. Social–cognitive research on the socialization of helplessness has rarely considered children's subjective responses to their parents' feedback, focusing instead on correlations between that feedback and children's behavior. In part this can be expected because research in this area is new, and several of the key studies have been conducted with very young children whose verbal skills are limited. It is also a function, though, of the attention the social–cognitive orientation gives to cognition and its relative lack of interest in affect and subjective experience.

From an object-relations perspective, Bornstein (1992, 1996) and Blatt (1974, 1991) have highlighted the role of affect in dependency. Bornstein (1996) pointed to the anxiety and fear felt by dependent people when they are expected to function independently. Blatt linked dependency to fears of abandonment (1974) and to the development of depression (Blatt & Homann, 1992). Attachment theorists also suggest that different patterns of mother–infant attachment lead to distinctive internal working models of self and other, which have strong affective components (Bowlby, 1980; Main, Kaplan, & Cassidy, 1985). For example, a secure internal working model is thought to foster emotional openness in discussions of potentially painful or sad topics, whereas insecure internal working models lead to dismissiveness or unduly heightened emotions about the same topics (Cassidy, 1994; Main et al., 1985). Cassidy (1988) found that securely attached children were confident about the self and were emotionally comfortable and open about admitting normal imperfections. Insecurely attached children, however, held rigid views of themselves as perfect or showed extreme negativity about themselves. These examples show that in theory pertaining to dependency and to internal working models of attachment, the affective responses associated with thoughts about the self and others have central importance.

In contrast, social–cognitive theories of motivation often treat negative emotion as a component of a helpless reaction but do not attend to emotional factors that may precipitate the reaction. It is likely that thoughts about how others might judge one's achievement performance are highly emotional. If children believe, for example, that an achievement failure means that they are stupid or worthless, or if they anticipate the criticism or hostility a parent or teacher might show if the failure became known, the emotions accompanying these thoughts are likely to be very powerful indeed. Indeed, some forms of helplessness may well be caused by emotions as well as have emotional consequences. On the other hand, children who do not see their self-worth as threatened by achievement failure or do not worry they will be judged harshly would probably have far less painful emotions and might even have the opportunity to relish the challenge that a task presents. Consistent with the suggestions presented here, Matas, Arend, and Sroufe (1978) found that children who were securely attached to their mothers at age 12 months were more flexible and persistent than insecurely attached children in their attempts to solve two difficult achievement tasks at age 24 months. On the basis of attachment theory, Matas et al. (1978) argued that feelings of security enable children to explore freely but that feelings of insecurity inhibit free exploration. These results are consonant with the idea that affective processes related to beliefs about the self and others influence achievement motivation. Our understanding of how individual and gender differences in helplessness develop would be greatly enhanced by further research on how affective processes, especially as these pertain to beliefs about the self and other, shape children's responses to achievement tasks. Object-relations theory and attachment theory can provide the social–cognitive approach with a rich understanding of the emotional and interpersonal meaning individuals attach to their performance.

On the other hand, the advantage of the social–cognitive approach is in its detailed understanding of the cognitive mechanisms mediating achievement motivation. When attachment or object-relations studies uncover links between parent–child relationships and children's behavior in achievement settings, such as in Matas et al.'s (1978) study, there is typically little attempt to gather empirical evidence about the specific thoughts that occur as children encounter and react to the achievement task. Social–cognitive studies often focus directly on obtaining such evidence. Such studies have not yet related children's thoughts about themselves and the task to larger issues about how others judge them, but testable hypotheses can be generated readily. For example, children who are confident of their parents' love may be less concerned about how parents will judge or criticize their efforts, less likely to interpret their performance as reflecting negatively on the self, or both. Girls and boys may differ in the extent to which their feelings about their parents affect their achievement behavior. Such detailed predictions can illuminate future research on the mechanisms by which socialization processes affect development.

Our understanding of helplessness would benefit greatly from investigating how specific styles of parental interaction lead to cognitions and emotions about the self and others in children that in turn lead to particular achievement behaviors. Research asking how these processes may differ between girls and boys would be especially valuable. It is likely that all parents sometimes criticize their children and act in controlling ways and that all parents sometimes provide constructive praise of children's efforts. Object-relations theory can illuminate the means by which overt behaviors develop different emotional meanings in the context of different relationships. Social–cognitive theories in turn can specify the way in which these emotionally charged ideas about the self and others affect children's cognitive, affective, and behavioral responses when the children encounter challenging achievement tasks.

Conclusions

In this chapter I have described the helpless and mastery-oriented motivational patterns and argued that these arise from different beliefs about the nature of ability and different goals in achievement settings. Helpless individuals tend to emphasize performance goals and to see performance as a measure of their fixed ability, whereas mastery-oriented individuals tend to emphasize learning goals and to see performance as providing evidence about the usefulness of their strategies. Research in the last 10 years suggests that these patterns are also evident among young children and that, early in development, helplessness is related to performance concerns and beliefs about the global self. In elementary school and beyond, girls appear to be more vulnerable to helplessness than boys, but this difference has not appeared consistently among very young children.

Studies of the parent–child interaction patterns associated with different motivational styles indicate that helplessness is correlated with negative parental criticism of children's performance, especially criticism of their personal qualities, as well as with greater parental control and less autonomy granting as children work on achievement tasks. Moreover, parents appear more likely to give critical and controlling feedback to girls than to boys, which may explain girls' greater vulnerability to helplessness. Such critical and controlling feedback may lead children to question their ability or self-worth during failure and undermine children's efforts to find ways to meet and resolve challenges, although few studies to date provide direct evidence about how parent behaviors shape children's responses.

It is here that psychodynamic theory, specifically object-relations theory and closely related attachment theory, may enrich the social–cognitive approach to motivation. By offering an understanding of the emotional meaning of parental relationships for children, object-relations theory holds great promise for identifying the mechanisms by which parental behaviors lead to differences in children's motivational style.

The clinical implications of this work are numerous. For example, the social–cognitive approach suggests that helpless individuals would benefit from training in which they learn to reinterpret achievement outcomes as reflecting effort rather than ability (see also Dweck, 1975, 1999). The social–cognitive approach also suggests that family therapists should look for the combination of parental criticism of children's personal traits and high control without autonomy granting as predictors of helplessness in children. These parental behaviors can be directly targeted for intervention. Therapists influenced by object-relations theory can benefit from understanding how self-judgment processes influence achievement behavior. Object-relations theory, in turn, suggests that therapies influenced by the social–cognitive approach should also consider the manner in which family relationships contribute to certain types of self-beliefs and introjects, rather than simply addressing the beliefs themselves.

I now return to the case of Tanya, whose helpless episode I described at the outset of this chapter. Social–cognitive theory and evidence suggest that, although Tanya may be too young to have an implicit view of intelligence as a fixed entity, she probably holds performance goals of obtaining positive judgments or avoiding negative judgments of her personal qualities when she approaches challenging learning situations. She may also think that failure has implications for her global worth. Because she is a girl rather than a boy, she may be especially likely to feel concern for or awareness of others' opinions of her and to blame her personal qualities for her performance. Her parents may criticize her work and behavior in a negative manner that refers to her personal qualities, and they may also praise her ability frequently when she succeeds. Moreover, their interactions with her in achievement settings may be intrusive and controlling. Parental criticism and intrusive control are associated with helplessness in children generally, but parents of girls are especially likely to show these behaviors. Object-relations theory suggests that Tanya believes her parents will judge her poor performance harshly and that this belief has strong emotional ramifications.

To understand Tanya's response more fully and with greater confidence, though, it is necessary to conduct research on numerous additional topics. We need to know more about the stability of helplessness in young children and about the causal relations between parents' and children's behavior. We also need to understand more fully the issue of whether and how gender differences in helplessness become more prevalent in later childhood and the mechanisms by which this may happen. More research on how fathers as well as mothers influence individual differences in responses to failure is needed. Finally, children's beliefs about their parents' judgments, and the emotional meaning of parental standards for children, need to be examined. These unresolved questions should add a note of caution to attempts to translate the work reviewed here into therapeutic strategies, but they also suggest interesting and potentially fruitful ideas for future research.

References

Abramson, L. Y., Seligman, M. E. P., & Teasdale, J. D. (1978). Learned helplessness in humans: Critique and reformulation. *Journal of Abnormal Psychology, 87*, 49–74.

Adler, A. (1927). *Understanding human nature.* Garden City, NY: Doubleday Anchor.

Adler, A. (1930). *The education of children.* South Bend, IN: Gateway.

Adler, A. (1973). Advantages and disadvantages of the inferiority feeling. In H. L. Ansbacher & R. R. Ansbacher (Eds.), *Superiority and social interest* (pp. 50–58). New York: Viking.

Alessandri, S. M., & Lewis, M. (1993). Parental evaluation and its relation to pride and shame in young children. *Sex Roles, 29*, 335–343.

Ames, C., & Archer, J. (1988). Achievement goals in the classroom: Students' learning strategies and motivational processes. *Journal of Educational Psychology, 80*, 260–267.

Ansbacher, H. L., & Ansbacher, R. R. (1956). *The individual psychology of Alfred Adler.* New York: Basic Books.

Bandura, A., Barbaranelli, C., Caprara, G. V., & Pastorelli, C. (1996). Multifaceted impact of self-efficacy beliefs on academic functioning. *Child Development, 67*, 1206–1222.

Bandura, M., & Dweck, C. S. (1985). *The relationship of conceptions of intelligence and achievement goals to achievement-related cognition, affect, and behavior.* Unpublished manuscript, Harvard University.

Barrett, K. C., Zahn-Waxler, C., & Cole, P. M. (1993). Avoiders vs. amenders: Implications for the investigation of shame and guilt during toddlerhood? *Cognition and Emotion, 7,* 481–505.

Bartsch, K., & Wellman, H. (1989). Young children's attribution of action to beliefs and desires. *Child Development, 60,* 946–964.

Belsky, J., Domitrovich, C., & Crnic, K. (1997). Temperament and parenting antecedents of individual differences in three-year-old boys' pride and shame reactions. *Child Development, 68,* 456–466.

Blatt, S. J. (1974). Levels of object representation in anaclitic and introjective depression. *Psychoanalytic Study of the Child, 29,* 107–157.

Blatt, S. J. (1991). A cognitive morphology of psychopathology. *Journal of Nervous and Mental Disease, 179,* 449–458.

Blatt, S. J., & Homann, E. (1992). Parent–child interaction in the etiology of dependent and self-critical depression. *Clinical Psychology Review, 12,* 47–91.

Bornstein, R. F. (1992). The dependent personality: Developmental, social, and clinical perspectives. *Psychological Bulletin, 112,* 3–23.

Bornstein, R. F. (1996). Beyond orality: Toward an object relations/interactionist reconceptualization of the etiology and dynamics of dependency. *Psychoanalytic Psychology, 13,* 177–203.

Bornstein, R. F., Manning, K. A., Krukonis, A. B., Rossner, S. C., & Mastrosimone, C. C. (1993). Sex differences in dependency: A comparison of objective and projective measures. *Journal of Personality Assessment, 61,* 169–181.

Bowlby, J. (1980). *Attachment and loss: Vol. 3. Loss: Sadness and depression.* New York: Basic Books.

Brooks-Gunn, J., & Peterson, A. C. (1991). Studying the emergence of depression and depressive symptoms during adolescence. *Journal of Youth and Adolescence, 20,* 115–119.

Burhans, K. K., & Dweck, C. S. (1995). Helplessness in early childhood: The role of contingent self-worth. *Child Development, 66,* 1719–1738.

Cain, K. M., & Dweck, C. S. (1995). The relation between motivational patterns and achievement cognitions through the elementary school years. *Merrill–Palmer Quarterly, 41,* 25–52.

Cain, K. M., Gallagher, M., Staneck, C. H., & Myers, G. F. (1997, April). Shame and patterns of mother–child interaction among two- and three-year-olds. In P. A. Smiley (Chair), *Socialization of individual differences in achievement motivation.* Symposium conducted at the biennial meeting of the Society for Research in Child Development, Washington, DC.

Cain, K. M., Heyman, G. D., & Walker, M. E. (1997). Preschoolers' ability to make dispositional predictions within and across domains. *Social Development, 6,* 53–75.

Cain, K. M., & Staneck, C. H. (1999, April). *Shame, helplessness, and social cognition in preschoolers.* Poster presented at the biennial meeting of the Society for Research in Child Development, Albuquerque, NM.

Cantor, N., & Sanderson, C. A. (1998). The functional regulation of adolescent dating relationships and sexual behavior: An interaction of
goals, strategies, and situations. In J. Heckhausen & C. S. Dweck
(Eds.), *Motivation and self-regulation across the lifespan* (pp. 185–215).
New York: Cambridge University Press.

Cassidy, J. (1988). Child–mother attachment and the self in six-year-olds.
Child Development, 59, 121–134.

Cassidy, J. (1994). Emotion regulation: Influences of attachment relationships. *Monographs of the Society for Research in Child Development, 59*(2–
3, Serial No. 240).

Coulson, S. L. (2001). *Relations between parental emotional support and control,
children's cognitive ability, and children's helplessness: The mediating and
moderating role of self-concept.* Unpublished doctoral dissertation, Claremont Graduate University, Claremont, CA.

Deaux, K. (1976). Sex: A perspective on the attribution process. In J. H.
Harvey, W. J. Ickes, & R. F. Kidd (Eds.), *New directions in attribution
research* (Vol. 1, pp. 335–352). Hillsdale, NJ: Erlbaum.

Deci, E. L., & Ryan, R. M. (1987). The support of autonomy and the control
of behavior. *Journal of Personality and Social Psychology, 53,* 1024–1037.

Diener, C. I., & Dweck, C. S. (1978). An analysis of learned helplessness:
Continuous changes in performance, strategy, and achievement cognitions following failure. *Journal of Personality and Social Psychology,
36,* 451–461.

Diener, C. I., & Dweck, C. S. (1980). An analysis of learned helplessness
II: The processing of success. *Journal of Personality and Social Psychology, 39,* 940–952.

Duda, J. L. (1992). Goal orientations and beliefs about the causes of sport
success among elite skiers. *Sports Psychologist, 6,* 334–343.

Dweck, C. S. (1975). The role of expectations and attributions in the alle-
viation of learned helplessness. *Journal of Personality and Social Psychology, 31,* 674–685.

Dweck, C. S. (1999). *Self-theories: Their role in motivation, personality, and
development.* Philadelphia: Psychology Press.

Dweck, C. S., & Bush, E. S. (1976). Sex differences in learned helplessness:
(I) Differential debilitation with peer and adult evaluators. *Developmental Psychology, 12,* 147–156.

Dweck, C. S., Davidson, W., Nelson, S., & Enna, B. (1978). Sex differences
in learned helplessness: (II) The contingencies of evaluative feedback
in the classroom, and (III) An experimental analysis. *Developmental
Psychology, 14,* 268–276.

Dweck, C. S., & Elliot, E. S. (1983). Achievement motivation. In P. Mussen
& E. M. Hetherington (Eds.), *Handbook of child psychology* (pp. 643–
691). New York: Wiley.

Dweck, C. S., Goetz, T. E., & Strauss, N. (1980). Sex differences in learned
helplessness: (IV) An experimental and naturalistic study of failure

generalization and its mediators. *Journal of Personality and Social Psychology, 38,* 441–452.

Dweck, C. S., & Leggett, E. L. (1988). A social–cognitive approach to motivation and personality. *Psychological Review, 95,* 256–273.

Dweck, C. S., & Reppucci, N. D. (1973). Learned helplessness and reinforcement responsibility in children. *Journal of Personality and Social Psychology, 25,* 109–116.

Eccles, J. S., Adler, T. F., Futterman, R., Goff, S. B., Kaczala, C. M., Meece, J., et al. (1983). Expectancies, values and academic behaviors. In J. T. Spence (Ed.), *Achievement and achievement behaviors* (pp. 75–146). San Francisco: W. H. Freeman.

Eccles, J., Wigfield, A., Harold, R. D., & Blumenfeld, P. (1993). Age and gender differences in children's self- and task perceptions during elementary school. *Child Development, 64,* 830–847.

Erdley, C. A., Cain, K. M., Loomis, C. C., Dumas-Hines, F., & Dweck, C. S. (1997). The relations among children's social goals, implicit personality theories, and response to social failure. *Developmental Psychology, 33,* 263–272.

Erdley, C. A., & Dweck, C. S. (1993). Children's implicit theories as predictors of their social judgments. *Child Development, 64,* 863–878.

Erikson, E. H. (1963). *Childhood and society* (2nd ed.). New York: Norton.

Fincham, F. D., Hokoda, A., & Sanders, R. (1989). Learned helplessness, test anxiety, and academic achievement: A longitudinal analysis. *Child Development, 60,* 138–145.

Flink, C., Boggiano, A. K., & Barrett, M. (1990). Controlling teaching strategies: Undermining children's self-determination and performance. *Journal of Personality and Social Psychology, 59,* 916–924.

Freud, S. (1953). Three assays on the theory of sexuality. In J. Strachey (Ed.), *The standard edition of the complete psychological works of Sigmund Freud* (Vol. 7, pp. 125–143). London: Hogarth. (Original work published 1905)

Freud, S. (1955). From the history of an infantile neurosis. In J. Strachey (Ed.), *The standard edition of the complete psychological works of Sigmund Freud* (Vol. 17, pp. 3–122). London: Hogarth. (Original work published 1918)

Freud, S. (1961a). The ego and the id. In J. Strachey (Ed.), *The standard edition of the complete psychological works of Sigmund Freud* (Vol. 19, pp. 3–66). London: Hogarth. (Original work published 1923)

Freud, S. (1961b). Some psychical consequencies of the anatomical distinction between the sexes. In J. Strachey (Ed.), *The standard edition of the complete psychological works of Sigmund Freud* (Vol. 19, pp. 243–258). London: Hogarth. (Original work published 1925)

Freud, S. (1964). An outline of psycho-analysis. In J. Strachey (Ed.), *The standard edition of the complete psychological works of Sigmund Freud* (Vol. 23, pp. 141–207). London: Hogarth. (Original work published 1940)

Heckhausen, J., & Dweck, C. S. (1998). Introduction: A developmental and process-oriented approach to motivation and self-regulation. In J. Heckhausen & C. S. Dweck (Eds.), *Motivation and self-regulation across the life span* (pp. 1–11). New York: Cambridge University Press.

Henderson, V., & Dweck, C. S. (1990). Achievement and motivation in adolescence: A new model and data. In S. Feldman & G. Elliott (Eds.), *At the threshold: The developing adolescent* (pp. 308–329). Cambridge, MA: Harvard University Press.

Heyman, G. D., & Dweck, C. S. (1998). Children's thinking about traits: Implications for judgments of self and others. *Child Development, 64,* 391–403.

Heyman, G. D., Dweck, C. S., & Cain, K. M. (1992). Young children's vulnerability to self-blame and helplessness. *Child Development, 63,* 401–415.

Heyman, G. D., & Gelman, S. A. (1998). Young children use motive information to make trait inferences. *Developmental Psychology, 34,* 310–321.

Heyman, G. D., & Gelman, S. A. (1999). The use of trait labels in making psychological inferences. *Child Development, 70,* 604–619.

Hoffman, L. W., & Kloska, D. D. (1995). Parents' gender-based attitudes toward marital roles and child rearing: Development and validation of new measures. *Sex Roles, 32,* 273–295.

Horney, K. (1937). *The neurotic personality of our time.* New York: Norton.

Horney, K. (1939). *New ways in psychoanalysis.* New York: Norton.

Horney, K. (1945). *Our inner conflicts.* New York: Norton.

Horney, K. (1967). *Feminine psychology.* New York: Norton.

Jacklin, C. N., DiPietro, J. A., & Maccoby, E. E. (1984). Sex-typing behavior and sex-typing pressure in child/parent interaction. *Archives of Sexual Behavior, 13,* 413–425.

Kamins, M. L., & Dweck, C. S. (1999). Person vs. process praise and criticism: Implications for contingent self-worth and coping. *Developmental Psychology, 35,* 835–847.

Keenan, K., & Shaw, D. (1997). Developmental and social influences on young girls' early problem behavior. *Psychological Bulletin, 121,* 95–113.

Kelley, S. A., Brownell, C. A., & Campbell, S. B. (2000). Mastery motivation and self-evaluative affect in toddlers: Longitudinal relations with maternal behavior. *Child Development, 71,* 1061–1071.

Klein, M. (1981). On Mahler's autistic and symbiotic phases: An exposition and evaluation. *Psychoanalysis and Contemporary Thought, 4,* 69–105.

Kohut, H. (1977). *The restoration of the self.* New York: International Universities Press.

Leggett, E. (1985, March). *Children's entity and incremental theories of intelligence: Relationships to achievement behavior.* Paper presented at the annual meeting of the Eastern Psychological Association, Boston.

Lenney, E. (1977). Women's self-confidence in achievement settings. *Psychological Bulletin, 84,* 1–13.

Lewis, H. B. (1971). *Shame and guilt in neurosis*. New York: International Universities Press.

Lewis, M. (1992). *Shame: The exposed self*. New York: Free Press.

Lewis, M. (1993). Self-conscious emotions: Embarrassment, pride, shame, and guilt. In M. Lewis & J. M. Haviland (Eds.), *Handbook of emotions* (pp. 563–573). New York: Guilford Press.

Lewis, M., Alessandri, S., & Sullivan, M. W. (1992). Differences in shame and pride as a function of children's gender and task difficulty. *Child Development, 63,* 630–638.

Licht, B. G., & Dweck, C. S. (1983). Sex differences in achievement orientations: Consequences for academic choices and attainments. In M. Marland (Ed.), *Sex differentiation and schooling* (pp. 72–97). London: Heinemann Educaitonal Books.

Licht, B. G., & Dweck, C. S. (1984). Determinants of academic achievement: The interaction of children's achievement orientations with skill area. *Developmental Psychology, 20,* 628–636.

Licht, B. G., & Shapiro, S. H. (1982, August). *Sex differences in attributions among high achievers*. Paper presented at the 90th Annual Convention of the American Psychological Association, Washington, DC.

Lytton, H., & Romney, D. M. (1991). Parents' differential socialization of boys and girls: A meta-analysis. *Psychological Bulletin, 109,* 267–296.

Maccoby, E. E., & Jacklin, C. N. (1974). *The psychology of sex differences*. Stanford, CA: Stanford University Press.

Mahler, M., Pine, F., & Bergman, A. (1975). *The psychological birth of the human infant*. New York: Basic Books.

Main, M., Kaplan, N., & Cassidy, J. (1985). Security in infancy, childhood, and adulthood: A move to the level of representation. *Monographs of the Society for Research in Child Development, 50*(1–2, Serial No. 209).

Matas, L., Arend, R. A., & Sroufe, L. A. (1978). Continuity of adaptation in the second year: The relationship between quality of attachment and later competence. *Child Development, 49,* 547–556.

McClelland, D., Koestner, R., & Weinberger, J. (1989). How do self-attributed and implicit motives differ? *Psychological Review, 56,* 690–702.

Miller, A. T. (1985). A developmental study of the cognitive basis of performance impairment after failure. *Journal of Personality and Social Psychology, 49,* 529–538.

Mueller, C. M., & Dweck, C. S. (1998). Intelligence praise can undermine motivation and performance. *Journal of Personality and Social Psychology, 75,* 33–52.

Nicholls, J. G. (1975). Causal attributions and other achievement-related cognitions: Effects of task outcome, attainment value, and sex. *Journal of Personality and Social Psychology, 31,* 379–389.

Nicholls, J. G. (1978). The development of the concepts of effort and ability, perception of academic attainment and the understanding that difficult tasks require more ability. *Child Development, 49,* 800–814.

Nicholls, J. G., & Miller, A. T. (1984). Development and its discontents: The differentiation of the concept of ability. In J. G. Nicholls (Ed.), *The development of achievement motivation* (pp. 185–218). Greenwich, CT: JAI Press.

Nolen-Hoeksema, S. (1990). *Sex differences in depression*. Stanford, CA: Stanford University Press.

Nolen-Hoeksema, S., & Girgus, J. S. (1994). The emergence of gender differences in depression during adolescence. *Psychological Bulletin, 115,* 424–443.

Nolen-Hoeksema, S., Girgus, J. S., & Seligman, M. E. P. (1986). Learned helplessness in children: A longitudinal study of depression, achievement, and explanatory style. *Journal of Personality and Social Psychology, 51,* 435–442.

Nolen-Hoeksema, S., Girgus, J. S., & Seligman, M. E. P. (1992). Predictors and consequences of childhood depressive symptoms: A 5-year longitudinal study. *Journal of Abnormal Psychology, 101,* 405–422.

Nolen-Hoeksema, S., Larson, J., & Grayson, C. (1999). Explaining the gender difference in depressive symptoms. *Journal of Personality and Social Psychology, 77,* 1061–1072.

Nolen-Hoeksema, S., Wolfson, A., Mumme, D., & Guskin, K. (1995). Helplessness in children of depressed and nondepressed mothers. *Developmental Psychology, 31,* 377–387.

Osofsky, J. D. (1995). Perspectives on attachment and psychoanalysis. *Psychoanalytic Psychology, 12,* 347–362.

Parsons, J. E., & Ruble, D. N. (1977). The development of achievement-related expectancies. *Child Development, 48,* 1075–1079.

Phillips, D. A. (1987). Socialization of perceived academic competence among highly competent children. *Child Development, 58,* 1308–1320.

Pomerantz, E. M., & Ruble, D. N. (1997). Distinguishing multiple dimensions and conceptions of ability: Implications for self-evaluation. *Child Development, 68,* 1165–1180.

Pomerantz, E. M., & Ruble, D. N. (1998). The role of maternal control in the development of sex differences in child self-evaluative factors. *Child Development, 69,* 458–478.

Rholes, W. S., Blackwell, J., Jordan, C., & Walters, C. (1980). A developmental study of learned helplessness. *Developmental Psychology, 16,* 616–624.

Rholes, W. S., Jones, M., & Wade, C. (1988). Children's understanding of personal dispositions and its relationship to behavior. *Journal of Experimental Child Psychology, 45,* 1–17.

Rholes, W. S., Newman, L. S., & Ruble, D. N. (1990). Understanding self and other: Developmental and motivational aspects of perceiving persons in terms of invariant dispositions. In E. T. Higgins & R. M. Sorrentino (Eds.), *Handbook of motivation and cognition: Foundations of social behavior* (Vol. 2, pp. 369–407). New York: Guilford Press.

Roberts, T. (1991). Gender and the influence of evaluation on self-assessments in achievement settings. *Psychological Bulletin, 109,* 297–308.

Rothbart, M. K., & Bates, J. E. (1998). Temperament. In W. Damon (Series Ed.) & N. Eisenberg (Vol. Ed.), *Handbook of child psychology: Vol. 3. Social, emotional, and personality development* (5th ed., pp. 105–176). New York: Wiley.

Ruble, D. N., Boggiano, A. K., Feldman, N. S., & Loebl, J. H. (1980). Developmental analysis of the role of social comparison in self-evaluation. *Developmental Psychology, 16,* 105–115.

Ruble, D. N., Greulich, F., Pomerantz, E. M., & Gochberg, B. (1993). The role of gender-related processes in the development of sex differences in sex differences in self-evaluation and depression. *Journal of Affective Disorders, 29,* 97–128.

Sears, R. R., Maccoby, E. E., & Levin, H. (1957). *Patterns of child rearing.* Evanston, IL: Row Peterson.

Sears, R. R., Rau, L., & Alpert, R. (1965). *Identifications and child rearing.* Stanford, CA: Stanford University Press.

Slomkowski, C. (1993, March). *The relationship between young children's response to criticism and social cognitive and moral development.* Poster presented at the biennial meeting of the Society for Research in Child Development, New Orleans, LA.

Smiley, P. A., & Dweck, C. S. (1994). Individual differences in achievement goals among young children. *Child Development, 65,* 1723–1743.

Smiley, P. A., & Tan, S. J. (2001, April). *Temperament and parenting influences on achievement in young children.* Poster presented at the biennial meeting of the Society for Research in Child Development, Minneapolis, MN.

Stipek, D. J. (1984). Young children's performance expectations: Logical analysis or wishful thinking. In J. G. Nicholls (Ed.), *The development of achievement motivation* (pp. 33–56). Greenwich, CT: JAI Press.

Stipek, D. J., & Gralinski, J. H. (1991). Gender differences in children's achievement-related beliefs and emotional responses to success and failure in mathematics. *Journal of Educational Psychology, 83,* 361–371.

Stipek, D. J., & Hoffman, J. (1980). Development of children's performance-related judgments. *Child Development, 51,* 912–914.

Stipek, D. J., Recchia, S., & McClintic, S. (1992). Self-evaluation in young children. *Monographs of the Society for Research in Child Development, 57*(1, Serial No. 226)

Updegraff, K. A., McHale, S. M., & Crouter, A. C. (1996). Gender roles in marriage: What do they mean for girls' and boys' school achievement? *Journal of Youth and Adolescence, 25,* 73–88.

Weiner, B. (1986). *An attributional theory of motivation and emotion.* New York: Springer-Verlag.

Weissman, M. M., & Klerman, G. L. (1977). Sex differences in the epidemiology of depression. *Archives of General Psychiatry, 34,* 98–111.

Wentzel, K. (1996). Social goals and social relationships as motivators of school adjustment. In J. Juvonen & K. Wentzel (Eds.), *Social motivation* (pp. 226–247). New York: Cambridge University Press.

Westen, D. (1998). The scientific legacy of Sigmund Freud: Toward a psychodynamically informed psychological science. *Psychological Bulletin*, 333–371.

Zahn-Waxler, C., Cole, P. M., & Barrett, K. C. (1991). Guilt and empathy: Sex differences and implications for the development of depression. In K. Dodge & J. Garber (Eds.), *Emotional regulation and dysregulation* (pp. 243–267). New York: Cambridge University Press.

Chapter 2

Gender Differences in Primary Process Thinking and Creativity

Sandra W. Russ

Consistent gender differences in primary process thinking have been found in the research literature both in the amount of primary process expressed and in the relation between primary process and creativity. In general, primary process thinking has been found to relate to creativity in males, but not in females. In this chapter I review the role of primary process in creativity from the perspectives of psychoanalysis and cognitive psychology. I also review the research literature with a focus on gender differences and discuss possible theoretical explanations for gender differences in primary process thinking.

Primary Process Thinking

S. Freud (1915/1958) first conceptualized primary process thought as an early, primitive system of thought that was drive laden and

53

not subject to rules of logic or oriented to reality. One example is the kind of thinking that occurs in dreams. Dreams are illogical, are not oriented to the rules of time and space, and frequently include affect-laden content and images. Dudek (1980) thought of primary process as the surfacing of unconscious instinctual energy in the form of images and ideas. Holt (1977) categorized the drive-laden content in primary process thought as oral, aggressive, and libidinal.

Primary process has usually been regarded as a blend of cognitive and affective processes (Martindale, 1981; Zimiles, 1981). As Holt (1977) developed a system to measure primary process thinking, he defined both *content properties*, which include affect-laden oral, aggressive, and libidinal content, and *formal properties*, which include qualities of illogical thinking, *condensation* (fusion of two ideas or images), and loose associations. Formal expressions of primary process may or may not go together. These definitions of primary process thinking imply a cognitive component and an affective component.

Affect is theoretically a major component of primary process thinking. The concepts of drive-laden and instinctual energy bring one into the realm of affect. Rapaport (1951) used the phrase *affect-charge* in discussing primary process thought. S. Freud (1895/1966), in "The Project for a Scientific Psychology," stated that primary process thought is frequently accompanied by affect. I (Russ, 1987) proposed that primary process is a subtype of affective content in cognition. Primary process content is material around which the child has experienced early intense feeling states (e.g., oral, anal, aggressive). Learning to regulate these intense emotions and affect-laden thoughts and images is a major developmental task. Broad individual differences exist in how people think about primary process content, express it in fantasy and play, and integrate it into fantasy and imagination. Pine and Holt (1960) suggested that primary process becomes a kind of cognitive style that reflects how one deals with affective material. I (Russ, 1987) proposed that current primary process expressions may reflect either current affect or a kind of "affective residue" in cognition left over from earlier developmental stages.

Primary Process Thinking and Creativity

Psychoanalytic Theory

Psychoanalytic theory has long postulated a relation between access to primary process thinking and creativity. S. Freud's (1926/1959) formulation that repression of "dangerous" drive-laden content leads to a more general intellectual restriction predicts that individuals with less access to affect-laden thoughts would have fewer associations in general. The psychoanalytic concept of repression involves the warding off of the feeling of instinctive impulses or the ideational representations of instincts (A. Freud, 1936/1966). Both the feeling and the thought associated with the feeling are repressed. The purpose of repression is to reduce the anxiety and conflict by reducing the awareness of the "dangerous" content. If there is too little repression, then the individual can be overwhelmed by inappropriate images and affects, such as in the manic phases associated with bipolar disorder. If there is too much repression, then a major constriction of thinking can occur. Individuals who have the ability to access primary process ideation in a controlled fashion (i.e., not be overwhelmed) should theoretically have many associations.

In psychoanalytic theory, S. Freud focused on sublimation as an important factor in creativity. As Arieti (1976) discussed, the concept of *sublimation*, or diversion of sexual energy from the original aim, was central to Freud's conceptualization of creativity. Sexual or libidinal energy is displaced in creative endeavors, and wish fulfillment is essential in creative work. Arieti pointed out that this approach focused on the motivation behind creative work, not on the actual process itself. However, S. Freud's writings on repression and intellectual restriction provide a framework for understanding the creative processes involved, and he (1907/1989) recognized the similarity between processes involved in children's play and creative work.

In classic psychoanalytic theory, access to primary process thought has been hypothesized to relate to creative thinking because associations are fluid and primitive images and ideas can be accessed and used. According to classic psychoanalytic theory, primary process thinking is characterized by "mobility of cathexis"; that is, the energy behind the ideas and images is easily displaced (Arlow & Brenner, 1964), leading to a free flow of energy not bound by specific ideas or objects. In this mode of thinking ideas are easily interchangeable, and attention is widely and flexibly distributed. Consequently, access to primary process thinking should facilitate a fluidity of thought and flexibility of search among all ideas and associations. Martindale (1989) stated that "because primary process cognition is associative, it makes the discovery of new combinations of mental elements more likely" (p. 216).

Much similarity exists between characteristics of primary process thinking and characteristics of two of the most important cognitive processes involved in creative thinking. According to Guilford (1968), divergent thinking and transformation abilities are the major cognitive processes that are unique to the creative process. *Divergent thinking* refers to the ability to generate a variety of associations to a word or solutions to a problem, and it flows in a number of directions. A typical item on a divergent-thinking test would be "How many uses for a brick can you think of?" A high scorer on this test would generate many different, acceptable uses for the object. Individuals who can use primary process and the fluidity of thought and breadth of associations inherent in it should be highly divergent thinkers. They should also score high on tests of Guilford's second important cognitive process: *transformation abilities*, which involve the ability to transform or revise what one knows into new patterns or configurations and to be flexible and break out of an old set. Again, the broad associations and flexible thinking characteristic of primary process should facilitate transformation abilities. Although there are cognitive processes involved in creative thinking other than divergent-production and transformation abilities, the role of primary process thinking has been thought to be most important in these two categories. Most of the research that has investigated the relation between primary process and creativity has focused on these two cognitive processes.

Kris's (1952) concept of "regression in the service of the ego" stresses the importance of control of primary process thinking. Kris postulated that creative individuals could regress, in a controlled fashion, and tap into primary process thinking. The individual could go back and forth between early, primary process thought and more mature, rational, secondary process thinking. Regression was an important concept because the individual could, at will, go back to an earlier, primitive mode of thought and use it adaptively for creative purposes. Creative individuals, as distinguished from individuals with thought disorders, are in charge of this regressive process and can logically evaluate the loose, primitive associations and images. I (Russ, 1993) presented creative individuals' descriptions of the creative process that describe getting in touch with primary process thinking. One good example is a description of the free flow of associations in a monologue by the comedian Robin Williams. In commenting about the process, he said,

> And sometimes there are times when you're just on it when you say the muse is with you and it's just flowing and that's when you stand back and say "yes"—you're in control but you're not —the characters are coming through you." (quoted in Culbane, 1988, pp. 1–5)

Several features of the conceptualization of primary process thinking according to classic psychoanalytic theory have limited the influence of primary process theory on current creativity research. First, as Urist (1980) pointed out, primary process thinking is based on the energy model. Most contemporary approaches have moved away from this conception of instinctual energy. A second feature, regression, has also been difficult to operationalize and test. However, recent discussions have moved away from both the energy model and the concept of regression. Holt (1967) proposed a structural model for primary process thought, with primary process as a group of structures having its own course of development. Noy (1969) also viewed primary process as developing its own structure. Arieti (1976) and Suler (1980) have suggested that the concept of regression to an earlier mode of thought may not be necessary. They both proposed that primary process may be a separate entity that develops simultaneously with secondary process thought. Arieti proposed the tertiary process, which integrates primary process thinking into secondary process thought. Rothenberg (1994) also proposed different processes that would transform primary process material. On the basis of interviews with novelists, poets, and playwrights, he proposed three ego processes important in creativity that are logic-transcending operations: (a) homospatial processes, in which visual images are superimposed on one another; (b) Janusian processes, in which the person simultaneously conceives of opposites; and (c) articulation, joining, and separating elements in a constant reworking process. Fischer and Pipp (1984) thought of primary process as a separate mode of thought that followed its own systematic developmental line. The implications of these conceptualizations are that the mechanism for access to primary process may be not regression but an entirely different kind of system.

Recent Conceptualizations

Contemporary theories in cognitive psychology explain the relation between primary process thinking and creativity without concepts of energy and regression. I (Russ, 1996) placed the primary process and creativity link within current theoretical models in cognitive psychology.

Recent research on the role of affective processes in creative production has found relations between access to affect-laden thoughts and divergent thinking (Russ & Grossman-McKee, 1990) and facilitation effects for positive emotional states on divergent thinking (Isen, 1999; Isen, Daubman, & Nowicki, 1987). The involvement of emotion theoretically broadens the search process for associations in creative problem solving by triggering associated memories and thoughts (Isen, 1999; Russ, 1993, 1999). Isen, Daubman, and Nowicki (1987) were the first to apply Bower's (1981) associative network theory to creative thinking. Bower's theory proposed that each emotion is a memory unit—each emotion has a special node or unit in memory. The activation of the emotion unit aids the retrieval of events associated with it. It primes emotional thematic imagery for use in free association, fantasies, and perceptual categorization. Rholes, Riskind, and Lane (1987) expanded Bower's theory and discussed mood-related cognitions. Affect states activate a set of relevant, mood-related cognitions, and a cognitive priming process occurs. Primary process can be conceptualized as mood-relevant cognition (Russ, 1993) that triggers related associations in memory.

A more recent theoretical model is Getz and Lubart's (1999) emotional resonance model of creativity, in which emotions contribute to the access and association of cognitively remote concepts in memory. In this model emotions become attached to concepts or images labeled *endocepts*. Associations are emotion based and may resonate with each other when triggered. Endocepts attached to concepts resonate with each other and link concepts in memory.

I (Russ, 1993) speculated that individuals open to affect states and affect-laden cognition benefit in carrying out creative tasks in two ways. First, they have access to more cues that activate other nodes in the search process. More associations occur. Second, more emotionally salient material is coded and stored when an individual is in an emotional state. For individuals open to affect, more would "get in," thus providing a richer network of affect-relevant associations. This storing of affective content is especially important for artistic creativity, where one is often dealing with affect and the transformation of affect content into universal symbols. Evidence shows that creative people are more sensitive and open to experience than are noncreative people (McCrae & Costa, 1987; Richards, 1990). Affective processes could then guide the search process for associations (Russ, 1999). The triggering of networks of mood-relevant associations would access sets of associations especially relevant to the problem on which one is working. This would be especially true of artistic creativity. For example, a painter attempting to capture the pain of loneliness would search a set of mood-relevant images and memories. Affect would partially determine which set of associations was triggered.

Affect could guide the search process in another way. As ideas, associations, or images are generated, some are more salient than others. Affect would guide the selection process. Consistent with Damasio's (1994) hypotheses of the somatic marker, a constant interaction exists between cognition and emotion in decision making. Affect would guide the generation of associations and the continual evaluation of the emerging associations.

In Damasio's (1994) somatic-marker hypothesis cognitive images become marked with physiological responses that reflect emotions. Damasio applied his model to decision making, and it is also applicable to divergent thinking. As associations occur, they are highlighted (or made salient) by positive and negative emotional responses. These emotional and physiological responses are rapid and often out of awareness, or unconscious (Damasio, 1994; Simon, 1998). Damasio quoted the creative mathematician Henri Poincarè, who described a nonrandom process of associations. Poincarè (Ghiselin, 1952) stated that creation involves making "useful" combinations of ideas. One sifts through a minority of useful possibilities, as though a preselection process had already occurred. Only potentially useful associations are considered. This may oversimplify the process, but it is consistent with the concept of a guided-association process.

A third way in which affect can guide the generation of variations is in the transformation of personal experiences, memories, and images into universal images that occurs in truly great art. Often artists incorporate early conflicts and traumas into their art (Niederland, 1976). Understanding exactly how these complex transformations occur is a task for future researchers.

Primary process thinking might be conceptualized as mood-relevant cognition, occurring when emotion nodes are activated. Perhaps emotion and cognition are fused in many primary process thoughts. If, as I (Russ, 1987) proposed, primary process is a subtype of affect in cognition that consists of content around which the child had experienced early intense feeling states (e.g., oral, anal, aggressive), then current primary process expressions could reflect these early encodings of fused affect and cognition. The primary process content was stored when emotion was present. Access to this content would activate nodes and associations, thus broadening the search process.

It also is possible that some cognitive and affective components of primary process are separate dimensions. This conceptualization would be consistent with Zajonc's (1980, 1990) view that affect and cognition can at times be two separate processes. Affective reactions can occur without prior involvement of cognitive processes. Cognition and affect are two interacting but independent functions. Furthermore, some stimuli pull for affective responses without cognitive involvement.

Zajonc's (1980, 1990) hypothesis is consistent with recent work by LeDoux (1989). In research with rats, LeDoux found that the amygdala triggers an emotional reaction before the thinking brain has fully processed the nerve signals. The amygdala can receive input from the senses before the input goes through the cortex. LeDoux, in regard to the existence of emotional memories, discovered neural pathways that do not pass through the cortex. Thus, the emotional system can act independently of the cognitive system. LeDoux suggested that these precognitive emotions are functional in infants during the early formative years. Behavior is affected with no conscious memory of the events.

Primary process thinking could involve pure cognitive components. For example, Martindale (1989) theorized that creative individuals engage more than noncreative individuals in states of defocused attention, during which many nodes (neurons or groups of neurons) are activated simultaneously. Defocused attention is more likely to occur during low cortical arousal, with evidence that primary process thinking involves defocused attention and low cortical arousal (Martindale, 1981).

Primary process could be a mode of thinking dominant in processing stimuli that are unconscious or below the level of awareness. In a review of the literature on subliminal perception, Masling (1992) concluded that the spread of associations is greater when stimuli do not quite reach awareness. Spence and Holland (1962) found that subliminal presentation of a word resulted in greater recall of associated words than either no presentation or above-threshold presentation of the word. They speculated that a different pattern of cognitive activity with different associative processes operated when awareness is reduced. Masling hypothesized that a "subliminal message stimulates a broad band of association pathways, allowing a spread of activation over a wide area of association traces" (p. 273). This broad band would facilitate tasks requiring divergent thinking and transformation abilities.

None of the various theoretical approaches—classic psychoanalytic theory or more recent conceptualizations—predict gender differences in the role of primary process thinking in creativity. However, gender differences in the relation between primary process and creativity have been repeatedly found. In the rest of this chapter I focus on gender differences in the research literature and possible explanations for them.

Gender Differences in Empirical Studies

Primary process thinking has been investigated in samples of narrative expression, dream reports, play samples, drawings, and Rorschach responses. In most of those studies, primary process thinking was related to creativity in males, but not in females. Much of the research investigating primary process thinking and creativity has used Holt's Scoring System for Primary Process Responses on the Rorschach (Holt, 1977; Holt & Havel, 1960). Researchers have not attempted to separate the cognitive dimension from the affective dimension of primary process thinking. Most of the research in the area has been reviewed by Holt (1977), Suler (1980), and myself (Russ, 1993, 1996).

Holt (1977) made a major contribution to the field by operationalizing the construct of primary process thinking and developing a scoring system for the Rorschach that could achieve good interrater reliability and convincing validity data. As I (Russ, 1993) described, the Holt system scores the responses that contain primary process content (aggressive and libidinal content that actually encompasses a broad range of affective content). The system measures the percentage of primary process content in the Rorschach protocol and the effectiveness of the control of that content. A controlled response expresses primary process content in a way that fits the form of the blot and is appropriately qualified. For example, two talking bugs can be made into a more appropriate response by making them cartoon figures. Holt's system also measures formal characteristics of thought, such as condensation and illogical associations. Although the scale was developed by Holt for use with adults, when used with children, it largely measures primary process content and adaptiveness of that content. Scorings of formal characteristics are a very small percentage in children's protocols (Dudek, 1975; Russ, 1982). Major scores in Holt's scoring system include the percentage of primary process responses in the entire protocol; the Defense Demand score, which measures the intensity of the content; the Defense Effectiveness score, which measures the control and cognitive integration of primary process responses; and the Adaptive Regression (AR) score, which measures both the intensity of the primary process content and the integration of the content. The Holt system measures both access to affect-laden material and the cognitive integration of that material. Scores on Holt's system show whether an individual can allow affect-laden content to surface and be expressed and how well controlled and well integrated that content is in cognition.

In adults, the AR score on the Rorschach has been significantly positively related to several measures of creativity (Cohen, 1961; Pine & Holt, 1960) and to problem-solving efficiency (Blatt, Allison, & Feirstein, 1969). The AR score was related to divergent thinking in Pine and Holt's (1960) study and to the ability to make remote associations (Murray & Russ, 1981). Gamble and Kellner (1968) found that creative individuals had greater access to primary process. Dudek (1968) reported more primitive primary process content (Level I in Holt's system) in artists than in nonartists and more primitive primary process in good artists than in poor artists. She also found that top-ranked creative architects produced more libidinal primary process content than did lower ranked architects (Dudek, 1984).

Gender differences consistently have been reported in studies of adults. Holt (1977) stated that, in general, in studies that relate AR with creativity criteria, "negative findings from well-executed studies came entirely from samples of females" (p. 413). The relation between AR and divergent thinking (Pine & Holt, 1960) and between AR and associational fluency (Murray & Russ, 1981) occurred in adult men but not in adult women. In Murray and Russ's (1981) study, the correlation between AR and the Remote Associates Test was $r = .36$, $p < .05$, for men, and $r = -.27$ for women. Suler's (1980) thorough review of the literature also concluded that gender is an important moderator variable. C. Martindale (personal communication, May 10, 2001) measured undergraduate students' primary process on the Thematic Apperception Test (TAT) with his software scoring system, a computerized content analysis (Martindale & Dailey, 1996) and found that primary process thinking related to creativity in men but not in women (C. Martindale, personal communication, May 10, 2001).

In children, age, gender, and specific measures and scores emerge as important factors. Dudek (1975), one of the first researchers to study children in this context, found no relation between primary process thinking on the Rorschach and divergent thinking on the Torrance Tests of Creative Thinking (Torrance,

1968) in fourth graders. However, primary process expression on a drawing task was related to divergent thinking. Dudek concluded that the relation between primary process and creativity is ambiguous in childhood and that children have not yet learned to use adaptively primary process. Dudek and Verreault (1989) found that creative children (fifth and sixth graders) gave significantly more total primary process ideation than did noncreative children, as measured by Holt's system as applied to the Torrance tests. Creative children also demonstrated more effective use of regression in the service of the ego than did noncreative children when popular responses were used to determine defense effectiveness. Dudek (1975) and Dudek and Verreault (1989) did not report possible gender differences.

Rogolsky (1968) found no relation between AR scores and artistic creativity in third-grade children; however, a new adaptive regression score that combined the amount of primary process with control measures for the entire Rorschach protocol (including populars) did significantly relate to artistic creativity for third-grade boys but not for girls.

My (Russ, 1980, 1981, 1982, 1988) investigations of primary process on the Rorschach, achievement, and creativity in children have obtained positive results (a full review of my research can be found in Russ, 1993). However, gender differences repeatedly occurred, with different scores within Holt's system predicting creativity in different studies. In all of the studies each child was individually administered the Rorschach according to Exner's (1974) system. Holt's (1970) scoring manual for primary process was followed exactly, except for two minor adaptations for use with a child population. There was no affect inquiry. However, affective expressions, verbal and nonverbal, were noted by the examiner and considered in the scoring. Also, the percept of spider was scored as an aggressive percept and given a low intensity rating, except for the common spider on Card X, which was not scored. Typical aggressive content in children's protocols were fighting animals, monsters, exploding volcanoes, blood, and scary insects. Typical oral responses were people eating, food, and mouths. In my studies the mean percentage of primary process content in the entire Rorschach protocol was about 50% for these child populations.

In the first study (Russ, 1980) I found a significant positive relation between AR scores and reading achievement in second-grade children, $r(37) = .54$, $p < .001$. This relation remained significant ($r = .45$) after IQ was partialed out and when productivity and general perceptual accuracy (F+ %) were partialed out. In a follow-up with these children when they were in the third grade the size of the relation between third-grade AR scores and reading achievement remained consistent, $r(39) = .52$, $p < .001$ (Russ, 1981). Although reading achievement does not specifically speak to creativity, the underlying rationale for using this criterion was that children who had access to primary process thinking and integrated it well would be flexible problem solvers and be open to ideas. Thus, they should be better learners than children with less access to primary process content. There were no significant gender differences between the means on the primary process measures. There was a noteworthy, although not significant, difference in the strength of the correlation between AR scores and reading in the second grade (boys, $r = .66$; girls, $r = .24$).

In my next series of studies I specifically investigated the relation between primary process thinking and creativity. In the first of these studies (Russ, 1982) I focused on the relation between primary process thinking and transformation abilities in third-grade children using Holt's scoring system for the Rorschach as the primary process measure. For a measure of flexibility of thinking for young children, I adapted the Luchins's Water-Jar Test (Luchins & Luchins, 1959). The task requires the child to break out of an old set in solving a problem and to discover a new, more adaptive approach. The child must see new relations in old patterns and be able to shift sets.

I found that, for boys, the AR score was significantly related to flexibility of shifting sets in both samples of children (Russ, 1982); that is, the ability to express well-controlled primary process content on the Rorschach was related to the ability to shift problem-solving strategies. I replicated this result with a second sample of children, which suggests the stability and robustness of this relation. When samples were combined, the size of the correlation was .39 ($df = 34$), $p < .01$. This relation was independent of IQ. For girls in both samples, AR was not related to the Luchins and Luchins's (1959) task. In the second sample the pure percentage of primary process predicted flexibility of shifting sets, $r(17) = .43$, $p < .05$, for girls.

In the next study (Russ, 1988) I investigated the relation between divergent thinking and primary process in a follow-up study of 53 fifth-grade children who remained from the third-grade samples. The results were significant for boys but not for girls. AR scores and percentages of primary process were significantly related to the Alternate Uses Test (Wallach & Kogan, 1965) for boys: $rs(27) = .34$ and $.33$, $p < .05$, respectively. Primary process scores did not predict divergent thinking for girls.

Russ and Grossman-McKee (1990) obtained the same pattern of gender differences in a study of second-grade children. For boys, percentage of primary process on the Rorschach predicted divergent thinking on the Alternate Uses Test, $r(20) = .72$, $p < .001$, a relation independent of intelligence. There was no significant relation for girls. AR did not predict divergent thinking for either gender. Perhaps, in children this young, the frequency of primary process expression rather than the integration of primary process is the more important aspect of primary process in creativity. Dudek and Verreault (1989) also made this point. Rogolsky (1968) speculated that young children do not yet show primary process and good control in the same response.

In all of my studies with the Rorschach I have found gender differences in the magnitude of the correlations between primary process and creativity. At times, the differences between the correlations for boys and girls were significant, and at other times the differences approached significance. The pattern was consistent. For boys, primary process was significantly related to divergent thinking and to transformation abilities. The integration of primary process material (AR) was usually the best predictor, but percentage of primary process content was also a significant predictor in several studies. For girls, there was generally no significant relation between any primary process scores and creativity. In one study (Russ, 1982), percentage of primary process did predict flexibility on Luchins and Luchins's (1959) Water-Jar Test.

The studies with children have shown the same gender differences in the pattern of correlations between primary process and creativity as research with adults. The one study with children that reported a relation for girls (Russ, 1982) identified percentage of primary process expression as the predictor, a finding consistent with that of Pine and Holt (1960), who concluded that the amount of primary process expressed was a better predictor for a variety of creativity tasks for women, whereas integration of primary process was the better predictor for men.

An important finding in my research is that boys usually expressed more primary process content than did girls. In both samples with the third-grade population (Russ, 1982) boys had a significantly greater percentage of primary process content than did girls. Specific analysis of the content revealed that boys had significantly more aggressive content than did girls. Boys also had more oral content in both samples, but the differences were not significant. This was also true in the study of fifth graders (Russ, 1988), in which there was a trend ($p < .07$) for boys to have a greater percentage of primary process responses. Kleinman and Russ (1988) also found that fourth- and fifth-grade boys expressed significantly more primary process content on the Rorschach than did girls. These results are consistent with those of other studies in the child literature. Boys are consistently more aggressive in their behavior and play (Maccoby & Jacklin, 1974). Girls recall fewer details of aggressive modeling (Bandura, 1965) and require longer tachistoscopic exposures than do boys for the aggressive scenes (Kagan & Moss, 1962). I (Russ, 1980) speculated that there may be more cultural taboos against expression of primary process material for girls than for boys.

Primary Process in Play Narratives

What happens if one investigates primary process expression in the context of children's play? As Waelder pointed out in 1933, *play* is a "leave of absence from reality" (p. 222). Play is a place to let primary process thinking occur, and play could be important in helping children learn to express primary process, integrate it, and use it adaptively.

S. Freud (1907/1989) viewed play as a precursor to the creative daydreams of the adult: "Might we not say that every child at play behaves like a creative writer, in that he creates a world of his own, or, rather, rearranges the things of his world in a new way that pleases him?" (p. 437). Freud saw creative writers as doing the same thing as children at play. Adults, instead of playing, use fantasy and daydreams. Freud went on to say that "a piece of creative writing, like a daydream, is a continuation of and a substitute for, what was once the play of childhood" (p. 442).

I was especially interested in investigating affective dimensions of play and creativity. To do so, I developed the Affect in Play Scale (APS), designed to meet the need for a standardized measure of affect in pretend play in children ages 6–10 years. Play sessions are individually administered 5-min standardized puppet play sessions. In the play task two neutral-looking puppets, one boy and one girl, are used, with three small blocks laid out on a table. The instructions are standardized and direct the children to play with the puppets any way they like for 5 min in a free-play period. The play task and instructions are unstructured enough to allow individual differences in the use of affect in pretend play. The play session is videotaped so that coding can occur later.

The APS measures the amount and types of affective expression in children's pretend play. It also assesses cognitive dimensions of the play, such as quality of fantasy and imagination. In a conceptual sense, the APS taps three dimensions of affect in fantasy: (a) *affect states*—actual emotional experiencing through expression of feeling states; (b) *affect-laden thoughts*—affective content themes that include emotional content themes and primary process themes; and (c) *cognitive integration of affect*.

These categories are three of the five affective dimensions I proposed to be important in the creative process (Russ, 1993). This conceptualization of affect and creativity guided the development of the scale. Holt's (1977) Scoring System for Primary Process on the Rorschach and Singer's (1973) play scales also were used as models. Details of the instructions and scoring system for the APS can be found in Russ (1993).

There are six major scores for the APS:

1. *Total frequency of units of affective expression*. A *unit* is defined as one scorable expression by an individual puppet. A unit can be the expression of an affect state, an affect theme, or a combination of the two.
2. *Variety of affect categories*. There are 11 possible affect

categories, the last 6 of which are primary process categories. The categories are Happiness/Pleasure, Anxi-
ety/Fear, Sadness/Hurt, Frustration/Displeasure, Nur-
turance/Affection, Aggression, Oral, Oral Aggression,
Anal, Sexual, and Competition. The categories can also
be divided into positive and negative affect groups.
3. *Mean intensity of affective expression* for each affective
   unit (1–5 rating).
4. *Comfort in play score* (1–5 global rating). This captures
   the child's enjoyment of and involvement in the play.
5. *Mean quality of fantasy*, based on subscores of organization, elaboration, imagination, and repetition.
6. *Affective integration score*. This captures the cognitive integration of affective material. The most useful combination of scores has been the Mean Quality of Fantasy
   × Frequency of Affect score.

Russ, Grossman-McKee, and Rutkin (1984) conducted pilot research on the APS to ensure that the task was appropriate for
young children and would result in adequate individual differences among normal school populations. By 1984, the basics of the
task and scoring system were in place. Recent studies have resulted
in refinement of the scoring criteria and a shortening of the play
period from 10 min to 5 min. Children with a high frequency of
affect in their play typically have the puppets playing competitive
games, fighting with each other, having fun together, eating (oral
content), and expressing affection.

APS and Creativity

In each of the validity studies my colleagues and I carried out with
the APS we obtained interrater reliabilities on 15 or 20 respondents.
Interrater reliabilities have been good, usually in the .80s and .90s,
using a variety of raters. We also obtained an adequate split–half
reliability of .85 for frequency of affective expression, comparing
the second and fourth minutes with the third and fifth minutes
(Russ, 1993; Russ & Peterson, 1990).

In the first study in the affect and creativity area Russ and
Grossman-McKee (1990) investigated the relations among the APS,
divergent thinking, and primary process thinking on the Rorschach

in 60 first- and second-grade children. As predicted, affective expression in play was significantly positively related to divergent thinking, as measured by the Alternate Uses Test. All major scores on the APS were significantly correlated with divergent thinking, with correlations ranging from $r(58) = .23$, $p < .05$, between comfort and divergent thinking to $r(58) = .42$, $p < .001$, between frequency of affective expression and divergent thinking. All correlations remained significant when IQ was partialed out, because IQ had such low correlations with the APS. The lack of relation between intelligence and any of the play scores is consistent with the theoretical model for the development of the scale and is similar to Singer's (1973) results. Also, there were no gender differences in the pattern of correlations between the APS and divergent thinking; specifically, primary process expression (frequency of primary process units) was related to divergent thinking for boys ($r = .38$, $p < .05$) and for girls ($r = .48$, $p < .01$).

Russ and Grossman-McKee (1990) also found a relation between the amount of primary process thinking on the Rorschach and APS scores. Children with more primary process responses on the Rorschach had more primary process in their play, more affect in their play, and higher fantasy scores than did children with less primary process on the Rorschach. This is an important finding, because it shows consistency in the construct of primary process expression across two types of situations. Again, there were no gender differences in the correlations between the Rorschach and the play measures; the Rorschach was equally predictive for boys and girls. This is important because the construct of primary process on the Rorschach was valid for both genders in that it related to primary process expression in play, although primary process on the Rorschach was related to divergent thinking for boys ($r = .72$, $p < .001$) but not for girls ($r = .27$, ns).

The relation between affect in play and divergent thinking (Russ & Grossman-McKee, 1990) was replicated by Russ and Peterson (1990; Russ, 1993), who used a larger sample of 121 first- and second-grade children. Once again, all the APS scores were significantly positively related to the Alternate Uses Test, independent of intelligence. Again, there were no gender differences in the correlations. Thus, with this replication one can have more confidence in the robustness of the finding of a relation between affect in pretend play and creativity in young children. There were no gender differences in the pattern of correlations in these two studies.

Russ and Schafer (2001) studied first- and second-grade children and found gender differences in the pattern of correlations between the APS and creativity. The measure of creativity was a divergent-thinking task. For boys, frequency of primary process was significantly related to divergent thinking ($r = .51$, $p < .01$) and to originality of the response ($r = .65$, $p < .01$). For girls, primary process thinking was not related to divergent thinking ($r = .01$, ns) or to originality ($r = .25$). The difference between the size of the correlations approached significance ($ps < .08$ and $< .10$, respectively). It is interesting that for girls, nonprimary process content was significantly related to originality ($r = .37$, $p < .001$). For boys, most of the play measures significantly predicted divergent thinking and originality. For girls, none of the play measures predicted divergent thinking, but they significantly predicted originality (except for primary process). The sample size was small (22 boys and 24 girls), and the results should be interpreted with caution.

In most studies with the APS there were no gender differences for the means on the major scores. Boys and girls usually express similar amounts of emotion in play; however, boys consistently express more aggressive content in their play than do girls. The aggressive content is a major component of the primary process content score. In Russ and Schafer's (2001) study, however, boys had both a significantly larger frequency of affect scores and larger primary process scores. The difference in expression of aggressive content accounts for the difference in primary process scores. Boys gave an average of 4.86 aggressive expressions in a 5-min play period, whereas girls gave an average of 0.63. These means are similar to those in Russ and Peterson's (1990) study, in which boys expressed 4.2 units and girls expressed 1.6 units. In the literature, boys have consistently shown more aggression in play (Maccoby & Jacklin, 1974) and recall more details of aggressive modeling (Bandura, 1965) than do girls.

In both Rorschach and play studies, boys express more aggressive content, increasing their primary process scores. This has been observed in recent samples as well as in samples from 25 years ago. In Rorschach studies, for males primary process thinking consistently relates to measures of creativity. In play research the results are mixed, with two of three studies showing no gender differences. In general, it may be that the medium of puppet play is a more natural form of expression for girls than are other test situations. Also, the APS measures a broader range of affect than does the Rorschach, so girls can "compensate" for their low aggressive responses with other kinds of affect expressions.

The type of affect content expressed in play could also be different than that expressed on the Rorschach. Although the primary process content categories on the APS were modeled on Holt's system for the Rorschach, the nature of the task is different. The correlations between primary process on the Rorschach and play scores were significant but of low magnitude (in the .30s and low .40s), which suggests not only overlapping variance but also specific variance in the constructs. The primary process content response on the Rorschach is a cognitive–perceptual response to a stimulus that reflects ideation. Primary process in play, as measured by the APS, is affect ideation expressed in a narrative and includes, in some responses, actual expression of emotion. The construct itself could be different in the two tasks.

Summary of Gender Differences

The following is a summary of the gender differences that have been observed in my research program.

1. On the Rorschach, in three studies, primary process was related to creativity measures for boys but not for girls. In only one subsample in one study was percentage of primary process related to creativity in girls.
2. In play, in two studies, primary process was related to creativity in both boys and girls. In one study primary process was related to creativity for boys but not for girls.
3. In both the Rorschach and play studies, boys expressed more aggressive ideation. At times, they expressed more oral content as well, but not a significantly higher amount.

When the Rorschach was used as the measure of primary process the hypothesized relation between primary process and creativity was supported for boys but not for girls. This conclusion is consistent with the adult literature. Thus, psychoanalytic theory seems to be applicable to males but not to females.

When primary process was measured in a play narrative the theory was supported for both boys and girls in two studies. In the third study gender differences again occurred. In general, boys expressed more primary process content; specifically, boys expressed more aggressive ideation on the Rorschach and in play.

Explanations of Gender Differences

Psychoanalytic theory would not predict gender differences in the role of primary process in creativity; neither would recent cognitive–affective conceptualizations. The involvement of emotion should result in a broader network of associations in the search process on creativity tasks for both males and females.

In 1980 I speculated that in U.S. culture, boys are freer than are girls to express primary process thinking in play, and they thereby learn to use it more effectively in adaptive pursuits (Russ, 1980). This explanation is still viable, in spite of 30 years of feminism. Thirty years after the beginning of the women's movement, girls still express significantly less primary process, especially aggression, in play and on the Rorschach. One might theorize that a child who is not expressing primary process ideation will not learn to "play" with it, integrate it, and have easy access to it when necessary. This speculation is consistent with the findings of West, Martindale, and Sutton-Smith (1985), who found, with a group of 106 children ages 2–11 years, gender differences in age trends of primary process content in children's spontaneous fantasy narratives. They found that boys conformed to psychoanalytic theory more than did girls. The developmental trends for girls suggested increasing influence of external controls. West et al. concluded that girls "appear to become increasingly indoctrinated with cultural values, and hence establish greater impulse control" (p. 403). They speculated that the greater importance of social relationships to girls could cause cognitive development to be more strongly shaped by social controls than for boys.

Reis (1999) reviewed the many factors that interfere with creativity in women and concluded that cultural demands still prevail. There continues to be pressure to be conventional and polite. The talented women she studied wanted to create and produce quietly in an environment where differences do not appear obvious. Sternberg and Lubart (1995) pointed to the need for women to minimize differences.

The important question is how these cultural pressures to be polite and conventional could affect children's play. It is logical to deduce that girls' play would be inhibited and constricted as a result of these cultural pressures. This empirical question needs investigation. The other important question is whether inhibition in expression of primary process leads to repression. Does it affect what a child lets herself think? And does that inhibit creativity?

It is important to point out that Baer's (1999) review of the literature found no consistent gender differences in divergent-thinking ability. Similarly, in my own research I have found no gender differences in most studies on creativity tasks. Of course, measuring creativity is always a challenge. The actual production of a creative object or idea is multidetermined: Many cognitive, affective, and personality processes within the individual are involved, and several external factors, such as chance, opportunity, and life experiences, are important elements. However, in many literatures, divergent thinking and flexibility of thought emerge as central to the act of generating a creative product, and there are valid measures of these cognitive processes. Thus, these kinds of measures have been used in many research studies. Nevertheless, it is essential that longitudinal studies of creativity follow children into adulthood and then assess their real-life creative accomplishments.

Other possible explanations exist for the gender differences. Hormonal differences could account for less aggression in girls. It is also possible that brain physiology differs for males and for females. There could be gender differences in how emotion is processed in the brain and how the emotion network functions. Goleman (1995) reports on gender differences in the amount of brain activity and in the location of brain activity in response to different emotions. The brains of men and women have different patterns of activity associated with different emotions. With the use of positron emission tomography scan technology Mark George found differences in the processing of emotion (Goleman, 1995). For example, women, when sad, activate the anterior limbic system more than do men. It is too soon to know whether these kinds of gender differences could affect the relation between emotion and the network of associations to which the individual has access.

From an evolutionary biological perspective it is possible that gender differences exist in the processing of emotions based on a history of different adaptive consequences. Slavin and Kriegman (1992) discussed psychoanalytic theory from an evolutionary biological perspective. They viewed some structures proposed by psychoanalytic theory as adaptive psychological deep structures that have been favored by natural selection. Slavin and Kriegman integrated many of Freud's concepts into this evolutionary framework. For Freud, affective states of all kinds become incorporated into the mind and become affective symbols. What evolves is a universal way of organizing experience. Although Slavin and Kriegman did not discuss possible gender differences, it is logical to assume that different affective symbol systems and ways of organizing affective experience could have evolved for men and women. As new technology enables researchers to learn about these possible differences, they can learn about differences in how emotion interacts with creative cognitive processes, such as divergent thinking, in men and women. Research in this area will, I hope, expand rapidly to investigate this area.

The integration of primary process has consistently related to creativity in males. In some studies the pure amount of primary process has also related to creativity. For females, the results are mixed. In most adult studies, when females are included, primary process does not predict creativity. In most studies with the Rorschach with children, primary process does not relate to creativity. In studies in which play has been the medium, primary process expression has related to creativity in two of the three samples. Play may be a more natural form of expression for girls and therefore a more valid measure of primary process, or the nature of the primary process construct could be different in play than in the Rorschach task. In addition, girls express less primary process, especially aggression, on the Rorschach and in play. In this respect girls may be at a disadvantage for creativity. They do not learn to express and integrate primary process ideation and affect as easily as do boys. They do not "play" with it as much as do boys, practice with it, and integrate the associations and memories. They cannot access it and use it as well as do boys in creative tasks. However, this reduced primary process thinking could be an advantage in other areas, such as cooperative interpersonal functioning.

I anticipate that if researchers identify highly creative girls, they will find that such girls have high amounts of well-integrated primary process thinking. Investigation of this hypothesis should be a top priority.

It is also important that researchers determine whether increasing access to primary process increases creative thinking. Play sessions would be one way to investigate this question. Several researchers (e.g., Isen, 1999) have found that inducing positive affect increases creativity. No gender differences have been found in those mood-induction studies. By investigating the mechanisms by which creativity is facilitated researchers can focus more definitively on whether the role of primary process in creativity is the same or different for males and females.

References

Arieti, S. (1976). *Creativity: The magic synthesis.* New York: Basic Books.

Arlow, J., & Brenner, C. (1964). *Psychoanalytic concepts and structural theory.* Madison, CT: International Universities Press.

Baer, J. (1999). Gender differences. In M. Runco & S. Pritzker (Eds.), *Encyclopedia of creativity* (pp. 753–758). San Diego: Academic Press.

Bandura, A. (1965). Influence of models' reinforcement contingencies in the acquisition of imitative responses. *Journal of Personality and Social Psychology, 1,* 589–595.

Blatt, S., Allison, O., & Feirstein, A. (1969). The capacity to cope with cognitive complexity. *Journal of Personality, 37,* 269–288.

Bower, G. H. (1981). Mood and memory. *American Psychologist, 36,* 129–148.

Cohen, I. (1961). Adaptive regression, dogmatism, and creativity. *Dissertation Abstracts International, 21,* 3522–3523.

Culbane, J. (1988, January 10). Throw away the script. *Cleveland Plain Dealer,* pp. 1–5.

Damasio, A. (1994). *Descartes' error: Emotion, reason, and the human brain.* New York: Grosset/Putnam.

Dudek, S. (1968). Regression and creativity. *Journal of Nervous and Mental Disease, 147,* 535–546.

Dudek, S. (1975). Regression in the service of the ego in young children. *Journal of Personality Assessment, 39,* 369–376.

Dudek, S. (1980). Primary process ideation. In R. H. Woody (Ed.), *Encyclopedia of clinical assessment* (Vol. 1, pp. 520–539). San Francisco, CA: Jossey-Bass.

Dudek, S. (1984). The architect as person: A Rorschach image. *Journal of Personality Assessment, 48,* 597–605.

Dudek, S., & Verreault, R. (1989). The creative thinking and ego functioning of children. *Creativity Research Journal, 2,* 64–86.

Exner, J. (1974). *The Rorschach: A comprehensive system.* New York: Wiley.

Fischer, K., & Pipp, S. (1984). The unconscious and psychopathology. In K. S. Bowers & D. Meichenbaum (Eds.), *The unconscious reconsidered* (pp. 88–148). New York: Wiley.

Freud, A. (1966). *The ego and the mechanisms of defense.* New York: International Universities Press. (Original work published 1936)

Freud, S. (1958). The unconscious. In J. Strachey (Ed. and Trans.), *The standard edition of the complete psychological works of Sigmund Freud* (Vol. 14, pp. 159–215). London: Hogarth Press. (Original work published 1915)

Freud, S. (1959). Inhibition, symptoms, and anxiety. In J. Strachey (Ed. and Trans.), *The standard edition of the complete psychological works of Sigmund Freud* (Vol. 20, pp. 87–172). London: Hogarth Press. (Original work published 1926)

Freud, S. (1966). Project for a scientific psychology. In J. Strachey (Ed. and Trans.), *The standard edition of the complete psychological works of Sigmund Freud* (Vol. 1, pp. 283–413). London: Hogarth Press. (Original work published 1895)

Freud, S. (1989). Creative writers and day-dreaming. In P. Gay (Ed.), *The Freud reader* (pp. 436–443). New York: Norton. (Original work published 1907)

Gamble, K., & Kellner, H. (1968). Creative functioning and cognitive regression. *Journal of Personality and Social Psychology, 9,* 266–271.

Getz, I., & Lubart, T. (1999). The emotional resonance model of creativity: Theoretical and practical extensions. In S. Russ (Ed.), *Affect, creative experience and psychological adjustment* (pp. 41–56). Philadelphia: Brunner/Mazel.

Ghiselin, B. (1952). *The creative process.* Berkeley: University of California Press.

Goleman, D. (1995, March 28). The brain manages happiness and sadness in different centers. *New York Times,* pp. B9–B10.

Guilford, J. P. (1968). *Intelligence, creativity and their educational implications.* San Diego, CA: Knapp.

Holt, R. (1967). The development of the primary process: A structural view. In R. Holt (Ed.), *Motivation and thought* (pp. 344–384). Madison, CT: International Universities Press.

Holt, R. (1970). *Manual for the scoring of primary process manifestations in Rorschach responses* (10th ed.). New York: Research Center for Mental Health, New York University.

Holt, R. R. (1977). A method for assessing primary process manifestations and their control in Rorschach responses. In M. Rickers-Ovsiankina (Ed.), *Rorschach psychology* (pp. 375–420). New York: Kreiger.

Holt, R. R., & Havel, J. (1960). A method for assessing primary and secondary process in the Rorschach. In M. Rickers-Ovsiankina (Ed.), *Rorschach psychology* (pp. 283–315). New York: Wiley.

Isen, A. (1999). On the relationship between affect and creative problem solving. In S. Russ (Ed.), *Affect, creative experience and psychological adjustment* (pp. 3–17). Philadelphia: Brunner/Mazel.

Isen, A., Daubman, K., & Nowicki, G. (1987). Positive affect facilitates creative problem solving. *Journal of Personality and Social Psychology, 52*, 1122–1131.

Kagan, J., & Moss, H. A. (1962). *Birth to maturity: A study in psychological development*. New York: Wiley.

Kleinman, M., & Russ, S. (1988). Primary process thinking and anxiety in children. *Journal of Personality Assessment, 52*, 538–548.

Kris, E. (1952). *Psychoanalytic exploration in art*. Madison, CT: International Universities Press.

LeDoux, J. E. (1989). Cognitive–emotional interaction in the brain. *Cognition and Emotion, 3*, 267–289.

Luchins, A., & Luchins, E. (1959). *Rigidity of behavior*. Eugene: University of Oregon Books.

Maccoby, E., & Jacklin, C. (1974). *The psychology of sex differences*. Stanford, CA: Stanford University Press.

Martindale, C. (1981). *Cognition and consciousness*. Homewood, IL: Dorsey Press.

Martindale, C. (1989). Personality, situation, and creativity. In J. Glover, R. Ronning, & C. R. Reynolds (Eds.), *Handbook of creativity* (pp. 211–232). New York: Plenum.

Martindale, C., & Dailey, A. (1996). Creativity, primary process cognition, and personality. *Personality and Individual Differences, 20*, 409–414.

Masling, J. (1992). What does it all mean? In R. Bornstein & T. Pittman (Eds.), *Perception without awareness* (pp. 259–276). New York: Guilford.

McCrae, R. R., & Costa, P. T., Jr. (1987). Validation of the five-factor model across instruments and observers. *Journal of Personality and Social Psychology, 52*, 81–90.

Murray, J., & Russ, S. (1981). Adaptive regression and types of cognitive flexibility. *Journal of Personality Assessment, 45*, 59–65.

Niederland, W. (1976). Psychoanalytic approaches to artistic creativity. *Psychoanalytic Quarterly, 45*, 185–212.

Noy, P. (1969). A revision of the psychoanalytic theory of the primary process. *International Journal of Psycho-Analysis, 50*, 155–178.

Pine, R., & Holt, R. (1960). Creativity and primary process: A study of adaptive regression. *Journal of Abnormal and Social Psychology, 61,* 370–379.

Rapaport, D. (1951). *Organization and pathology of thought.* New York: Columbia Unviersity Press.

Reis, S. M. (1999). Women and creativity. In M. Runco & S. Pritzker (Eds.), *Encyclopedia of creativity* (Vol. 2, pp. 699–708). San Diego, CA: Academic Press.

Rholes, W., Riskind, J., & Lane, J. (1987). Emotional states and memory biases: Effects of cognitive priming and mood. *Journal of Personality and Social Psychology, 52,* 91–99.

Richards, R. (1990). Everyday creativity, eminent creativity, and health: After-view for CRT issues on creativity and health. *Creativity Research Journal, 3,* 300–326.

Rogolsky, M. M. (1968). Artistic creativity and adaptive regression in third grade children. *Journal of Projective Techniques and Personality Assessment, 32,* 53–62.

Rothenberg, A. (1994). Studies in the creative process: An empirical approach. In J. Masling & R. Bornstein (Eds.), *Empirical perspectives on object relations theory* (pp. 195–245). Washington, DC: American Psychological Association.

Russ, S. (1980). Primary process integration on the Rorschach and achievement in children. *Journal of Personality Assessment, 44,* 338–344.

Russ, S. (1981). Primary process on the Rorschach and achievement in children: A follow-up study. *Journal of Personality Assessment, 46,* 473–477.

Russ, S. (1982). Sex differences in primary process thinking and flexibility in problem solving in children. *Journal of Personality Assessment, 45,* 569–577.

Russ, S. (1987). Assessment of cognitive affective interaction in children: Creativity, fantasy, and play research. In J. Butcher & C. Spielberger (Eds.), *Advances in personality assessment* (Vol. 6, pp. 141–155). Hillsdale, NJ: Erlbaum.

Russ, S. (1988). Primary process thinking on the Rorschach, divergent thinking, and coping in children. *Journal of Personality Assessment, 52,* 539–548.

Russ, S. (1993). *Affect and creativity: The role of affect and play in the creative process.* Hillsdale, NJ: Erlbaum.

Russ, S. (1996). Psychoanalytic theory and creativity: Cognition and affect revisited. In J. Masling & R. Bornstein (Eds.), *Psychoanalytic perspectives on developmental psychology* (pp. 69–103). Washington, DC: American Psychological Association.

Russ, S. (1999). An evolutionary model for creativity: Does it fit? *Psychological Inquiry, 10,* 359–361.

Russ, S., & Grossman-McKee, A. (1990). Affective expression in children's fantasy play, primary process thinking on the Rorschach, and divergent thinking. *Journal of Personality Assessment, 54,* 756–771.

Russ, S., Grossman-McKee, A., & Rutkin, Z. (1984). [Affect in Play Scale: Pilot project]. Unpublished raw data.

Russ, S., & Peterson, N. (1990). *The Affect in Play Scale: Predicting creativity and coping in children.* Unpublished manuscript.

Russ, S., & Schafer, E. (2001). *Affect in play, divergent thinking, and emotional memories.* Manuscript in preparation, Case Western Reserve University.

Simon, V. (1998). Emotional participation in decision-making. *Psychology in Spain, 2,* 100–107.

Singer, J. L. (1973). *Child's world of make-believe.* New York: Academic Press.

Slavin, M., & Kriegman, D. (1992). *The adaptive design of the human psyche.* New York: Guilford.

Spence, D., & Holland, B. (1962). The restricting effects of awareness: A paradox and explanation. *Journal of Abnormal and Social Psychology, 64,* 163–174.

Suler, J. (1980). Primary process thinking and creativity. *Psychological Bulletin, 88,* 144–165.

Sternberg, R. J., & Lubart, T. I. (1995). *Defying the crowd: Cultivating creativity in a culture of conformity.* New York: Free Press.

Torrance, E. P. (1968). A longitudinal examination of the 4th grade slump in creativity. *Gifted Child Quarterly, 12,* 195–197.

Urist, J. (1980). The continuum between primary and secondary process thinking: Toward a concept of borderline thought. In J. Kwawer, H. Lerner, P. Lerner, & A. Sugarman (Eds.), *Borderline phenomena and the Rorschach test* (pp. 133–154). Madison, CT: International Universities Press.

Waelder, R. (1933). Psychoanalytic theory of play. *Psychoanalytic Quarterly, 2,* 208–224.

Wallach, M., & Kogan, N. C. (1965). *Modes of thinking in young children: A study of the creativity–intelligence distinction.* New York: Holt, Rinehart, & Winston.

West, A., Martindale, C., & Sutton-Smith, B. (1985). Age trends in the content of children's spontaneous fantasy narratives. *Genetic, Social, and General Psychology Monographs, 111,* 389–405.

Zajonc, R. (1980). Feeling and thinking: Preferences need no inferences. *American Psychologist, 35,* 151–175.

Zajonc, R. (1990, August). *Emotions and brain temperature.* Paper presented at the 98th Annual Convention of the American Psychological Association, Boston.

Zimiles, H. (1981). Cognitive–affective interaction: A concept that exceeds the researcher's grasp. In E. Shapiro & E. Weber (Eds.), *Cognitive and affective growth* (pp. 49–63). Hillsdale, NJ: Erlbaum.

3

The Study of Defense Mechanisms:
Gender Implications

Phebe Cramer

Interest in the concept of the defense mechanism has been increasing among research psychologists (see Cramer & Davidson, 1998). The importance of understanding the contribution of certain defense mechanisms to psychiatric diagnosis also has been increasingly recognized (see *Diagnostic and Statistical Manual of Mental Disorders*, 4th ed., *DSM–IV*, American Psychiatric Association, 1994; Perry et al., 1998; Skodol & Perry, 1993; Soldz & Vaillant, 1998). Defense mechanisms are one of the most important ideas in classical psychoanalytic theory and contemporary psychoanalysis has expanded their conceptualization and function. In addition to inhibiting the expression of instincts and drives and thus protecting the individual from anxiety, in current theory, defenses also function to protect the self—self-esteem and self-integration (e.g., Cooper, 1998). Furthermore, some defenses are seen as fostering healthy adaptation: Defenses are no longer uniquely associated with psychopathology (cf. Vaillant, 1993).

Some years ago, I became interested in the question of how children develop and use defense mechanisms. My thinking about this topic was strongly influenced by the work of Rene Spitz (1957) who, in exquisite detail, theorized about the chronological progression in the infant of the development of the concept of "no" —from a physiological reflex to a cognitive, linguistic mental operation. Although some people might criticize the research methods Spitz used, his theoretical conception of a mental operation evolving from a physiological reflex guided my thinking about defense mechanism development.

The work of Anna Freud (1936/1946), who had begun to classify defenses in terms of their chronological development, also influenced my thinking. She wrote that "possibly each defence mechanism is first evolved in order to master some specific instinctual urge and so is associated with a particular phase of infantile development" (p. 55) and that

> it is meaningless to speak of repression when the ego is still merged with the id. Similarly, we might suppose that projection and introjection were methods which depended on the differentiation of the ego from the outside world. The expulsion of ideas or affects from the ego and their regulation to the outside world would be a relief to the ego only when it had learnt to distinguish itself from that world. . . . Sublimation, i.e., the displacement of the instinctual aim in conformity with higher social values, presupposed the acceptance or at least the knowledge of such values, that is to say, presupposed the existence of the super-ego. (pp. 55–56)

Although A. Freud eventually abandoned the attempt to order defenses chronologically, both she and Spitz believed that defense mechanisms did emerge in a consistent developmental pattern. Thus Spitz (1961) wrote, "under normal circumstances certain defense mechanisms will emerge at given points of the child's development" (p. 630), with which Freud (1965) agreed when she wrote, "Defenses have their own chronology, even if only an approximate one" (p. 177). The idea of a chronology of defense mechanism development had also been discussed by Glover (1937),

Hartmann (1950), and Nunberg (1932/1955); various theoretical classifications had been proposed by Anthony (1970), Blum (1953), Engel (1962), Gedo and Goldberg (1973), Lichtenberg and Slap (1972), and Vaillant (1977), among others. The basis for these models was a combination of theoretical preconceptions plus selected clinical observations.[1] Although the particulars of the models differed, there were also points of consensus regarding the position of specific defenses in the chronological hierarchy. For example, there was general agreement that denial was a simple defense and would be normative in young children, whereas intellectualization was a complex defense that would not emerge until adolescence. Most important, however, was the consensus among these theoreticians that it was reasonable to expect defense mechanisms to emerge according to a developmental chronology. The possibility of gender differences was not, and has not been, considered, as I discuss later in this chapter.

Although the developmental point of view is theoretically interesting, empirical evidence to support or refute it was missing. As a developmental psychologist, I am experienced in working with children. As a clinical psychologist, I have knowledge of defense mechanisms and training in clinical assessment methods. As a research psychologist, I was familiar with the most popular research tool of the time for studying defenses, the Defense Mechanism Inventory (DMI; Gleser & Ihilevich, 1969), a semiprojective method in which individuals are asked to read descriptions of several stressful situations and to choose one of several possible reactions to each situation. These predetermined reactions were designed to represent one of five defense mechanisms. Although providing prearranged situations and responses has some disadvantages—for example, it lacks ecological validity—the methodological advantages (standard stress situations, objective assessment of responses) make this approach appealing to researchers. However, both in content and format, the method is not appropriate for children. A search of the research literature revealed no other well-developed method for studying children's defense mechanisms.

---

[1] Vaillant (e.g., 1976) has also carried out intensive empirical studies of defense mechanisms with men.

Developing a Method to Study Defenses in Children

Video Vignettes: An Analogue to the DMI

My first task was to develop a method for studying children's defense mechanisms. I began by trying to create a children's analogue to the DMI. The initial step was to create a series of dramatic vignettes depicting some unpleasant situation that a child might encounter in everyday life. After I wrote a set of these vignettes, I enlisted local children as actors, taught them the scripts, and coached them in acting out the scripts while their performance was videotaped. After repeated practice, I created a final set of eight video test vignettes. I used the same eight vignettes to test boys and girls; the "boy" version was filmed using boys as actors, whereas in the "girl" version girls acted out the scripts.

For example, in one vignette an adult man and woman are sitting in a living room, reading the newspaper. A child enters the room and asks if he may go to the movies with a friend. The man responds by saying no, it is raining outside, and he doesn't think it would be a good idea. He adds that he, the child's uncle, and the woman, the child's aunt, have been taking care of the child since his parents were killed in an auto accident, and they really don't think it would be a good idea for him to go out. The aunt nods agreement, while the child looks disappointed. As the adults go back to reading their papers, the child sneaks to the corner of the room, picks up his coat, and is about to go out the door, when the uncle says he hears something, finds the child trying to leave, and sternly tells him he is not to go.

In my research investigation (Cramer, 1983), children from two age groups were studied. The youngest group of children were first and second graders, with an average age of 7 years, 0 months; the older group were fifth and sixth graders, with an average age of 10 years, 1 month. After each child participant watched a video vignette, he or she was asked, "What would you do if you were (the child actor)?" and "How would you feel?" After children had provided their own free response for each vignette, they were presented with a series of four prearranged reactions and were asked to choose the reaction that they would most likely do (or feel).

I created the four response alternatives to correspond to the defense alternatives represented in the DMI. As defined by the DMI,
reversal (REV) includes the defenses of denial, negation, and reaction formation; *projection* (PRO) represents attributing one's own
thoughts of feelings to others; *turning against the object* (TAO) includes identification with the aggressor and displacement, and
turning against the self (TAS) is based on directing negative affect
inward. Each child's defense responses to the question "What
would you do?" and to "What would you feel?" were summed
over the eight vignettes.

The findings of the study are presented in Figure 3.1. One can
see that the REV defense of denial, negation, and reaction formation was chosen most often; this was true for both younger and
older children. Age differences are seen in the greater use of TAS
by the younger children and TAO by the older ones, although the
latter difference was not statistically significant. The two age
groups did not differ in their choice of PRO.

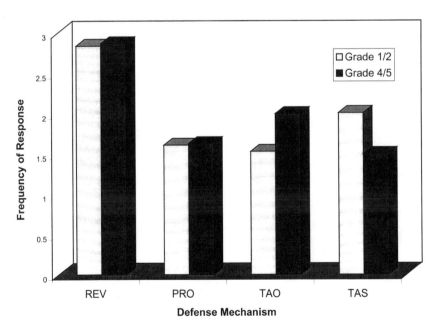

Figure 3.1.   Video vignettes: defense mechanism choice. REV =
reversal; PRO = projection; TAO = turning against the object; TAS =
turning against the self.

In their free responses, 96% of the children indicated they would feel mad, sad, or some other negative emotion, confirming that the video vignettes did arouse negative affect. Fifty-nine percent of their free responses to the question "What would you do?" were rated as representing one of the four defenses, with REV (28%) and TAO (24%) being most frequent. The remaining responses were coded as representing one of four coping strategies. Furthermore, when a child's free response did indicate the use of either REV or TAO, there was strong agreement between this freely given response and the child's choice of the prescribed alternatives. The correlation between the free responses of REV and the prescribed alternative choice of REV was .53 for boys and .66 for girls; both correlations were statistically significant at the $p < .005$ level. Likewise, the correlation between free-response TAO and prescribed-alternative TAO was .47 ($p < .005$) for boys and .36 ($p < .05$) for girls.

Although these results—that the video vignette method could produce results comparable to those obtained from children's free responses—were encouraging, the method did not seem satisfactory in several ways. First, the free-response data indicated that 41% of the children's responses to unpleasant situations and their consequent negative emotions did not involve the use of defense mechanisms. This meant that by requiring children to choose a defense response I was forcing them to respond uncharacteristically. Related to this was the further limitation that the procedure constrained the child's response to the defense alternatives offered. Furthermore, the whole idea of "choosing" defense mechanisms is not ecologically valid. According to theory, the defense mechanisms that one uses are not consciously chosen; their functioning occurs automatically and is outside of awareness. Perhaps, as a consequence of these limitations, the method failed to show much in the way of developmental, or age differences.

Coding Narrative Material for Defenses

For these reasons, it seemed clear that a better method for assessing children's defenses was needed. This method should allow the child's thought patterns to emerge freely and not be limited to pre-established response alternatives. It should allow for a range of content to be expressed in an undirected fashion, in a situation for which no stereotyped response is readily available. Although the mental processes involved in defense mechanisms cannot be observed directly, they may be inferred from verbal behavior. Thus, the assessment method should arouse thought processes, produce relatively extensive samples of verbal behavior rather than single-word responses, and be sufficiently emotionally arousing to stimulate the use of defenses. Also, because I was interested in developmental differences, it was important to have a method that was both standard and equally appropriate across a range of ages. In terms of method, it was critical that there be some means for two or more independent observers to determine whether a defense had been used.

The method that best met these requirements was the Thematic Apperception Test (TAT; Murray, 1943). The TAT consists of a standard set of dramatic pictures presented to an individual, one at a time, with the request that a story be told about the picture. Instructions regarding the story are minimal and include asking the storyteller to describe who the characters are, what they are thinking and feeling, what led up to the present situation, and how the story turns out.

To determine the feasibility of this approach I conducted a derivation study with 42 children of different ages (Cramer, 1987). The 168 stories collected were tape recorded, transcribed, and then closely studied for themes and response styles that both illustrated the use of a defense mechanism and differentiated between younger and older children. Because I was interested in developmental differences in defense use I decided to focus on three defenses that were theoretically expected to show developmental differences in frequency of use. Denial, a simple defense, would be expected to occur most frequently in young children but to decline with age. Projection, a more complex defense, was expected to increase during later childhood and early adolescence, whereas identification, related to the important adolescent issue of identity development, was expected to occur most frequently during later adolescence.[2]

---

[2] I have provided an extensive discussion of the theory behind this hypothesized developmental pattern (Cramer, 1991b).

For each of these three defenses I developed scoring categories representing different manifestations of the defense. These categories illustrated some aspect of the theoretical nature of the defense, as described in the literature (e.g., Fenichel, 1945; A. Freud, 1936/1946); a few had been used previously to establish scoring criteria for defenses with projective test responses (Bellak, 1975; Haworth, 1963; Schafer, 1954). Eventually, I established a set of seven categories for each defense. Each category represented a different aspect of the defense, and each had a set of coding rules, with examples, that indicated the type of story content and style that could be coded as indicating use of that defense. On the basis of this work I developed a detailed coding manual. The coding rules of the Defense Mechanism Manual (DMM; Cramer, 1991b) are sufficiently explicit that other investigators may instruct themselves and use the coding method in their independent research, as has been done by Avery (1985); Blaess (1998); Brody, Rozek, and Muten (1985); Hibbard et al. (1994); Luciano (1999); and Porcerelli, Thomas, Hibbard, and Cogan (1998).

Here are some examples of children's stories that illustrate the use of the three defenses. Each story was told in response to TAT Card 17BM, which depicts a man clinging to a rope. A 5-year-old told the following story, which illustrates the use of denial.

> A statue . . . climbing down a rope. He falls and then breaks. And then somebody builds him back up, and he does the same thing over again. The people have to build him back up and put him back up on the rope, and then he swings down and breaks. [How is he feeling?] He's made of clay. He doesn't.

This narrative is unusual in that the central figure, who is almost always seen as a live man, is turned into a statue. Given the plot of the story, it appears that that the storyteller is anxious about the possibility of the central figure falling. To alleviate this anxiety she turns the figure into something inanimate: If it is not alive, it cannot be hurt and cannot die. Even when it does fall, the child's denial that this is a man, and turning it into a statue, make it possible that the figure may be put back together. Thus, there is nothing to be feared. However, the anxiety about falling is not put to rest, and the whole process is repeated. The use of denial is made most explicit in the child's closing statement: Because the figure is made out of clay, he does not have any feelings and so is not afraid and is not hurt.

Consider now another story to the same TAT card, told by a 10-year-old. In this case, the defense of projection is prominent.

> A man was being chased by a bunch of soldiers who wanted to kill him. He's climbing up the rope, and if he doesn't make it up he'll get chopped to death with swords. So he is hanging as tight as he can, and when he gets to the top he'll be on the border—that's a secret place underground. There is this hatch that is on the border so they can't get him.

Although this story was told to the same stimulus picture, which shows only a single figure clinging to a rope, the storyteller has added numerous hostile soldiers as well as the need for protection from that hostility. The image of being chopped to death with swords comes entirely from the psyche of the storyteller, as do the soldiers and swords. Concern about places to hide, to protect himself, lead to the cognitive confusion about being either on the top or underground. The focus on others being out to get him continues throughout.

Finally, consider a third story told to the same picture by an 8-year-old. Although the defense of identification is not the most prominent defense at this age, it is beginning to increase in frequency, as in the following story.

> This is a man that was climbing up a rope, and he's kind of like Tarzan, but he's a different man, though. And he fights crime, and he was climbing up a rope to watch a parade. Then he saw somebody kidnapping a lady. And now he's climbing down a rope and going down to stop the man. Then he got down and he found some witnesses, and they said he went off into a cave. And the man went down to the cave and found the man and brought him to the police. [How is he feeling?] He's very proud because he fought one of his first crimes.

Although this story still involves some projection, the focus is different. Now the main character is identified as being like another well-known hero. He behaves in ways that show a clear internalization of and identification with the laws and mores of our society: fighting crime, saving a victim, assisting the police, and deriving self-esteem from this identification.

Using the DMM to Study the Development of Defenses

Once this coding method was established I collected new stories from more than 300 children, ranging in age from 5 to 16 years, who represented four age groups: primary (mean age = 5 years, 8 months); intermediate (mean age = 9 years, 10 months); early adolescent (mean age = 14 years, 6 months); and late adolescent (mean age = 16 years, 0 months; Cramer, 1987). Without knowledge of age or gender, I coded each story using the DMM to determine the incidence of the three defenses. A subset of the stories from each of the four age groups was coded by two independent raters; the high rate of agreement between the coders indicated satisfactory reliability for the coding method.

My main interest, of course, was whether the four age groups would show developmental differences in the use of the three defenses. Because the adolescents typically told longer stories than the younger children, thus increasing the likelihood of receiving a defense score, I converted each child's defense scores into relative scores, with the use of each individual defense expressed as a proportion of total defense use. In this way, story length did not influence the defense score.

The relative use of the three defenses for each of the four age groups is shown in Figure 3.2. As predicted, denial occurred most frequently with the youngest children and then sharply decreased across the other three age groups. In contrast, the use of projection increased after age 5, remained prominent in the two middle age groups, and then slightly decreased in late adolescence. Identification was used infrequently by the youngest children and then steadily increased until it became the most frequently used defense in late adolescence. Porcerelli et al. (1998) conducted a similar study 10 years later at a different laboratory with children of similar age groups but from a different geographical region of the country (see Figure 3.3). When Figures 3.2 and 3.3 are superimposed, they show very similar results for the comparable age

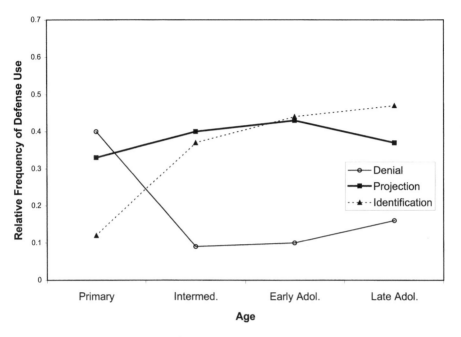

Figure 3.2.   Relative use of defense mechanisms, by age. Intermed. = intermediate; Adol. = adolescent.

groups of the two investigations. Over the age span from 7 to 17 years, denial decreases sharply after age 7, projection continues at a high level until late adolescence, and identification continues to increase into late adolescence. This replication study also included college freshmen; as can be seen in Figure 3.3, identification continued to increase in this late adolescent group, whereas denial and projection continued a slight decrease.

My findings, and those of Porcerelli et al. (1998), indicate clear developmental differences in the use of defense mechanisms. From this one might infer that different defenses emerge at successive developmental periods in the life of children. However, because these data were cross-sectional—that is, they were based on different children studied at each age period—it is possible that the difference in defense use might in some way be due to cohort variations. To eliminate this possibility it was necessary to conduct a longitudinal study in which the same children were followed

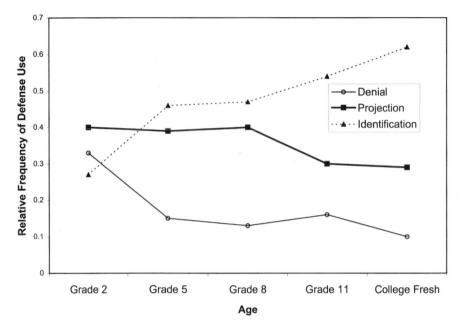

Figure 3.3.   Relative use of defense mechanisms, by age: replication study. Fresh = freshmen.

from early childhood. Thus, using a cohort longitudinal design, I studied the use of defense mechanisms by the same children from age 6 years, 6 months to age 9 years, 9 months (Cramer, 1997). Figure 3.4 shows the results of this study. As was found with the cross-sectional studies, the frequency of denial significantly decreased between age 6 years, 6 months and at age 7 years, 3 months ($p < .004$), whereas projection significantly increased between age 8 years, 0 months and age 8 years, 8 months ($p < .05$). As in the cross-sectional data, identification increased gradually; one can presume that if these children had been followed into late adolescence identification would become the predominant defense. The import of these results, however, is that children change from using denial as the predominant defense to using projection—that is, that the developmental differences found in the previous two studies do indeed represent the emergence of difference defenses at different developmental points in the life of the child.

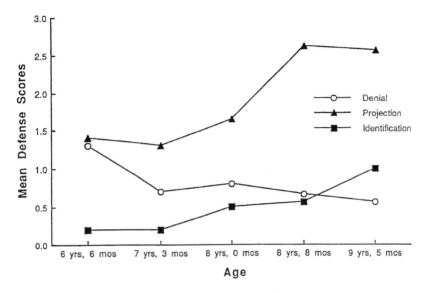

Figure 3.4. Longitudinal study of defense mechanisms. yrs = years; mos = months.

Why Does Defense Use Change With Development?

It is clear that cognitive development makes possible the operation of more cognitively complex defenses; however, this fact alone does not explain why defense use changes, only how it is possible. To understand the "why" of change I return to a consideration of the nature of the defense mechanism as a cognitive operation that functions outside of awareness. According to theory, lack of awareness is one of the reasons that defenses are successful—that is, one is unaware that one is "deceiving" oneself. In thinking about why children abandon certain defenses and replace them with others, it seemed that the issue of "awareness" might be critical; that is, it seemed likely that once a child consciously recognizes a defense and its function, the usefulness of that defense would decline. This in turn suggested the possibility that as children mature and develop cognitively they become able to "see through" a simple defense, such as denial. When that happens they may abandon that

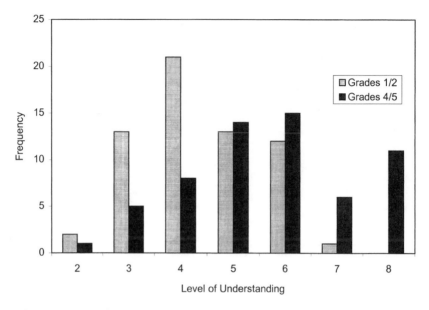

Figure 3.5.   Understanding denial: Grades 1 and 2 and Grades 4 and 5.

defense and in its place adopt another that is more complex and not yet understood.

To investigate this possibility, Cramer and Brilliant (2001) studied children's use of defenses in conjunction with their understanding of how defenses function. We studied children from two age groups: one (mean age = 7 years, 6 months) in which the shift from denial to projection should be occurring, and another (mean age = 10 years, 5 months) in which projection should be the predominant defense among the majority of the children. Both groups provided TAT stories that were subsequently coded with the DMM for defense use. Each child also was queried to assess the degree of his or her defense understanding—that is, how well he or she understood the way in which the defenses of denial and projection function. Defense use was subsequently plotted as a function of defense understanding.

Looking first at Figure 3.5,[3] one sees that the defense of denial was better understood by the older children than by the younger

---

[3]These figures were also reported by Cramer and Brilliant (2001).

children, as one would expect. The majority of the older children were rated as understanding at Level 5 or above, indicating that their comprehension varied between partial and complete understanding. In contrast, the majority of the younger children were rated at Level 4 or below, indicating minimal or no understanding.

Comparable results for the defense of projection are provided in Figure 3.6. The majority of the older children were rated at 4 or above, indicating at least minimal understanding, whereas the majority of the younger children were rated at 3 or below, indicating a level of comprehension between minimal and none.

There was, however, variability in the level of understanding of denial and projection within the two age groups, ranging from no to full understanding. If our hypothesis that understanding a defense will preclude its use is correct, then children who understand the defense should use it less. Looking at Figure 3.7, one sees that children in Grades 1 and 2 who had at least partial understanding of denial (Levels 6 and 7) were less likely to use denial than children who had no understanding (Levels 2 and 3) or those who had

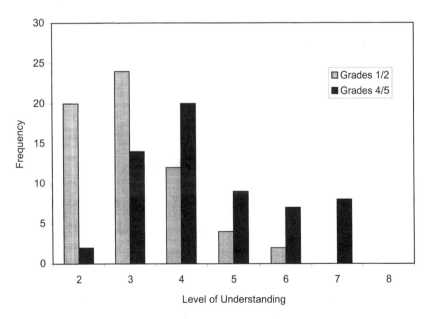

Figure 3.6.   Understanding projection: Grades 1 and 2 and Grades 4 and 5.

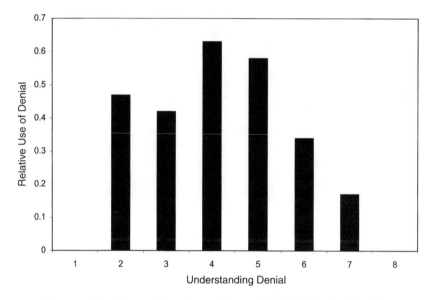

Figure 3.7. Use and understanding of denial: Grades 1and 2.

minimal to partial understanding (Levels 4 and 5; quadratic trend analysis, $p < .008$). Likewise, as seen in Figure 3.8, children in Grades 4 and 5 who did not understand (Level 2) projection were more likely to use projection than those who had some understanding of the defense (Levels 4 and above; linear trend analysis, $p < .01$). These findings support the theoretical assumption that the usefulness of a defense depends on its not being consciously understood. Once the function of the defense is consciously realized, its usefulness declines, and a new, cognitively more complex and not-yet-comprehended defense takes its place.

How Does One Know One Is Assessing Defenses?

The previously discussed studies have demonstrated developmental differences, developmental change, reliability of assessment, and a relation between defense use and defense understanding. However, how do researchers know that what they are assessing

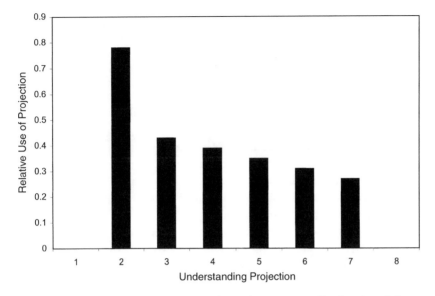

Figure 3.8.   Use and understanding of projection: Grades 4 and 5.

are defense mechanisms? How do they know their assessment method is valid?

On the basis of theory, one can identify three conditions that should be met if one's method is indeed assessing defenses. First, the use of defense mechanisms should increase under conditions of negative affect arousal or threat to the self. Second, defenses should protect the individual from psychological upset. Third, excessive reliance on age-inappropriate defenses should be associated with psychopathology. For each condition relevant research exists.

Use of Defenses Should Increase Under Negative Affect Arousal .

In a first test of this hypothesis Cramer and Gaul (1988) created an experiment in which children experienced a mildly stressful situation and observed the effect of this stress on their use of defenses. Sixty-four elementary school children participated in this two-session study. During the first session they told stories to TAT pictures, which were then coded with the DMM for defense use under minimal stress. We used this coding to create groups matched for defense use within each grade. Having established these groups, which were equivalent in their level of defense use, we then provided each group with a different experience during the second testing session; one group experienced success and one group experienced failure. To accomplish this, each child participated in a game that involved placing a marble at the top of a wooden rollway; the object of the game was to see how rapidly the marble could roll down a multilevel wooden track to exit from a chute at the bottom. The task was described to the child as one that depended on personal ability—skill and motor coordination—and that each child should try to get the marble to roll down the track fast enough to beat the (fictitious) time that "most kids your age could beat." The children also were told that if they did beat that time, their name, attached to a big gold seal, would be placed on the "Honor Board" along with those of other children who had done well. This Honor Board, with awards attached, was placed in the child's clear view.

To create the situation of success or failure, the experimenter used a stopwatch to measure the time elapsed between placement of the marble onto the track and its exit from the chute. Regardless of the actual time elapsed, children in the success condition were told they had beaten the time, and their names were put on the Honor Board. Children in the failure condition were told they had not beaten the necessary time and that their name could not be put on the Honor Board. In a previous pilot study we had determined that this experimental procedure elicited positive emotions among children experiencing success but negative affect among those experiencing failure.

After the experience of success or failure, the children again told TAT stories, which were coded with the DMM for defense use. Our interest here was in whether children who had experienced failure would tell stories in which there was a higher incidence of defense use. If so, then we might conclude that the increased use of these defenses occurred as a way to protect the child from potential upset associated with the arousal of negative emotions. After the storytelling, all children in the failure condition were given another chance with the marble rollway; all of them were "successful" this time and had their names put on the Honor Board.

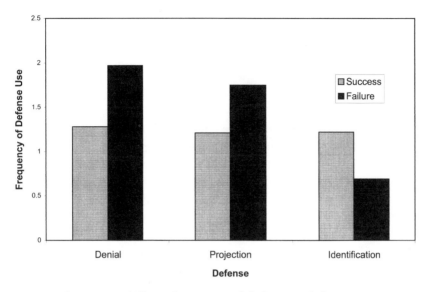

Figure 3.9. Effect of success and failure on defense use.

As one can see in Figure 3.9, the results confirmed the prediction that the failure condition would result in greater use of defenses. Although the success and failure groups had not differed in defense use prior to the game-playing session, after the experimental treatment children in the failure group used more denial and more projection than did children in the success group, who made greater use of identification. Thus, under conditions of negative affect arousal, the children used age-characteristic defenses; in contrast, the experience of success appeared to promote the use of a higher level defense.[4]

In a second study, I (Cramer, 1991a) applied this experimental paradigm to a group of college students. Students were individually escorted to the experimental room, where they lay on a cot with a videorecording camera focused directly at them. The experimenter explained that this was a study of creative imagination in college students. Standard TAT instructions were given, and again the use of imagination was emphasized. The student was

---

[4]The findings with identification may alternatively indicate that failure reduced the likelihood of using a more advanced defense.

then given four TAT cards, one at a time, and asked to tell a story in response to each card. During this time, the experimenter responded to each story neutrally, saying "all right" or "OK." However, after the fourth story for students in the negative affect group, the experimenter became extremely critical, saying "These stories are about the worst I have ever heard. Could you try to get some better ones?" After the fifth story the criticism continued, as it did after the sixth and seventh stories. At the end of the eighth story students sat up and completed a questionnaire describing their emotional experience during the experiment. They were then debriefed; the purpose of the criticism was explained, and assurance was given that the stories they told were quite adequate. In contrast to the experience of the criticized students, those in the control condition continued to receive the neutral reaction of the experimenter for all eight stories. For both conditions, stories were coded with the DMM for defense use during the first four and the second four stories.

As in the children's study (Cramer & Gaul, 1988), the hypothesis was that the experimental creation of a negative affect situation would increase the use of age-appropriate defenses. As one can see in Figure 3.10, this is what happened. Although the stress (anger) and control groups did not differ in defense use for the first four stories, students who were then criticized significantly increased their use of projection and identification. Denial also increased, but the increase was not statistically significant.

A third study, conducted with college students, focused on threatening a specific aspect of the students' self-image: their sex-role orientation (Cramer, 1998b). Again, the prediction was that this threat to self would increase the use of defenses. After providing an initial set of TAT stories, each student was given the Bem Sex-Role Inventory (BSRI; Bem, 1974), from which a student's predominant sex role orientation can be assessed. After each student completed the BSRI, its purpose was explained, and the examiner left the room for a few minutes, ostensibly to score the student's answer sheet. When the experimenter returned the student was presented with a complicated table of statistics and was told that his or her score was either extremely high on the Masculine scale or extremely high on the Feminine scale. Half of the students were given gender-consistent feedback (i.e., men were told they

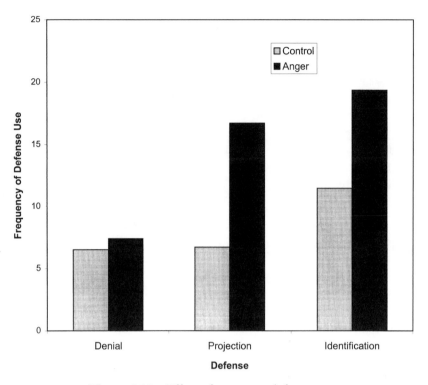

Figure 3.10.   Effect of anger on defense use.

scored high on the Masculine scale, and women were told that they scored high on the Feminine scale), and half were given gender-inconsistent feedback (i.e., men were told they scored high on the Feminine scale, and women were told that they scored high on the Masculine scale). The experimenter than engaged the student in a brief discussion in which the student was asked to explain his or her BSRI results.

Each student subsequently told three more TAT stories. My interest was in whether, having been provided with (bogus) feedback regarding their sex-role orientation, students who had received gender-inconsistent feedback would, as a result of a threat to the self, increase their use of defenses. The results of the study were very clear: Students who had received the gender-inconsistent feedback showed a dramatic increase in the use of identification, the defense that is both age appropriate and appropriate to the nature of the threat to self; that is, the threat to an aspect of the students' identity was responded to by an increase in the defense that is associated with identity (Erikson, 1968; see Figure 3.11).

These three studies (Cramer, 1991a, 1998b; Cramer & Gaul, 1988), then, demonstrate that the TAT-based measure of defense mechanisms, as coded by the DMM, produces the results that defense mechanism theory would predict: that under conditions of negative affect arousal or threat to the self individuals will increase their use of defenses.

Use of Defense Mechanisms Should Protect the Individual From Psychological Upset

According to theory, the function of a defense mechanism is to protect the individual from anxiety and emotional upset. The op-

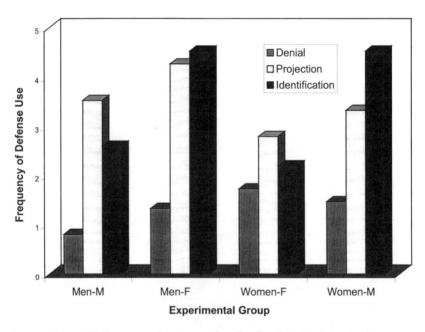

Figure 3.11. Defense mechanisms after feedback. Men-M = Male participant, masculine feedback; Men-F = male participant, feminine feedback; Women-F = female participant, feminine feedback; Women-M = female participant, masculine feedback.

portunity to test this assumption using the DMM arose in connection with a naturally occurring disaster (Dollinger & Cramer, 1990). A group of preadolescent boys were engaged in a soccer game when a thunderstorm began. After an extended halftime spent in their parents' cars, the boys resumed playing. Shortly into the second half, a lightning bolt struck the playing field. All the players were knocked to the ground; one boy was hit directly by the strike and died. A child clinical psychologist, Stephen Dollinger, undertook a clinical assessment of these boys. As part of this assessment he rated their level of emotional upset. This rating of upset was subsequently found to predict the parents' report of psychological problems in the boys (Dollinger, O'Donnell, & Staley, 1984). It also significantly predicted which boys avoided playing soccer in the subsequent 2-year interval (Dollinger, 1985).

At the time of the assessment, the boys told two TAT-like stories to pictures depicting lightning. Several years later these stories were coded with the DMM to determine the use of defense mechanisms. We predicted (Dollinger & Cramer, 1990) that boys with higher defense scores at this time—that is, close to the stressful incident—would be clinically assessed as showing less psychological upset. That is, using defenses would protect them from psychological upset. This prediction was supported. Boys who had higher defense scores (denial + projection + identification) were less upset than those with lower defense scores (multiple regression analysis; B = $-.41$, $p < .03$). Furthermore, when the incidence of only the two more mature defenses of projection and identification was considered, the relation between defense use and lack of upset was even stronger (multiple regression analysis; B = $-.68$, $p < .0006$). Thus, the use of defense mechanisms, as determined by the DMM, was consistent with theory: Boys who used more defenses at this time of psychological stress showed fewer signs of psychological upset.

Excessive Reliance on Age-Inappropriate Defenses Should Be Associated With Psychopathology

Both theory and research demonstrate that the defense of denial characterizes young children. It is age appropriate, or normative, and is not expected to imply the presence of a psychological disorder or pathology. However, frequent and persistent use of the immature defense of denial by an adult is a different matter. Indeed, the adult use of perceptual denial, in the absence of organic brain pathology, is a likely indication of psychosis. Thus, one should expect to find indications of psychopathology among adults whose TAT stories, when coded using the DMM, show strong use of the defense of denial.

Data from a study of patients at a small, psychodynamically oriented hospital offering intensive treatment are informative here (Blatt & Ford, 1994). All of these patients provided TAT stories on admission to the hospital and again after 15 months of treatment. These stories were coded for defense use with the DMM. A comparison of patients diagnosed as psychotic with those diagnosed with borderline personality disorder (BPD) indicated that the more seriously disturbed patients had higher overall defense scores; most significant is that the psychotic patients used more denial than did the patients with BPD. Also informative was the finding that, after treatment, the psychotic patients significantly reduced their defense use, especially denial. Furthermore, when the patients were independently rated by clinicians for degree of improvement after 15 months of treatment, those who were rated most improved had lower defense scores, and especially lower denial scores, than those who were rated as least improved (Cramer, 1999).

Thus, in these several ways, one sees that, among adults, relying on denial was especially associated with a more severe form of psychopathology. Furthermore, the abandonment of this immature defense was especially associated with a decrease in psychopathology.

I have shown that three theoretical assumptions about defense mechanisms—that negative affect arousal or threat to self increases the occurrence of defenses, that the use of defenses protects one from undue psychological upset, and that the use of immature defenses by adults is associated with psychopathology —are all supported when defenses are assessed on the basis of narrative stories coded with the DMM. It turn, these results support the validity of the DMM as a measure of defense mechanisms.

Immature Defense Use by Adults: Regression or Fixation?

The use of immature defenses by seriously disturbed adults raises the question of how this arises. Does it result from regression to a lower level of functioning, or have these individuals failed to develop more mature forms of defense and instead have remained fixated at an early stage of defense development? A definitive answer to this question requires a long-term longitudinal study in which defense use is continually assessed from early childhood to the point in adulthood at which pathology was manifest. No such study has yet been conducted. However, longitudinal studies of development have been conducted that contain extensive information regarding psychological functioning at early and later ages. In one of these (described by J. H. Block & Block, 1980), the study began when the children were age 3 years and has continued until age 23, when the participants provided TAT stories. It was thus possible to compare carefully collected ratings of the participants' psychological functioning when they were preschoolers with their adult defense functioning (Cramer & Block, 1998).

Coding the TAT stories of these 90 young adults from the San Francisco Bay area for defense use indicated that the predominant defense was projection. Compared to college students, identification was used less often. Whether this dissimilarity is due to differences between a college population and a mixed, not necessarily collegiate group, or whether the importance of the defense of identification diminishes after late adolescence is a matter to yet be determined. At any rate, identification was not as predominant in this young adult group as is generally the case in college samples.

As would be expected for 23-year-olds, denial was relatively rare. However, for some individuals this defense was predominant. These were not hospitalized patients, but they relied on an immature defense rather than a more developmentally appropriate one. Is there some way to understand this anomaly?

Because information regarding the participants' earlier defense use is not available, one cannot know whether the current use of denial reflects a regression from a higher to a lower level of defense functioning. However, information is available about the psychological status of these young adults when they were in early child-hood, when denial was age appropriate; this information might illuminate the fixation hypothesis. It is possible that, if these individuals were excessively stressed early in their development, they would use the defense of denial excessively. As a consequence of this overuse, denial might become firmly embedded in the child's personality, just as other stressors during critical periods of development have had lasting effects on children's physical and mental development. One must look, then, to discover what these adults who relied on denial were like as preschoolers.

In undertaking this exploration it soon became apparent that it was necessary to study the male and female participants separately, for the relation of early personality to later defense use differed by gender. Considering the males first, we (Cramer & Block, 1998) found that those who used denial as young adults had evidenced numerous signs of psychological distress as youngsters. These young boys had been described by their preschool teachers as being emotionally labile and inappropriate, lacking intellectual competence, having poor impulse control and poor interpersonal relationships, and lacking prosocial skills. In addition, the boys were more likely to be depressed and were rated as having low ego resilience. The single best predictor ($p < .0001$) of use of denial at age 23 was to have been described at age 3 as "appears to feel unworthy; thinks of self as bad." It is clear that the young boys had a strong need to protect themselves from excessive anxiety and to guard self-esteem; denial is the defense available at this age to carry out such a protective function. If, through intensive and continual use, this defense became ingrained in the child's personality, then its continued occurrence in adulthood may indicate a kind of defense fixation.

What about the females who were found to rely on denial at age 23? Although the use of denial by females is more socially approved, especially in certain social subgroups, it still is developmentally inappropriate. In this case one should expect to find evidence of psychological distress during the preschool years of these women. Looking to the descriptions provided by the female participants' preschool teachers, we found that this was indeed the case. However, the way in which distress was manifest differed from that occurring in the boys. The young girls were described as reacting to external stress by withdrawing into an inner private world, and as being involved in fantasy activity while avoiding interaction with others. This withdrawal was further accompanied by immobility, brooding, unusual mannerisms, daydreaming, and nonverbal communication. As with the boys, the girls showed signs of psychological distress, although the form this took was different from that shown by the boys. Also, in contrast with the boys, there was no relation between the girls' early ego resilience, prosocial behavior, or depression and the later occurrence of denial.

Taken together, these findings are consistent with the theoretical assumption that psychological upset at an early age will increase the use of the age-appropriate defense of denial and that under these conditions children will continue to rely on that defense into young adulthood, when it is no longer age appropriate.

Gender Differences and Defenses

When one begins to think about possible relations between gender and defense mechanisms, one obvious question is whether males and females generally use the same or different defenses. In addition to the possibility that males and females might differ in the particular defenses they use, it is also possible that using the same defense has different implications for males and females. For example, Cramer and Block's (1998) findings indicate that relying on the same defense—denial—in young adulthood by men and by women was related to very different personality features when they were young. In this section I consider these two issues: (a) gender differences in the use of defenses and (b) gender differences in the implications of using the same defenses.

It is curious that the theoretical literature on defense mechanisms has ignored, by and large, the idea that gender differences in personality might result in gender differences in defense use. Proponents of defense mechanism theory have also failed to consider the possibility that the use of defenses may have different consequences for the two genders. These omissions are true for classical psychoanalytic theory (e.g., A. Freud, 1936/1946; Fenichel, 1945) as well as for contemporary treatises (e.g., Cooper, 1998; Cramer, 1991b; Vaillant, 1976, 1977).

Still, among the psychoanalytic theories that address the general question of gender differences and personality there are aspects from which one may extrapolate to develop hypotheses relevant to the issue of gender and defense. For example, both S. Freud (1932) and Helene Deutsch (1944) theorized that female sexual identity included a component of turning aggression inward, from which one might predict that females would be likely to use defenses such as TAS. More generally, both Deutsch (1944) and Erikson (1964) emphasized women's sexual identity as based on a proclivity to focus inward toward their internal worlds, whereas men's sexual identity involved an outward orientation, focusing on the external world. Extrapolating from these theoretical positions, one might hypothesize that females would rely more on defenses that modify inner thoughts and feelings, even if this results in falsifying external perception, whereas males would depend more on defenses that place conflict in the external world, even if this means falsely attributing inner motivations to that external world. In this section I examine empirical research relevant to these theoretical positions.

Defense Use by Adult Men and Women

I turn now to the issue of defense use by each gender. As noted earlier, theory suggests that defenses that are directed outward and that externalize conflict and affect, such as projection or turning against the object, should characterize males more than females. In contrast, defenses that involve a modification of internal reality— such as denial, reversal, or reaction formation—or that direct aggression inward—such as turning against the self—should characterize females more than males.

"Masculine" defenses. Research findings generally support these predictions. In many studies, when defense use was assessed by semistructured projective techniques, such as the DMI, adult men consistently used projection and turning against the object more frequently than did adult women.

It is interesting that males and females who are independently determined to have a masculine orientation both make strong use of turning against the object (e.g., Evans, 1982). Thus sexual orientation, rather than biological gender, appears to be the important determining factor in the gender-associated difference in the use of turning against the object. In contrast, projection was found to be associated with a masculine orientation in males but not in females. Here biological gender, in consort with a masculine orientation, rather than sexual orientation alone, was the critical factor for the use of projection. (See Cramer, 1991b, for a review of relevant studies.)

When defense is assessed from TAT narratives, the findings again largely support the predictions. Among upper-level college students, projection is more frequent in men than in women (Cramer, 1991a, 1998a). This result has also been found in children and is discussed later.

However, not all research using the TAT approach to assessing defenses has found gender differences in the use of projection. Among young adults in the longitudinal study conducted in the San Francisco Bay area,[5] men and women did not differ significantly in the occurrence of projection (Cramer & Block, 1998). Likewise, male and female college freshmen have not differed statistically in their use of this defense (Cramer, 1995).

At first glance, one might be tempted to explain these exceptions to the general finding that projection characterizes males more than females as being due to some special factors in the nonconfirming samples. However, continuing study of these same college freshmen indicated that by the time they became seniors they showed the typical pattern: Men scored higher on projection than did women (Cramer, 1998a). Although it is unclear why the gender-based difference in projection was not present on entry to college, previous research has found a similar dedifferentiation between men and women when they are assessed for sexual identity during the freshman year, with a clear return to gender-based sexual differentiation among seniors (Cramer, 1980).

"Feminine" defenses. On the basis of theory, one expects that inwardly directed defenses, such as turning against the self, or defenses that function by changing inner affect or perception, such

---

[5]See J. H. Block and Block (1980) for a description of this study.

as denial, will characterize females more than males. As with masculine defenses, the research results largely support these predictions.

Research with the DMI or similar assessment methods has consistently demonstrated that females use more turning against the self, are more likely to use reaction formation and, in some studies, are more likely to use reversal (including reaction formation and denial). (See Cramer, 1991b, for a review of these studies.) Again, sexual orientation, rather than biological gender, appears to be the important factor in determining these gender differences. Turning against the self and reversal occur most frequently among people with a feminine sexual orientation, regardless of whether they are biologically male or female (Cramer & Carter, 1978; Evans, 1982; Frank, McLaughlin, & Crusco, 1984; Gleser & Ihilevich, 1969; Levit, 1991; Lobel & Winch, 1986).

Defenses as assessed from TAT narratives follow the pattern suggested by gender-based predictions. Among upper-level college students, women typically use denial more than do men (Cramer, 1991a, 1998a); as before, this difference is not statistically significant during the first year in college or in post-college age young adults. In these cases the absence of a statistically significant gender difference for denial is caused in part by the overall low level of occurrence of this immature defense; nevertheless, where gender difference exists, it is in the predicted direction.

The defense of identification is not easily characterized as being either masculine or feminine; thus, one might not expect to find gender differences in the use of this defense. On the other hand, psychoanalytic theory might support the prediction that the defense of identification should be stronger among males than among females, insofar as (a) identification plays a crucial role in young boys' resolution of the Oedipal conflict and (b) the plight of the Oedipal-stage boy involves greater stress than that of the girl, because the boy needs to switch his identification from mother to father (Chodorow, 1978).

The research findings regarding gender differences in the frequency of use of identification are mostly consistent. Various samples of college students, both upper and lower level, and samples of adults from the general population do not show any difference in the use of identification by men and women.

Defense Use by Children and Adolescent Boys and Girls

Although adult gender differences in defense use may be explained by socialization processes that vary for males and females, such differences are also found for children and adolescents. It is significant that these dissimilarities are greater for young children than for older children whereas, if continuing social pressures were entirely responsible for gender divergences, one would expect to find the opposite result.

Using the DMI, or similar assessment procedures, researchers have found that both early and late adolescents (Grades 9–10 and 11–12) show the typical gender-related pattern (Cramer, 1979; Levit, 1991). Boys use turning against the object and projection more than girls, whereas girls rely on turning against the self more than do boys. Also, older adolescent girls use reversal more than do boys of the same age (Cramer, 1979; Levit, 1991). Among younger children, boys use turning against the object more than do girls. This difference is statistically significant for first- and second-grade boys and shows the same pattern among fourth- and fifth-grade boys, although it lacks statistical significance. In contrast, the use of reversal is greater among girls than among boys. Again, the difference is statistically significant for the first and second graders; the same but nonsignificant pattern is found among the fourth and fifth graders (from analysis of data in Cramer, 1983).

Using the narrative DMM approach, researchers have shown that the incidence of projection is higher among boys than among girls. Again, the difference is statistically significant only among the youngest children ([mean age = 5 years, 8 months]; Cramer, 1987). However, boys consistently use projection more than do girls across childhood and adolescence. In contrast, girls use denial more than do boys. This difference is statistically significant at the youngest age, but girls continue to use more denial than do boys throughout childhood and adolescence (Cramer, 1987; Cramer & Gaul, 1988).

Studies of identification, in contrast to the findings for college students and adults, have shown that in two samples of elementary school children, girls used more identification than did boys (Cramer & Brilliant, 2001; Cramer & Gaul, 1988). A similar tendency was found in a third study, in which adolescent males and females were compared (Cramer, 1987).

Thus, ample evidence demonstrates gender differences in defense use. For the defenses of denial and projection, these differences conform to the predictions made from psychoanalytic theory. Comparable results have been found using two distinctive paradigms to assess defense use. The diversity of these two methods —one that is more structured, with expert-based prepared response alternatives, and the other an open-ended narrative procedure subsequently coded by trained raters—lends assurance that the results are not method specific but rather represent gender-based differences.

Implications of Defense Use: Gender-Based Differences

I have demonstrated differences in the frequency of defense use by males and females. At the same time, one finds that both genders use a variety of defenses, albeit to a greater or lesser degree. In this connection one may ask whether the use of the same defense by males and females has the same implication for their psychosocial functioning. For example, if projection is typically associated with males, whereas denial is more typically associated with females, then what are the implications of males relying on denial or females relying on projection? In the previous section I noted that males who used the feminine defenses of TAS and reversal were also found to have a cross-gender, feminine sexual orientation; however, females who used the masculine defense of projection were not found to have a cross-gender masculine sexual orientation.

I now look at gender-based differences in the relation between defense use and personality functioning. We investigated this question in two groups of individuals. The first was a group of more than 300 college students from a New England liberal arts college that draws applicants from every state in the United States (Cramer, 1995, 1998a, 2001). The second was the sample of 90 young adults from the San Francisco Bay area who have been participating in a longitudinal study from ages 3 to 23 (Cramer, in press); extensive information on their development has been systematically collected over the years by Jack and Jeanne Block (see J. H. Block & Block, 1980, for a full description of the sample and study).

College students. Among college students, are there different implications for men and women who use the same defense mechanism? In one study of 172 male and female college students I assessed the students' identification with their parents and related this to the students' defense use (Cramer, 2001). To assess the degree of their identification with either the same-sex parent or the opposite-sex parent, I asked each student to first describe his or her ideal self, using a set of 70 adjectives pertaining to personality, values, morals, attitudes, and intellectual functioning. Each adjective was rated on a 7-point scale, indicating whether this trait was very much like one's ideal self or very unlike one's ideal self.[6] The students subsequently used the same 70 adjectives to describe either their same-sex or opposite-sex parent. I used the degree of similarity in the rating of each adjective for the ideal self and for the parent as a measure of identification with the parent: The more similar the ideal self to the parent, the greater the degree of identification; that is, the more the student ideally wished to be like the parent, the stronger the identification.

I then related this measure of parent identification to the students' use of defense mechanisms. I also compared DMM defense scores with the students' stage of identity development, as provided from an independent measure (Mallory, 1989) created to assess Erikson's (1968) four stages of identity: Diffusion, Foreclosure, Moratorium, and Achieved.

The results showed that for college men the defense of identification predicted the closeness of the male students' identification with their fathers (Cramer, 2001); however, for college women defense identification was unrelated to identification with either the father or mother. Also, for college men, defense identification occurred in conjunction with reaching the last stage of identity development—that is, an Achieved identity. For women, this relation between defense and Achieved identity was found only if the woman's identification with her father was weak. Thus, for women

---

[6] A Q-sort resulting in a rectangular forced seven-step distribution was used.

there was a reciprocal relation between defense identification and father identification in predicting an Achieved identity: Either strong defense or strong father identification, but not both, predicted the Achieved status.

A different study of college students (Cramer, 1995) indicated that the use of identification among freshman women was positively correlated with scores on the Narcissism Personality Inventory (Raskin & Terry, 1988). This relation was partly due to high scores on the Authority and Superiority subscales, which are generally considered to be positive, adaptive aspects of narcissism. However, the use of identification by these women was also associated with the Exploitative and Exhibitionistic subscales—features of narcissism seen as defensive and maladaptive. These relations were not found for men, and for the women they were no longer evident when the women were restudied during their senior year of college (Cramer, 1998a). In fact, for the men at senior year there was a negative association between identification and narcissism scores; this was largely due to aspects of narcissism that involve domination or control of others.

Another study found that men also differed from women at freshman year in the relation between identification and certain personality characteristics. For men, identification tended to be positively connected to ego resiliency and negatively connected to alienation—associations not found for the women (data from Cramer, 2001).

The relation of the defense of denial to identity status or to parent identification did not differ by gender. Neither for men nor for women was denial correlated to either parent identification or identity status (Cramer, 2001). Neither, among the college students, were the other personality variables studied (narcissism, ego control, ego resiliency, depression, and anxiety) associated with denial, for either men or women (Cramer, 1995, 2001).

However, for both genders projection was positively related to the Moratorium status and negatively related to the Foreclosure status (Cramer, 1995, 2001). There also was an interesting tendency for projection to be positively associated with women's identification with their mothers but negatively associated with men's identification with their fathers (Cramer, 2001). For men, there was a tendency for projection to be positively connected with depression, a result not found for the women. Instead, for the freshman women, narcissism was positively related to projection; this was due only to the positive, adaptive aspects of narcissism, including authority, superiority, and self-sufficiency (Cramer, 1995). This positive connection between projection and adaptive narcissism continued into the senior year of college (Cramer, 1998a). Consistent with this was the finding that, for women, the use of projection was negatively associated with a measure of ego overcontrol, indicating that the women who used projection were not overly rigid or "uptight" in their psychological functioning (Cramer, in press).

Differences in the implications of the use of projection were also found in an experimental study in which college students' self-esteem was threatened by critical remarks made by the experimenter (Cramer, 1991a). After the experiment, the students who had been criticized reported that the experimenter's remarks had made them angry. At the same time, their TAT stories indicated increased anger through the story content. For some students this content consisted of anger directed outward; for others, the content was of anger directed inward.

We (Cramer 1991a) then related the use of defenses to the direction of anger expression and found that, prior to criticism, projection in both men and women was positively correlated with the outward expression of anger. Also, for women only, projection was positively related to anger directed inward. However, after criticism, this changed: For men, there was a tendency for projection to be correlated with aggression directed inward, whereas for women projection was correlated only with aggression directed outward.

Two additional gender differences were found: Men who used the feminine defense of denial were less likely to direct aggression outward, a relation not found for the women. Instead, women who used denial were more likely to direct aggression inward after criticism. Also, in the absence of criticism, women who used identification were more likely to direct aggression inward, whereas men who used identification were more likely to direct aggression outward.

Young adult sample. In a slightly older, more diverse sample of young adults I showed even more clearly how the use of the same defense by men and women has different implications for personality (Cramer, in press). Each participant, in addition to providing TAT stories coded for defense use, participated in an extensive series of interviews and clinical assessments. On the basis of this information, experienced personality and clinical psychologists rated the personality, cognitive, and emotional functioning of the participants. These ratings were then related to the participants' defense use.

Gender differences were seen most clearly for the use of projection. Men who relied on projection were described by expert observers as having a wary, paranoid style of behavior. They were characterized as being distrustful of others; transferring blame to others; evaluating the motives of others; and tending to be guileful, manipulative, and hostile toward others. They also appeared both anxious and depressed. In contrast, women who relied on projection were described quite differently. They were seen as lively, positive, and extraverted and were rated as not showing the interpersonal wariness and mistrust shown by the men. They did not transfer blame to others and did not see themselves as victims. In addition, whereas men who used projection were characterized as anxious and depressed, there was a negative relation between projection and depressive tendencies in women. Furthermore, men who used projection tended toward a narcissistic and psychopathic personality, whereas for women projection was related to healthy adjustment. I further examine this gender difference in the implications of the use of projection later.

Identification as a defense also had different implications for men and women in the young adult group. Women who relied on identification were described quite positively and appeared socially competent. They communicated well, were sought out for their ideas, and were at ease with themselves and others. They were less likely to be depressed than women who used little identification. Overall, they appeared mature and well adjusted. The men in this sample showed few clear personality correlates of identification; however, different from the women, men who did rely on identification were characterized as lacking self-esteem and being low in ego control.

In contrast to the differential gender implications for the use of projection and identification by males and females, men and women who relied on the immature defense of denial were characterized in similar ways. They appeared to be inconsistent and unpredictable, with an unstable personality. For both men and women denial was associated with anxiety. They were also characterized as showing a weakness in cognitive functioning, engaging in what might be termed *fuzzy thinking*, and being unable to see to the heart of important problems. These men and women also had a strong egotistical quality; they were self-centered, self-indulgent, and self-dramatizing. The women, however, were rated as having some more positive features—being interesting, expressive, and initiating humor—that were not characteristic of the men. Overall, however, there was a high degree of similarity in the personality descriptions of men and women who relied on denial.

These results are also relevant to the previously raised issue of whether the use of an age-inappropriate defense, such as denial, would be associated with other indications of psychological difficulties. The findings indicate that this is indeed the case: Men and women who relied on denial were characterized by ego instability, inability to delay gratification, and self-centeredness. Although there had been gender differences at preschool age in the behavior of these heavy denial users, at age 23 they are described in remarkably similar terms (Cramer, in press). The main difference at age 23 appears to be that this combination of behavioral characteristics was more favorably perceived when it occurred in women than when it occurred in men, suggesting the possibility that aspects of this behavioral style fit more readily with a feminine gender stereotype.

Thus, it was with the defense of projection—the predominant defense style in this sample of young adults—that the most marked gender differences were found. For men, extensive use of projection was associated with an interpersonal wariness, in which guilt and blame are transferred to others, including both interpersonal hypersensitivity and mistrust. This behavioral description of the men shares many features with the clinical description of paranoid personality disorder (*DSM–IV*; American Psychiatric Association, 1994). These data demonstrate that men who display some of the behavioral characteristics associated with a paranoid personality are those who also use the defense of projection, the defense that characterizes this diagnosis (S. Freud, 1911/1958; Vaillant, 1994).

On the other hand, the use of projection by the young adult women in this sample is associated with quite a different picture. Perhaps the most striking finding here is that, for these women, projection is related to adaptive behaviors. Further examination of these results revealed that, in contrast to the men, only one facet of projection is related to women's adaptive behaviors—namely, the externalization of anger and other negative emotions. Women who externalized negative emotions were described as lively and poised; they are intellectually motivated and concerned with abstract issues. These are the women who are described as not having the wary, hypersensitive behaviors of the men who use projection, and they were not found to be anxious. Furthermore, projection in these women is a negative predictor for depression, in contrast to the men.

Synthesis: Gender Differences in Implications of Defense Use

In this section I synthesize these reported findings based on two participant groups: the young adults from the general population of the San Francisco Bay area and the college students at a highly selective New England college.

The findings on denial as a defense may be summarized by three general points. First, college students do not use denial often, and it generally is not associated with their personality characteristics, for either men or women. However, in the case of handling anger, the use of denial by men and women has different implications. College men who use the feminine defense of denial do not show the typical male pattern of directing anger outward, whereas women who use the feminine defense of denial do show the feminine pattern of directing anger inward in response to criticism. Third, both young adult men and women from the general population who rely on denial have immature, egotistical, and unstable personalities, although the women who use denial are perceived more favorably than are the men.

For both genders the defense of identification is related to their gender-typed handling of anger; men who use identification direct anger outward, but women who use identification direct anger inward, consistent with psychoanalytic theory. For both genders, identification is related to reaching an Achieved identity, as suggested by Erikson (1968). However, this occurs somewhat differently for men and women. For men, there is a direct positive relation between the defense of identification and an Achieved identity; there is also a direct relation between defense identification and identification with one's father. For women, defense identification is related to an Achieved identity only if the woman's identification with her father is weak; otherwise, defense identification is not related to her identification with either parent.

The use of identification also appears to have different implications for the way males and females perceive themselves and the way they are perceived by others. Late adolescent females who rely on identification are high in narcissism—both the adaptive and defensive types. This connection, however, no longer holds as these young women mature to their last year in college. By young adulthood, women who use identification are seen as socially competent, mature, and well adjusted.

The picture is rather different for males. Among late adolescent males, identification is positively related to ego resiliency and negatively related to alienation. As they mature, males who use identification are low in narcissism, especially the type involving domination and control of others. As young adults, they also lack ego control. In a society in which male domination is rewarded, it is likely these associations contribute to the finding that young adult men who rely on identification are also lacking in self-esteem.

The most striking gender differences in the implications of defense use are seen for projection. Females who use projection are positively identified with their same-sex parent, whereas males who rely on projection are negatively identified with their same-sex parent. It is striking that when males who rely on projection are criticized they direct anger inward; this may explain the positive association for men between projection and depression in both the college and the young adult groups. These relations are not found for females: When criticized, females who rely on projection direct their anger outward. Furthermore, females who rely on projection are not depressed; rather, as seen in the late adolescents and continuing into young adulthood, females who use projection are characterized by healthy narcissism, lively sociability, and positive adjustment.

It is interesting to contrast the description of the women who use the masculine defense of projection with that of women who use the more typically feminine defense of turning against the self (e.g., Cramer, 1991b; Cramer & Carter, 1978; Gleser & Ihilevich, 1969; Massong, Dickson, Ritzler, & Layne, 1982).[7] Turning against the self is associated, for both men and women, with self-blame, low self-esteem, maladjustment, symptom distress, and suicide attempts (e.g., Frank et al., 1984; Ihilevich & Gleser, 1986; Scholz, 1973; Vaillant, 1983). As discussed earlier, turning against the self is also positively associated with a feminine sex-role orientation and especially with passive dependency (Cramer & Carter, 1978; Evans, 1982; Frank et al., 1984; Gleser & Ihilevich, 1969; Levit, 1991; Lobel & Winch, 1986). In contrast, projection is negatively associated with a feminine orientation (Levit, 1991).

As the studies I have discussed indicate, females who direct negative affect inward are more prone to psychological difficulties, especially depression. Using a defense that directs negative affect inward is also associated with feminine sex-role adoption. Thus, there is a stereotyped sex-role configuration in which the defense of turning of negative emotions inward is associated with low self-esteem, self-blame, and depression. In women, this orientation may garner a degree of social approval, for the "feminine" defense of turning against the self is positively correlated with social desirability in women; however, it is negatively correlated for men (Evans, 1979; Richert & Ketterling, 1978; Wilson, 1982).

This research-based configuration suggests a corollary: Women who fail to direct negative affect outward are more subject to depression. Support for this corollary is seen in the present study (Cramer, in press): Minimal use by women of the externally oriented defense of projection was associated with depression, sensitivity to criticism, vulnerability to threat, dependency, feeling victimized, and a tendency to withdraw when faced with difficulties. In contrast is the configuration, also found in the present study, in which the use of projection by women—that is, the externalization

---

[7]Portions of the following discussion appear in Cramer (in press).

of negative emotions—occurs in conjunction with lively sociability, communality, humor, and poise and with the absence of vulnerability, passivity, and depressive symptoms. Thus, women who use projection are less likely to experience psychological difficulties.

Conclusion

I have shown how one of the central concepts in psychoanalytic theory, the defense mechanism, has been studied empirically. Research has demonstrated a chronological pattern for the emergence of different defenses, as hypothesized by Anna Freud. It has also demonstrated a reason for this developmental change—namely, that as a child becomes cognitively capable of deciphering the functioning of a defense, that particular defense becomes less useful, and a new, cognitively more complex and not-yet-understood defense takes its place.

The research reported here also provides empirical support for the basic psychoanalytic concept of the defense mechanism. According to psychoanalytic theory, defenses are brought into play when a person is threatened by excessive negative affect or when there is a threat to the self. As reported, experimental studies designed to increase negative affect or to threaten the self-concept have clearly shown that the use of defense mechanisms increases under such circumstances.

The research also goes beyond psychoanalytic theory to explore the question of gender differences in the use of defenses and gender differences in the implications of defense use. In this chapter I have drawn together a variety of findings relevant to this issue. As an example, the defense of projection is consistently found to characterize males more than females, although there are some females for whom projection is a prominent defense. It is striking that the personality of males who rely on projection is quite different from that of females who use projection: The males are described as wary, mistrustful, and hostile, whereas the females are seen as sociable, lively, and well adjusted. There are fewer differences between males and females who rely on denial. Although females tend to use denial more than males and although the overall occurrence of denial among adults is at a low level, men and women who do rely on denial are described in strikingly similar ways. They are seen as narcissistic, unpredictable, and anxious. Furthermore, gender-related differences in the implications of the use of denial, projection, and identification were demonstrated in the ways in which anger is deployed, in the area of identity development, and in the association of defenses with narcissism and self-esteem.

It is heartening to see that the concept of the defense mechanism, for so many years ignored by empirical researchers,[8] has sparked renewed interest in empirical study. In addition to the work discussed here, other programs of research on defenses, such as those of Davidson (1996; Davidson & MacGregor, 1996), Hibbard and Porcerelli (Hibbard et al., 1994; Porcerelli, Thomas, Hibbard, & Cogan, 1998), Perry (1988; Perry & Hoglend, 1998; Perry et al., 1998), and Vaillant (1977, 1993, 1994), have demonstrated that defenses can be studied by systematic methods and that research with these methods increases understanding of both normal personality and psychopathology. These studies should continue to enrich understanding of human nature.

References

American Psychiatric Association. (1994). *Diagnostic and statistical manual of mental disorders* (4th ed.). Washington, DC: Author.

Anthony, E. J. (1970). The behavior disorders of childhood. In P. H. Mussen (Ed.), *Carmichael's handbook of child psychology* (Vol. 2, pp. 667–764). New York: Wiley.

Avery, R. R. (1985). *The place of self and object representations in personality organization and social behavior.* Unpublished doctoral dissertation, University of Rochester, New York.

Bellak, L. (1975). *The Thematic Apperception Test: The Children's Apperception Test and the Senior Apperception Technique in clinical use* (3rd ed.). New York: Grune & Stratton.

---

[8]For a discussion of the reasons for this, see Cramer and Davidson, 1998; 2000A.

Bem, S. J. (1974). The measurement of psychological androgyny. *Journal of Consulting and Clinical Psychology, 42*, 155–162.

Blaess, D. R. (1998). *The relationships among defense mechanisms, psychological and physical health symptoms, and electrodermal response to emotionally evocative stimuli.* Unpublished doctoral dissertation, California School of Professional Psychology, Los Angeles.

Blatt, S. J., & Ford, R. Q. (1994). *Therapeutic change: An object relations perspective.* New York: Plenum.

Block, J. H., & Block, J. (1980). The role of ego-control and ego-resiliency in the organization of behavior. In W. A. Collins (Ed.), *Minnesota Symposia on Child Psychology: Development of cognition, affect and social relations* (pp. 39–101). Hillsdale, NJ: Erlbaum.

Blum, G. S. (1953). *Psychoanalytic theories of personality.* New York: McGraw-Hill.

Brody, L. R., Rozek, M. K., & Muten, E. O. (1985). Age, sex, and individual differences in children's defensive styles. *Journal of Child Clinical Psychology, 14*, 132–138.

Chodorow, N. (1978). *The reproduction of mothering: Psychoanalysis and the sociology of gender.* Berkeley: University of California Press.

Cooper, S. H. (1998). Changing notions of defense within psychoanalytic theory. *Journal of Personality, 66*, 947–964.

Cramer, P. (1979). Defense mechanisms in adolescence. *Developmental Psychology, 15*, 476–477.

Cramer, P. (1980). The development of sexual identity. *Journal of Personality Assessment, 44*, 604–612.

Cramer, P. (1983). Children's use of defense mechanisms in reaction to displeasure caused by others. *Journal of Personality, 51*, 78–94.

Cramer, P. (1987). The development of defense mechanisms. *Journal of Personality, 55*, 597–614.

Cramer, P. (1991a). Anger and the use of defense mechanisms in college students. *Journal of Personality, 59*, 39–55.

Cramer, P. (1991b). *The development of defense mechanisms: Theory, research, and assessment.* New York: Springer-Verlag.

Cramer, P. (1995). Identity, narcissism and defense mechanisms in late adolescence. *Journal of Research in Personality, 29*, 341–361.

Cramer, P. (1997). Evidence for change in children's use of defense mechanisms. *Journal of Personality, 65*, 233–247.

Cramer, P. (1998a). Freshman to senior year: A follow-up study of identity, narcissism and defense mechanisms. *Journal of Research in Personality, 32*, 156–172.

Cramer, P. (1998b). Threat to gender representation: Identity and identification. *Journal of Personality, 66*, 335–357.

Cramer, P. (1999). Future directions for the Thematic Apperception Test. *Journal of Personality Assessment, 72*, 74–92.

Cramer, P. (2000a). Defense mechanisms in psychology today: Further processes for adaptation. *American Psychologist, 55*, 637–646.

Cramer, P. (2000b). Development of identity: Gender makes a difference. *Journal of Research in Personality, 34*, 42–72.

Cramer, P. (in press). Defense mechanisms, behavior and affect in young adulthood. *Journal of Personality.*

Cramer, P. (2001). Identification and its relation to identity development. *Journal of Personality, 69*, 667–688.

Cramer, P., & Block, J. (1998). Preschool antecedents of defense mechanism use in young adulthood. *Journal of Personality and Social Psychology, 74*, 159–169.

Cramer, P., & Brilliant, M. (2001). Defense use and defense understanding in children. *Journal of Personality, (69)*2, 297–322.

Cramer, P., & Carter, T. (1978). The relationship between sexual identification and the use of defense mechanisms. *Journal of Personality Assessment, 42*, 63–73.

Cramer, P., & Davidson, K. (Eds.). (1998). Defense mechanisms in current personality research. *Journal of Personality, 66*, 879–1157.

Cramer, P., & Gaul, R. (1988). The effects of success and failure on children's use of defense mechanisms. *Journal of Personality, 56*, 729–742.

Davidson, K. (1996). Self- and expert-reported emotion inhibition: On the utility of both data sources. *Journal of Research in Personality, 30*, 535–549.

Davidson, K., & MacGregor, M. W. (1996). Reliability of an idiographic Q-sort measure of defense mechanisms. *Journal of Personality Assessment, 66*, 624–639.

Deutsch, H. (1944). *The psychology of women* (Vol. 1). New York: Grune & Stratton.

Dollinger, S. J. (1985). Lightening-strike disaster among children. *British Journal of Medical Psychology, 58*, 375–383.

Dollinger, S. J., & Cramer, P. (1990). Children's defensive responses and emotional upset following a disaster: A projective assessment. *Journal of Personality Assessment, 54*, 116–127.

Dollinger, S. J., O'Donnell, J. P., & Staley, A. A. (1984). Lightening strike disaster: Effects on children's fears and worries. *Journal of Consulting and Clinical Psychology, 52*, 1028–1038.

Engel, G. L. (1962). *Psychological development in health and disease.* Philadelphia: Saunders.

Erikson, E. H. (1964). Inner and outer space: Reflections on womanhood. In R. J. Lifton (Ed.), *The woman in America* (pp. 1–26). Boston: Beacon Press.

Erikson, E. H. (1968). *Identity: Youth and crisis.* New York: Norton.

Evans, R. G. (1979). The relationship of the Marlowe–Crowne Scale and its components to defensive preferences. *Journal of Personality Assessment, 43*, 406–410.

Evans, R. G. (1982). Defense mechanisms in females as a function of sex-role orientation. *Journal of Clinical Psychology, 38*, 816–817.

Fenichel, O. (1945). *The psychoanalytic theory of neurosis.* New York: Norton.

Frank, S. J., McLaughlin, A. M., & Crusco, A. (1984). Sex role attributes, symptom distress, and defensive style among college men and women. *Journal of Personality and Social Psychology, 47,* 182–192.

Freud, A. (1946). *The ego and the mechanisms of defense.* New York: International Universities Press. (Original work published 1936)

Freud, A. (1965). *Normality and pathology in childhood.* New York: International Universities Press.

Freud, S. (1932). The psychology of women. In J. Strachey (Ed. & Trans.), *The standard edition of the complete psychological works of Sigmund Freud* (Vol. 22, pp. 112–135). London: Hogarth.

Freud, S. (1958). Psycho-analytic notes on an autobiographical account of a case of paranoia (dementia paranoides). In J. Strachey (Ed. & Trans.), *The standard edition of the complete psychological works of Sigmund Freud* (Vol. 12, pp. 9–34). London: Hogarth. (Original work published 1911)

Gedo, J., & Goldberg, A. (1973). *Models of the mind.* Chicago: University of Chicago Press.

Gleser, G. C., & Ihilevich, D. (1969). An objective instrument for measuring defense mechanisms. *Journal of Consulting and Clinical Psychology, 33,* 51–60.

Glover, E. (1937). Symposium on the theory of the therapeutic results of psychoanalysis. *International Journal of Psychoanalysis, 18,* 125–132.

Hartmann, H. (1950). Psychoanalysis and developmental psychology. In *Essays on ego psychology* (pp. 99–112). New York: International Universities Press.

Haworth, M. R. (1963). A schedule for the analysis of CAT responses. *Journal of Projective Techniques and Personality Assessment, 27,* 181–184.

Hibbard, S., Farmer, L., Wells, C., Difillipo, E., Barry, W., Korman, R., & Sloan, P. (1994). Validation of Cramer's Defense Mechanism Manual for the TAT. *Journal of Personality Assessment, 63,* 197–210.

Ihilevich, D., & Gleser, G. C. (1986). *Defense mechanisms: Their classification, correlates, and measurement with the Defense Mechanisms Inventory.* Owosso, MI: DMI Associates.

Levit, D. B. (1991). Gender differences in ego defenses in adolescence: Sex roles as one way to understand the differences. *Journal of Personality and Social Psychology, 61,* 992–999.

Lichtenberg, J. D., & Slap, J. W. (1972). On the defense mechanism: A survey and synthesis. *Journal of the American Psychoanalytic Association, 20,* 776–792.

Lobel, T. E., & Winch, G. L. (1986). Different defense mechanisms among men with different sex role orientations. *Sex Roles, 15,* 215–220.

Luciano, J. (1999). *Examining the cultural specificity of the Thematic Apperception Test through ego defense measurement.* Unpublished doctoral dissertation, Gallaudet University, Washington, DC.

Mallory, M. E. (1989). Q-sort definition of ego identity status. *Journal of Youth and Adolescence, 18,* 399–411.

Massong, S. R., Dickson, A. I., Ritzler, B. A., & Layne, C. C. (1982). Assertion and defense mechanism preference. *Journal of Counseling Psychology, 29*, 591–596.

Murray, H. A. (1943). *Thematic Apperception Test*. Cambridge, MA: Harvard University Press.

Nunberg, H. (1955). *Principles of psychoanalysis*. New York: International Universities Press. (Original work published 1932)

Perry, J. C. (1988). A prospective study of life stress, defenses, psychotic symptoms and depression in borderline and antisocial personality disorders and bipolar Type II affective disorder. *Journal of Personality Disorders, 2*, 49–59.

Perry, J. C., & Hoglend, P. (1998). Convergent and discriminant validity of overall defensive functioning. *Journal of Nervous and Mental Disease, 186*, 529–535.

Perry, J. C., Hoglend, P., Shear, K., Vaillant, G. E., Horowitz, M. J., Kardos, M. E., & Bille, H. (1998). Field trial of a diagnostic axis for defense mechanisms for *DSM–IV*. *Journal of Personality Disorders, 12*, 56–68.

Porcerelli, J. H., Thomas, S., Hibbard, S., & Cogan, R. (1998). Defense mechanisms development in children, adolescents and late adolescents. *Journal of Personality Assessment, 71*, 411–420.

Raskin, R., & Terry, H. (1988). A principal-components analysis of the Narcissistic Personality Inventory and further evidence of its construct validity. *Journal of Personality and Social Psychology, 54*, 896–902.

Richert, A. J., & Ketterling, R. (1978). Psychological defense as a moderator variable. *Psychological Reports, 42*, 291–294.

Schafer, R. (1954). *Psychoanalytic interpretation in Rorschach testing*. New York: Grune & Stratton.

Scholz, J. A. (1973). Defense styles in suicide attempters. *Journal of Consulting and Clinical Psychology, 40*, 70–73.

Skodol, A. E., & Perry, J. C. (1993). Should an axis for defense mechanisms be included in DSM-IV? *Comprehensive Psychiatry, 34*, 108–119.

Soldz, S., & Valliant, G. E. (1998). A 50-year longitudinal study of defense use among inner city men: A validation of the DSM-IV defense axis. *Journal of Nervous and Mental Disease, 186*, 104–111.

Spitz, R. (1957). *No and yes: On the beginnings of human communication*. New York: International Universities Press.

Spitz, R. (1961). Some early prototypes of ego defenses. *Journal of the American Psychoanalytic Association, 9*, 626–651.

Vaillant, G. E. (1976). Natural history of male psychological health: V. The relation of choice of ego mechanisms of defense to adult adjustment. *Archives of General Psychiatry, 33*, 535–545.

Vaillant, G. E. (1977). *Adaptation to life*. Boston: Little, Brown.

Vaillant, G. E. (1983). Childhood environment and maturity of defense mechanisms. In D. Magnusson & V. L. Allen (Eds.), *Human development: An interactional perspective* (pp. 342–352). New York: Academic Press.

Vaillant, G. E. (1993). *The wisdom of the ego*. Cambridge, MA: Harvard University Press.

Vaillant, G. E. (1994). Ego mechanisms of defense and personality psychopathology. *Journal of Abnormal Psychology, 103*, 44–50.

Wilson, J. F. (1982). Recovery from surgery and scores on the Defense Mechanism Inventory. *Journal of Personality Assessment, 46*, 312–319.

4

Exploring the Inner World of Severely Disturbed Bulimic Women:
Empirical Investigations of Psychoanalytic Theory of Female Development

J. Christopher Fowler, Ben Brunnschweiler, and
Johanna Brock

Since its inclusion as a distinct psychiatric disorder in the *Diagnostic and Statistical Manual of Mental Disorders*, 3rd ed. (*DSM–III*; American Psychiatric Association, 1980), bulimia nervosa has been under intense scientific scrutiny to delineate its core behavioral features and to explore its biological, psychological, and social causes. In this chapter we undertake a limited review of theory and empirical research and report on a recent project in which psychoanalytic formulations of bulimia were tested in a

We extend special thanks to Mark A. Blais for statistical consultation. We also thank Gary Harrington for his role in creating the electronic database used in this study and to the Erik H. Erikson Institute at the Austen Riggs Center for financial, technical, and conceptual support in conducting this project.

sample of 120 women with serious psychiatric disorders, approximately half of whom have been diagnosed with bulimia nervosa.[1] We use a psychoanalytic theory of eating disorders to review the literature and current results and to consider the role that gender-specific conflicts may play in the formation of bulimic symptoms. In this study we explored a broad range of unconscious processes and behaviors that may relate to bulimic women's internal conflicts, ego deficits, and defenses. This investigation did not address the major problems of causality; neither did it resolve major disagreements in this area of research. Rather, we examined to what extent aggression, dependency, object relations, and primitive defenses play in the current psychological makeup of severely disturbed bulimic women. An exploration of the day-to-day interpersonal behaviors of these inpatients may also clarify the behavioral correlates of bulimia. Given that bulimia afflicts predominately adolescent and young adult women, we consider the impact that gender-specific conflicts and cultural influences may have on the formation and maintenance of this symptom.

Historical Context

The enigma of pathological eating has long puzzled, intrigued, and concerned physicians, philosophers, and families of those afflicted. Historical reconstructions trace anorexic and bulimic activity as far back as the 11th century (Sours, 1980) in Persia, where a physician successfully treated an anorexic prince. Historians have debated the likelihood that psychopathology in the form of anorexia and bulimia were driving forces in the starvation rituals of 13th- and 14th-century Roman Catholic "holy women" (Bell, 1985; Brumberg, 1988). Later, more reliable medical texts (Gull, 1873; Morton, 1694)

---

[1] We originally set out to study anorexia nervosa, bulimia nervosa, and a well-matched comparison group, but because of underrepresentation of anorexic patients ($n = 10$), we were unable to statistically contrast anorexic and bulimic cases in this hospital population. The intriguing questions that arise regarding the potential intrapsychic differences between these groups must be postponed until adequate sampling can ensure adequate power for analyses.

documented cases of starvation with intermittent bingeing and purging secondary to starvation. Gull and his contemporary Lasegue (1873/1964) coined the term *anorexia* to classify patients whose illness had apparently caused them to lose their desire for food. Both physicians, independent and unknown to the other, struggled with the etiology of the disorder. Gull first postulated an organic cause (gastric nervous dysfunction) and then, on the basis of disconfirming physical evidence, turned to possible psychological causes. Descriptive psychiatry's shifting emphasis from organic to psychological cause has been apparent throughout the past 100 years as popular biological theories gave way to psychological theories, only to return to physical causes and thus begin another iteration of etiological theories (Sours, 1980).

Psychoanalytic formulations have also undergone a major paradigm shift in the past 100 years. Classic drive theorists attributed the meaning of eating disorders to a regressive, hysterical defense against sexual impulses, but with the emergence of alternative theories there is a growing recognition that eating disorders are complex syndromes that result from disturbances in object relations, ego functions, and personality development exacerbated, and perhaps caused, by disturbances in the family system and the social context in which they arise (Bruch, 1973; Cross, 1993; Jeammet & Chabert, 1998; Minuchin, Rosman, & Baker, 1978; Steiner-Adair, 1986).

Whereas researchers can draw on 100 years of investigations into the meanings and causes of anorexia, there is far less information available about the puzzling symptoms of bingeing and purging as a distinct disorder. Bulimia nervosa was distinguished as a separate form of pathology in 1980 when it was introduced in the *DSM–III*. Bulimic activity has long been seen as one of the features and subtypes of anorexia, but it emerged as a distinct disorder on the discovery that some individuals engaged in frequent bingeing and purging but maintained normal body weight. As with anorexia, the incidence of bulimia nervosa is far more prevalent in females, especially adolescents and young adults. *Bulimia*, as defined by the *DSM–III–R* (American Psychiatric Association, 1987), is characterized by recurrent episodes of uncontrolled binge eating frequently followed by self-induced vomiting, use of laxatives or diuretics, strict dieting or fasting, or vigorous exercise to prevent weight gain. The hallmarks of this disorder are binge eating followed by frantic attempts to counteract the effects of eating such massive quantities of food. There is persistent overconcern with body shape and weight, with relative success in maintaining normal body mass (within 15% of average weight for age and height).

Modern psychological theories have advanced from assessing single causal factors to incorporating biological, cultural, familial, and intrapsychic factors that interact to create and maintain eating disorders (Cross, 1993; Garfinkel & Garner, 1982), yet few empirical studies have explored multiple factors. An outstanding exception is a recent monozygotic twin study in which the primary causal factors for bulimia were investigated. Bulik, Wade, and Kendler (2001) tentatively concluded that additive genetic factors predisposed both siblings to bulimia, but personality factors, such as external locus of control and differential family treatment, contributed to the development of the disorder in only one of the twins.

Because bulimia is a relatively new disorder, many questions about it remain unanswered; therefore, studies of intrapsychic and behavioral factors may advance our knowledge in this early stage. The following review of the psychoanalytic theories and relevant empirical research draws, to some extent, on the study and treatment of anorexia, because we suspect that some formulations and findings regarding anorexia are applicable to bulimia.

Psychoanalytic Theory and Empirical Evidence

The study of bulimia crosses most schools of psychoanalysis, yet there are several specific ego deficits and psychic states common to most psychoanalytic treatments of the subject despite differences in language or emphasis. These include intense dependency conflicts, which usually are most problematic in relation to maternal objects (Bornstein, 1993; Bornstein & Greenberg, 1991; Bruch, 1973; Chasseguet-Smirgel, 1995; Jacobson & Robins, 1989; Pendleton, Tisdale, & Marler, 1991); pathological object relations marked by ill-defined and highly conflicted self–other boundaries that are expressed behaviorally by attempts to control outward appearance and the intake of sustaining needs (Bruch, 1966, 1973; Chasseguet-

Smirgel, 1995; Cross, 1993; Schwartz, 1988; Sugarman & Kurash, 1981); and ego deficits in the recognition and regulation of a broad range of internal bodily states, including affective experience (Bruch, 1973; Cross, 1993; Fonagy & Target, 2000; Krueger, 1988; Zerbe, 1993).

Conflicts over eating and sustaining adequate nutrition in a culture of excess and plentitude led psychoanalytic investigators working within the classic drive model to equate problems with nutritional intake with corresponding fixations at the oral stage of psychosexual development (for a contemporary view of drive theory and bulimia, see Schwartz, 1988). Although intriguing case reports have linked pathological eating to unconscious fantasies of oral impregnation and fixations at the earliest psychosexual stage, little empirical evidence permits generalization of these observations.

Modern object-relations theory and ego psychology have provided alternative models that have been empirically tested. Object-relations theories tend to stress the centrality of early failures and conflicts in the child's environment, particularly those that involve parental failures that subvert the child's natural inclination toward separation and individuation. It is often assumed that the fragility of parents' narcissism and their need to exert control over the child's moods and movements can cause a blurring of boundaries such that children come to experience themselves as an extension of one or both parents. Internalization of self- and object representations are then blurred and diffuse rather than distinct. The affective quality of internalizations are experienced as hostile and demanding but not clearly as emanating from within a well-bounded self. To the extent that the child remains emotionally and physically dependent on the parents, conflicts over dependency and autonomy will likely be lived out in attraction to and repulsion from sources of nurturance. From this perspective, problems for bulimic patients may arise from conflicted longings for nurturance and the fear that such longings will subvert the need for autonomy. This internal conflict may be expressed through efforts to control eating through excessive dieting, followed by giving in to intense dependency needs, then by a redoubling of the need to disavow such need. One can see that conflicted inner representations of objects and self-representations of independence and autonomy may be interrelated.

Most experts agree that patients with eating disorders are highly conflicted about inner stirrings of dependent longings and their outward expressions of dependency on others (Bornstein, 1993; Bornstein & Greenberg, 1991; Bruch, 1973; Chasseguet-Smirgel, 1995; Jacobson & Robins, 1989; Pendleton et al., 1991). French analyst Chasseguet-Smirgel (1995) viewed eating disorders as an enactment of pseudo-independence to ward off intense unconscious dependency conflicts, particularly in relation to the mother during the second phase of separation and individuation during adolescence. She, like Laufer (1996), considered the emergence of young girls' sexual development as precipitating a severe conflict in adolescents with vulnerabilities to feeling overtaken by forces they cannot control. Cross (1993) emphasized the role that female social and sexual development leads young women to feel alienated from their bodies in ways that make them feel like passive victims to their emotions, the changes in their bodies, and the power of others to influence them. She viewed the development of eating disorders and self-mutilation as an effort—misguided and pathological as it might be—to claim the body, to exert control over its activities, and to turn passive into active. All three authors have traced the vulnerability and fear of being overtaken to conflicted identifications with the mother and unstable identity formation at puberty. They postulate that confusions arising from sexual maturation can lead some women to experience their bodies as out of their control. Chasseguet-Smirgel observed that her bulimic patients compulsively clung to an illusion of absolute independence they developed in relation to fear of an omnipotent and engulfing maternal object. The adolescent, faced with the prospect of physically becoming like the mother whom she fears will overpower her, then develops an eating disorder both to halt the terrifying changes in her body while simultaneously controlling the emergence of powerful impulses and affects. The compensatory fantasies of exerting total control over impulses (including dependent longings, sexual impulses, and emotions) are enacted in the real battle to exert control over eating. If these observations are generalizable beyond case studies, then a review of the research literature should reveal some evidence for more intense conflicts along the dependency–autonomy continuum.

A steady series of empirical studies has indicated that patients with eating disorders express a higher number of dependency themes than do their peers. In a thorough review of dependency and psychopathology, Bornstein (1993) reviewed 11 studies reporting a statistical link between dependency and eating disorders. Bornstein and Greenberg (1991) used the Rorschach Oral Dependency Scale (ROD; Masling, Rabie, & Blondheim, 1967) to assess the level of dependency in a small mixed group of psychiatric inpatients with eating disorders. They found that anorexic and bulimic patients produced twice as many oral and dependent scores as did normal-weight inpatients and almost three times as many as did obese women. By contrast, no group differed in relation to the number of Rorschach percepts depicting food items. These findings provide evidence for the hypothesis that bulimic and anorexic women are preoccupied with dependency themes rather than fixated on food or physiological hunger.

Jacobson and Robins (1989) compared 23 normal-weight women with bulimia with 38 control women on self-report measures of social dependency and the availability of social supports. They found that bulimic women reported a higher need for social support and a greater sense of dependency than did a matched group of women without eating disorders. Although this type of study supports the greater preponderance of dependency themes among women with eating disorders—and, as such, highlights the likelihood that dependency conflicts are of greater concern to women with eating disorders—it does not directly address the nature of conflicted dependency.

Using the Millon Clinical Multiaxial Inventory (MCMI), Tisdale, Pendleton, and Marler (1990) found that bulimic women scored higher than did clinical and normal control women on scales assessing schizoid, avoidant, and dependent personality characteristics. This suggests that bulimic women are deeply conflicted about dependency. As the authors pointed out, "Elevations [on the MCMI] among the bulimic group illuminate a complex interplay of personality variables reflecting a strong conflict over autonomy. Avoidant characteristics would appear to collide with strong needs for nurturance reflected in the bulimic's dependent stance" (p. 482).

Similar patterns emerged in Friedlander and Siegel's (1990) study of bulimic women in which they used a variety of interrelated self-report measures. They found a conflict between the wish to be independent and the bulimic women's reliance on parents to manage aspects of their lives. Bulimic women complained more about their parents' interference in their lives but simultaneously relied on them more than did other women. Becker, Bell, and Billington (1987) found that bulimic women in a college sample reported greater fears of abandonment while simultaneously reporting a strong wish for independence and autonomy in their relationships.

Although these findings reveal an association between the wish for autonomy and the strong affective pull toward dependency, two studies have demonstrated a cause-and-effect relation between fear of abandonment and subsequent reactive overeating. On the basis of Margaret Mahler's theory of separation–individuation and object-relations theory, Patton (1992) hypothesized that bulimic activity may be triggered by unconscious fears of abandonment in women who have not successfully negotiated the subphase of separation–individuation such that the act of eating serves as a concrete action defense against internal sense of loss. She speculated that this developmental arrest results in the bulimic woman's inability to sustain viable internal representations of the other and self such that minor breaks in continuity bring about defensive efforts to repair any breach in the merger through eating.

Working from this model, Patton (1992) devised a subliminal psychodynamic activation experiment in which she exposed two groups of college women with high and low scores on a reliable self-report measure of bulimic behavior to test whether women with higher scores would react to subliminally perceived abandonment stimuli by eating significantly more food than the women with low scores. After exposing both groups to the subliminal stimulus "Mama is leaving me," she found that women with high bulimia scores ate twice as much food as did women with low scores. To test discriminant validity, she exposed the groups to a subliminal message similar in structure "Mama is loaning it" and found no differences in subsequent eating behavior. This methodologically sound experiment provides the first evidence of a causal relation between experimentally induced fear of abandonment and greater food consumption immediately afterward.

Gerard, Kupper, and Nguyen (1993) devised a similar experiment while exploring the dimension of depression and heightened affective arousal following the subliminal presentation of the "Mama is leaving me" stimulus. They found that college women who manifested higher bulimia scores, and who scored higher on a measure of dependency and depression, experienced greater anxiety after the presentation of the stimulus and ate more food than did the group of women with low scores on both measures. In addition to replicating Patton's (1992) findings, they were able to demonstrate that the subliminally activated message evoked anxiety in the college women with bulimic symptoms and that they subsequently ate significantly more food, apparently in reaction to the unconsciously stimulated fears of abandonment.

This last series of studies provides a segue to considering evidence supporting the role of object representations and ego boundaries in the development of bulimia. Psychoanalytic theories have proposed a distinctive link between failures to create self–other ego boundaries that are separate from the mother and the development of eating disorders. Although the development of ego boundaries has its roots in the earliest human interactions, particularly with the primary caregivers (Muller, 1996), the flashpoint for differentiation and individuation occurs for young girls during adolescence. It is during this critical phase of sexual and mental maturation that a young girl struggles most seriously with her sexual identity, her sense of control over and ownership of her body, and her identifications with women in her family (Chasseguet-Smirgel, 1995; Cross, 1993). Bruch (1966, 1973) was the first to speculate that anorexia is the manifestation of the struggle for psychic autonomy. She viewed eating disorders as developing around ego disturbances in distorted body image, in the perception and recognition of internal visceral and affective states, and in the sense of autonomy and effectiveness. Such distortions are lived out in a girl's massive efforts to control her body and, through this control, she attempts to declare herself as different than her mother; consolidates a temporary sense of identity; and experiences a sense of competence, no matter how illusory.

Other theorists have made finer distinctions and more complex formulations of the autonomy–dependence–affect conflict, but few have delineated a clearer description than Jeammet (Jeammet

& Chabert, 1998) who emphasized the role that archaic pathological structures play in the dependency–autonomy conflict. Individuals who, because of early environmental and intrapsychic failures,
cannot contain and metabolize affects or maintain coherent ego
boundaries conflate dependency with the need to control:

> An entire framework for dependency is thus likely to develop
> as a defense against affective dependency perceived as a threat
> to the subject's identity and an alienation from his objects of
> attachment. It is a system whereby the subject tries to substitute
> bonds of control and ascendancy to his affective, relational ones,
> which are experienced as so much more threatening in that they
> are so much more necessary. (p. 66)

From the vantage of object relations and ego psychology bulimic
patients conflate dependency–autonomy conflicts with devouring
food in a concrete sign of dependency, then go to great lengths to
purge or otherwise nullify the need for nurturance. Readers may
be reminded of Chasseguet-Smirgel's (1995) observation that her
bulimic patients compulsively clung to an illusion of absolute independence that they developed in relation to their fear of an omnipotent and dangerous maternal object.

Such theories are compelling, yet there is relatively limited evidence for these clinical observations. Although anorexia has been
linked to maternal overprotectiveness in twin studies (Walters &
Kinder, 1995), bulimic women report more experiences of parental
rejection (Stuart, Laraia, Ballenger, & Lydiard, 1990). Bulimic
women also report feeling that their parents single them out and
unfairly restrict their activity compared to their siblings and that
their parents are less affectionate toward them than toward their
siblings (Wonderlich, Ukestad, & Peracki, 1994). Becker et al.
(1987), using self-report measures of object-relations phenomena,
demonstrated that bulimic college women reported feeling a lack
of autonomy in their relationships and manifested more fears of
abandonment than did an equivalent cohort, and Friedlander and
Siegel (1990) showed that bulimic symptoms in a group of college
women were correlated with difficulties with both dependency and
poor self–other differentiation. A final source of self-report data is
Dykens and Gerrard's (1986) study of college students with eating
disorders, in which bulimic students and repeat dieters manifested

higher scores on a measure of external locus of control than did nondieters, which suggests that the former have a poorer sense of mastery and control over internal experiences.

Studies of intrapsychic processes have found support as well. Strauss and Ryan (1987) conducted a multimethod assessment of object relations in restrictor and bulimic subtypes of anorexia. In addition to self-report measures, the authors assessed object representations with the Mutuality of Autonomy Scale (MOA; Urist, 1977) and the Structural Analysis of Social Behavior (Benjamin, 1977). Assuming that patients with anorexia would manifest greater disturbance in autonomy than would matched control patients, they contrasted the groups on disturbance in self- and other-object representations. Their results confirmed that anorexic patients manifest more disturbances in autonomy, poorer self-concept, and more disturbed object representations marked by poor differentiation between self-representations and representations of others. Zakin (1989) found a similar pattern in 35 binge eaters who produced significantly higher scores on Fisher and Cleveland's (1958) Body Penetration Scale, reflecting a greater propensity for experiencing body boundaries as easily penetrated and fluid. Thus, binge eaters appear to experience autonomy as more precarious and easily disturbed. Finally, Parmer (1991), using the Separation–Individuation Theme Scale (Coonerty, 1986), found that bulimic college students manifest more primitive object representations marked by poor differentiation between self and other than did a matched group of college women. The bulimic respondents also manifested significantly greater psychopathology and ego weakness as measured by the Minnesota Multiphasic Personality Inventory.

Disturbances in boundary formation and pathological object relations may significantly impede the individual's capacity to regulate affective experience and to understand the precursors to emotionally evocative interactions. Bruch (1966, 1973) has discovered that, in addition to internal struggles of dependence and autonomy, her patients demonstrated serious ego deficits in their ability to identify and accurately articulate internal states. This disturbance is viewed as one of the primary factors in both restricting and binge eating. Zerbe (1993) approached eating disorders as a psychosomatic disorder and viewed failures by parents to "decode"

nascent affective and bodily experiences for a young child as leading to an inability in the growing child and adolescent to recognize
internal signals that could produce pacification and development
of the capacity to differentiate bodily sensations such as hunger,
anxiety, anger, and sexual excitement. Bulimic women, by contrast,
may experience internal states of emotions and tensions as confus-
ing and overwhelming sensations that are felt as foreign intrusions.
This failure in affect recognition and modulation is thought to interfere with the capacity to "mentalize" experiences, leading to an
impoverishment in the capacity to fantasize with a resultant expression of sensations through physical symptoms and action defenses (Fonagy & Target, 2000).

Empirical evidence supporting this proposition is mounting.
Herkov, Greer, Blau, McGuire, and Eaker (1994) found that bulimic
women had difficulty discriminating emotional responses from
bodily (visceral) reactions and concluded that bulimic patients may
misinterpret affective and visceral responses to physical hunger.
Researchers have demonstrated that bulimic women show a
greater incapacity to identify and express emotions and have more
limited imaginary lives than women without major psychological
disturbances (Cochrane, Brewerton, Wilson, & Hodges, 1993;
DeGroot, Rodin, & Olmstead, 1995; Taylor, Parker, Bagby, &
Bourke, 1996). It is interesting that most comparative studies have
shown that anorexic women are more alexithymic than are bulimic
women, leaving open the possibility that bulimic women are constrained in the expression and experience of emotions rather than
unable to recognize and decode emotions.

In later clinical formulations, Bruch (1988) described several patients whose anorexic symptoms were related to the conscious inhibition of anger and frustration as an aspect of the family culture.
More recent sociocultural formulations of eating disorders have
pointed to the acculturation of females from infancy onward to
inhibit and deny hostility in favor of more affiliative affects and
behaviors (DeGroot & Rodin, 1994). This restriction in perceiving,
signaling, and communicating hostile affects is believed to interfere
with normal development of interoceptive learning for these affects
and may be the main link between Bruch's (1973) formulation and
the role of acculturation.

Several studies have demonstrated a connection between eating disorders and difficulties in managing and regulating hostility, either through an overcontrolled inhibition of ordinary hostile reactions or through affective instability. Smith, Hillard, and Roll (1991), for example, found significant differences between 12 bulimic and 12 control adolescents on Rorschach indexes of depression, level of thought disorder, and aggressive themes. In a well-designed, large-scale Rorschach study, Weisberg, Norman, and Herzog (1987) examined the personality organization and functioning of 57 normal-weight bulimic women and compared this group's Rorschach results with those of a group of higher functioning women and of a group of outpatient depressed women. Among the findings were indications that bulimic and depressed patients differed significantly from the nonpatient group on indicators of emotional lability and impulsivity. Bulimic patients also manifested more anger and negative feelings than did either the depressed or the nonpatient participants.

A Study of Severely Disturbed Bulimic Women

In this study we explored a broad range of intrapsychic processes and behaviors that may be related to internal conflicts, ego deficits, and defenses associated with bulimia. Using the empirical findings and clinical theory, we assessed excessive dependency using the ROD and conflicted or hostile–dependent phenomena with a new scale, described later. Because the ROD assesses the presence or absence of dependent themes without attempting to differentiate conflicted from nonconflicted responses, it has built-in limitations for assessing conflicted dependency. Thus, the majority of Rorschach studies have reported a linear relation between dependency and eating disorders, demonstrating a positive correlation between higher levels of dependent imagery and eating disorders (cf. Bornstein, 1993). We anticipated that the new scale would be strongly associated with bulimia, whereas the ROD scale may be marginally related because the treatment environment stimulates dependent longings (all patients in this study were undergoing intensive treatment characterized by four-times-weekly psychoanalytic treatment and 24-hr nursing care).

Given the research findings relating poor self–object differentiation, we anticipated that bulimic patients may manifest more pathological object representations marked by a state of dedifferentiation in representations of self and other. We used the MOA (Urist, 1977) to assess patients' capacities to conceptualize object representations along a continuum of well-differentiated objects to highly diffuse and dedifferentiated percepts marked by malevolence and diffusion of self–other boundaries. We chose a composite score of all Level 5, 6, and 7 pathological scores because it has been found to be a robust and stable measure of poorly differentiated pathological object representations (Berg, Packer, & Nunno, 1993).

Clinical experience with patients with eating disorders highlights not only Bruch's (1966, 1973) formulation that such patients struggle to decode internal stimuli but also that specific internal states are more difficult to interpret and communicate, perhaps because these women are deeply conflicted about experiencing and expressing hostility and frustration. Therefore, we hypothesized that bulimic patients would manifest more primary and secondary process aggression scores (Holt, 1977) on the Rorschach than would other hospitalized women. Finally, we planned to explore the relation of primitive defenses and select behavioral indexes that have not been previously investigated.

We began selecting participants by pooling all available patient records, masking patient identity, and then downloading files from the Austen Riggs Center's database. Files contained patient identification numbers, diagnostic codes, and demographic data. The initial sample consisted of all 355 patients admitted to the center from January 1993 to April 2000. Fifty-six of these patients carried a *DSM–IV* diagnosis of bulimia nervosa (American Psychiatric Association, 1994). The diagnosis was confirmed in a consensus case conference at the culmination of the initial evaluation and treatment phase 4–6 weeks following admission. Diagnoses were made using available sources of information (Rorschach data were not available at the time), including an integration of interview data, initial contact with the therapist, consultations with outpatient therapists, prior hospital records, review of family history, life history, and premorbid level of functioning. This method of diagnostic practice approximates the LEAD (longitudinal expert evaluation using all data) standard of diagnosis (Pilkonis, Heape, Ruddy, &

Serrao, 1991; Spitzer, 1983). Although all patients in this study had multiple Axis I and Axis II disorders, we excluded those with a comorbid Axis I psychotic disorder. Criteria for inclusion required that all patients had a hospital stay of at least 30 days to complete the full diagnostic and treatment evaluation and complete the psychological testing.

The final sample consisted of 120 women with a mean age at admission of 31.5 years (SD = 10.54). Average educational level was 15.2 years (SD = 2.7), and the average Full Scale IQ was 107.33 (SD = 14.9). Eighty-nine patients were single, 25 were married, and 16 were widowed or divorced. Patients had an average of 4.2 (SD = 1.1) Axis I and II diagnoses.

The Rorschach measures we used were developed to assess psychodynamic constructs and phenomena. The ROD (Masling et al., 1967) was developed to assess oral–dependent imagery. A response is defined as oral dependent if it falls into any of the following categories: food and drinks, food sources, food objects, food providers, passive food receivers, food organs, supplicants, nurturers, gifts and gift givers, good luck symbols, oral activity, passivity and helplessness, pregnancy and reproductive anatomy, and negations of oral percepts (i.e., not pregnant, man with no mouth). Respondents receive 1 point for each "oral" response in their Rorschach protocol, so ROD scores can range from 0 to the maximum number of responses a patient gives to the Rorschach. The construct validity and reliability regarding this measure have been excellent in more than 90 experimental studies with various populations (Bornstein, 1996).

A new Rorschach scale was developed for this study (see Exhibit 4.1), because J. Christopher Fowler has observed that some dependent-laden percepts were qualitatively different because they were infused with aggressive themes. Following the trajectory of Kernberg's (1992) formulation of libidinal and aggressive affects as fused in more primitive character pathology, this Rorschach analogue scale captures the fusion of dependent and aggressive–sadistic themes. These "hostile–dependent" responses reflect a highly conflicted, counterdependent process that may be associated with bulimia. A common percept of "two girls smiling at each other" is strikingly different than the response "Dracula—his fangs are dripping with blood." The latter percept communicates

Exhibit 4.1

Austen Riggs Hostile–Dependency Scale

Score all Rorschach responses for percepts involving a fusion of oral and aggressive themes.

1. Foods and drinks that have been tainted (spoiled milk; goblet of poison; a gross, bloody hunk of meat; rotten or rotting food). Do not score for poisonous gases or other airborne toxins.
2. Food containers associated with aggressive themes (two witches dancing around a cauldron, a vial for storing poisons).
3. Aggressively infused oral organs (a snarling dog, a vicious alligator with sharp teeth, a bug with sharp mandibles, shark's teeth, a lion's mouth).
4. Aggressive human and animal percepts of an oral nature (vampire bat, Count Dracula, two cannibals, the witch from *Hansel and Gretel*, vultures, carrion birds, leeches, snakes with fangs, black widow spider, mosquitoes, tics, tapeworm and other parasites).
5. Aggressive and oral activity (worms eating the brains of a dead rabbit, alligator devouring a poodle, a praying mantis with a bug in its mouth, two men ripping apart a carcass).
6. Dangerous oral instruments (a blow gun, spitting poison, the kiss of death).
7. Oral percepts with clear negative affect (e.g., "That's fried chicken . . . I hate fried chicken"; "Big, disgusting lips, a perverted old man . . . his smile gives him away").

a persecutory fear of dangerous aggressive hunger that will drain the patient and others. Such a fear may lead to counterdependent behavior in the person's approach to all forms of nurturance, including attitudes toward eating.[2]

We assessed aggressive ideation using Holt's (1977) method for scoring primary and secondary process manifestations on the Ror-

---

[2] Prior to publication we learned of a scale by Holt that has similar constructs. The scale, part of the Holt Primary Process Scoring System, has been published in Italian.

schach. Holt's system differentiates two levels of aggressive content. Level 1 scores are related to primary process forms of primitive aggressive themes and specifically measure murderous or palpably sadomasochistic aggression. Level 2 scores are related to secondary process ideation and specifically measure indirect forms of aggression expressed in more socially acceptable ways. The Holt system has demonstrated high levels of test–retest (Gray, 1969) and interrater reliability (Fowler, Hilsenroth, & Handler, 1996), as well as construct validity, in many studies (Blatt & Berman, 1984; Hilsenroth, Hibbard, Nash, & Handler, 1993; Russ, 1988).

The MOA (Urist, 1977) assesses the thematic content of relationships (stated or implied) among animal, inanimate, and human objects in Rorschach percepts. The scale was developed to assess the degree of differentiation of object representations and focuses primarily on the developmental progression of separation–individuation from engulfing, fused relations to highly differentiated self–other representations. Scale Points 1 and 2 reflect the capacity to construe self- and other representations as structurally differentiated and engaged in mutually interactive or parallel activity (e.g., "two people pushing shopping carts"). Scale Points 3 and 4 capture dependent and mirroring object relationships and often reveal an emerging loss of autonomy between figures (e.g., "Siamese twins connected at the waist"). Scale Points 5, 6, and 7 reflect not only the loss of the capacity for separateness but also increasing malevolence (e.g. "an evil fog engulfing this frog . . . smothering it"). Reliability data are excellent (Tuber, 1989), and the scale has demonstrated a high degree of construct validity with behavioral ratings (Ryan, Avery, & Grolnick, 1985; Urist, 1977; Urist & Schill, 1982).

We assessed defenses with the Lerner Defense Scales (LDS; Lerner & Lerner, 1980), which are based on Kernberg's theoretical conceptualizations and clinical observations. We assessed primitive defenses of splitting, idealization, and devaluation represented in percepts of human, quasi-human, and human detail responses. The LDS has shown good construct validity and high interrater reliability (Lerner, 1991). To use more stringent parametric statistics in the analysis of defenses that are ranked on a continuum from high to low order (devaluation, 1–5; idealization, 1–5; and denial, 1–3), we weighted defenses according to rank, then collapsed them into an overall score for that category. For example, if there were three instances of idealization on a participant's protocol, one at Level 1 and the other two instances at Level 3, the participant would receive a total idealization score of 7 (1 + 3 + 3 = 7).

We gathered behavioral measures from an electronic database of daily activity logs for individual patients. Presence or absence was coded for discrete behaviors related to patient functioning. We chose variables to explore on the basis of their relevance to dependency and counterdependency. Behaviors that clearly indicate dependency needs and demand for direct and indirect forms of social support include patients' use of nursing staff time to manage crises and to air grievances toward staff and other patients. The use of multiple nursing staff members over the course of an 8-hour shift, hostile interactions with nursing staff, and the need for doctor-on-call visits may also be associated with counterdependent and indirect means of obtaining individualized nurturance from staff. Attendance at community groups and psychotherapy groups may also be related to dependency longings. Finally, instances of patients isolating themselves in their rooms and refusing direct contact with community members may be related to hostile or avoidant forms of dependency.

The administration and original scoring of Rorschach protocols followed the procedures articulated by Exner (1993). All patients were administered the Rorschach within 30 days of admission. The Rorschach protocols we used were drawn from an archival search of hospital psychological evaluation files. Protocols were then scored on the ROD, the hostile–dependency scale, the Urist MOA, Holt's primary and secondary process aggression scores, and the LDS. To assess rater reliability (Weiner, 1991), 20 Rorschach protocols were chosen at random and then independently rescored on the ROD and Oral Aggression scales by Ben Brunnschweiler and Johanna Brock. The two sets of scored protocols were compared, and intraclass correlation (ICC) values were calculated for the ROD (ICC = .96) and oral aggression (ICC = .89). J. Christopher Fowler independently scored all protocols on the Urist MOA, Holt's primary and secondary process aggression scores, and the LDS.

Statistical analysis followed a logical progression from global to more specific analyses to assess differences between the bulimic and clinical control groups. First, an analysis of variance contrast-

Table 4.1

Analysis of Variance on Demographic Variables

Variable	Bulimic patients ($n = 56$)		Clinical controls ($n = 64$)		df	F	p
	M	SD	M	SD			
Age	24.1	2.2	33.7	11.6	1, 119	9.1	.003
Education	14.9	2.6	15.3	2.7	1, 119	0.64	.43
FSIQ	107.7	16.8	107.9	16.8	1, 119	0.01	.93
Rorschach R	24.1	12.2	23.6	11.9	1, 119	0.04	.85
Total no. diagnoses	4.3	1.2	4.07	0.99	1, 119	1.6	.22

Note. FSIQ = Wechsler Full Scale Intelligence Quotient (1958); Rorschach R = total number of Rorschach responses.

ing the clinical groups (see Table 4.1) revealed that patients with eating disorders were, on average, younger, $F(1, 119) = 9.1$, $p = .003$, and were more likely to be single, $F(1, 119) = 4.9$, $p = .03$. By contrast, level of education, $F(1, 119) = 0.6$, $p = .43$; full scale IQ, $F(1, 119) = 0.0$, $p = .93$; and Rorschach productivity, $F(1, 119) = 0.0$, $p = .85$, were not significantly different. Because previous research findings have linked serious psychological impairment to multiple Axis I and Axis II disorders, we compared the patient groups on the total number of Axis I and Axis II disorders. No differences were found in relation to total number of diagnoses, $F(1, 129) = 1.6$, $p = .22$.

To provide a conservative estimate of Rorschach predictors we included total number of diagnoses as a potential covariate because the analysis indicated a trend toward significance. In the second phase of analysis we used stepwise logistic regression analyses to determine what, if any, Rorschach mean scores (see Table 4.2) differentiated bulimic female patients from the clinical control group. We used logistic regression because it is a more sensitive and conservative statistic when dichotomous and categorical variables are under investigation (Davis & Offord, 1997). Demographic variables

Table 4.2

Descriptive Statistics for Rorschach Variables

Variable	Bulimic participants (*n* = 56)		Clinical control participants (*n* = 64)	
	M	*SD*	*M*	*SD*
Rorschach oral dependency	5.5	3.6	6.0	3.4
Hostile dependency	1.3	1.4	1.0	1.3
Primary process aggression	1.0	1.5	0.7	1.0
Secondary process aggression	6.1	3.9	5.0	2.7
Mutuality of autonomy PATH	1.5	2.0	1.0	1.6
Splitting defense	0.9	1.5	0.7	0.9
Idealization defense	4.8	6.5	4.7	5.5
Devaluation defense	10.4	8.1	8.2	6.9

Note. PATH = Sum of all MOA 5, 6, 7 scores.

of age, marital status, length of hospitalization, and total number of diagnoses were entered in the first block under a stepwise conditional process. Table 4.3 indicates that patient age entered the regression equation as a salient predictor (B = −.0454), followed by length of hospitalization (B = .0044). No other demographic variables were entered. The second block consisted of Rorschach variables also entered under a stepwise conditional process; because demographic variables were entered in the first block, variance associated with demographic variables was covaried from the Rorschach variables. The first Rorschach variable to enter the regression model was secondary process aggression (B = .2212), followed by a negative predictor for ROD scores (B = −.2095) and hostile dependency scores (B = .3717).

To explore how bulimic patients may behave differently in their day-to-day relationships within the hospital, we first examined descriptive statistics (see Table 4.4). Inspection of mean scores suggests that bulimic patients may engage in all behaviors under investigation, with the exception of time they spend isolating

Table 4.3

Logistic Regression Analyses of Bulimic Status as a Function of Demographic and Psychiatric Variables and Rorschach Scale

Step	Dependent variable	-2 Log likelihood	Model χ^2	p
1	Age	6.7	6.6	.01
2	Length of hospitalization	3.1	3.2	.02
3	Secondary process aggression	5.4	5.4	.01
4	Oral dependency	4.4	4.3	.04
5	Oral aggression	3.2	3.2	.05

	Psychiatric variables		
	B	Wald	*P*	R
Age	$-.0454$	4.3	.04	$-.1297$
Length of hospitalization	.0044	4.2	.04	.1281
Secondary process aggression	.2212	5.425	.02	.1589
Oral aggression	.3717	3.034	.08	.0873

Note. Variables included age, marital status, length of hospitalization, total number of diagnoses, primary and secondary process aggression, Rorschach oral dependency, oral aggression, pathological object relations, splitting, idealization, and devaluation.

themselves in their rooms. These data can be somewhat misleading, because the length of hospitalization varies tremendously. As a result, length of hospitalization directly affects the number of nursing records available for analysis and therefore may spuriously inflate behavioral indexes. For this reason we computed proportional scores by dividing behavioral counts by the patient's length of hospitalization. We then conducted a second logistic regression analysis, again entering demographic variables in a stepwise procedure, followed by a second block of behavioral data entered in the same stepwise condition. The final regression model (see Table 4.5) indicates that bulimic patients are diagnosed with more psychopathology (B = .6641), are younger (B = −.0328), and

Table 4.4

Descriptive Statistics for Behavioral Variables

Variable	Bulimic participants (*n* = 56)		Clinical control participants (*n* = 64)	
	M	*SD*	*M*	*SD*
Group hours	165.0	224.9	92.0	83.4
Informal group hours	173.5	155.3	131.1	116.1
One-to-one contacts	37.3	41.4	25.3	28.4
Doctor-on-call contacts	4.8	8.3	1.7	3.1
Multiple nursing contacts	5.9	8.7	3.2	5.0
Isolative behavior	20.2	29.1	23.9	54.3
Conflicts with nursing staff	19.6	24.7	13.4	21.6
Limit setting	3.0	5.9	1.2	2.7
Suicide threat	1.5	3.0	0.42	1.3

are less isolative (B = −6.072) but are less likely to engage in informal social gatherings with patients and staff (B = −2.337). Bulimic women also engaged in more conflict-laden interactions with nurses (B = 14.2625) than did other female patients.

Taken together, these results suggest that there are subtle rather than dramatic differences between bulimic women and female patients without an eating disorder. It appears that bulimic women are far more conflicted about their dependency on others, expressing their longings and neediness through more hostile interactions with nursing staff. They spend less time in their rooms than do other women patients, but they do not socialize comfortably with others when informal gatherings spontaneously emerge in the hospital's community center. When they do make contact with nursing staff, bulimic women tend to engage in more heated and argumentative conversations than do other female patients. This gives the impression that these young women can neither be alone nor engage easily in interpersonal relationships—instead, they manage closeness through friction that may allow them to feel autonomous despite their longings.

Parallel undercurrents of intrapsychic conflict emerged in the

Table 4.5

Logistic Regression Analyses of Bulimic Status as a Function of
Demographic and Psychiatric Variables and Behavioral Variables

Step	Dependent variable	−2 Log likelihood	Model χ^2	p
1	Age	118.87	5.87	.01
2	Total no. diagnoses	115.48	9.2	.01
3	Conflictual interactions with nursing staff	106.75	17.99	.000
4	Isolative behavior	100.21	24.53	.000
5	Informal group hours	94.76	30.07	.000

	Final regression model			
	B	Wald	p	R
Total diagnoses	.6641	6.3	.01	.19
Age	−.0328	1.6	.20	.00
Isolative behavior	−6.07	6.5	.01	−.20
Informal group hours	−2.34	4.9	.02	−.16
Conflictual interactions with nursing staff	14.26	3.2	.05	.10

Note. Variables included demographic variables and all behavioral data listed in Table 4.4. Proportional scores were computed by dividing behaviors by length of hospitalization. R = Rorschach Oral Dependency score.

Rorschach findings, according to which bulimic women produced fewer purely dependent responses yet produced more responses indicative of hostile dependency. Because the latter finding emerged from a new measure, it is unclear to what extent the scale measures a conflict over dependency or a deficit in affect regulation, in which case the hostile–dependent responses are indicative of a fusion and confusion of dependent and aggressive affects. Our impression is that bulimic women are more conflicted than confused about their dependency, because their greater preponderance of secondary process aggression responses suggests that they are more aware than unaware of their hostility. If bulimic women had manifested more primary process aggression scores it would have indicated less control and containment. Whatever the final outcome, it is clear that bulimic women express high degrees of hostility and dependency and that this intrapsychic conflict may be largely responsible for their difficulty in tolerating closeness.

Discussion

Clinicians who treat bulimic patients are often stunned by the dramatic and apparently inexplicable symptoms, in part because these young women often have little or no understanding of the motivations or triggers for bingeing and purging. As a result, clinicians and theorists must rely on clinical inference to grapple with its meaning and function, making the empirical study of eating disorders all the more relevant. Although evidence is mounting for the biological, psychological, and social implications of bulimia, the knowledge base is limited. When considering questions of etiology and intrapsychic functioning, one must contend with two crucial questions: Why does this disorder primarily afflict females, and in what way is the developmental phase of adolescence implicated in the expression of bulimia?

Although much of this discussion focuses on the evidence for intrapsychic correlates, it is far more difficult to assess empirically the gender specificity of the disorder. Thus far, no one has assessed this question adequately, and it was not possible to make empirical comparisons with bulimic males in our population. After searching our database, we found only four males with eating disorders, all of whom were anorexic. The exceedingly low base rate of male bulimics has made empirical comparison unfeasible. For this reason we turn to psychoanalytic theories when considering the impact of gender, sexuality, and cultural influences on pathological developments.

Analytic observers (Bruch, 1966, 1973; Chasseguet-Smirgel, 1995; Cross, 1993; Sugarman & Kurash, 1981; Tabin & Tabin, 1988) mark adolescence as a turbulent developmental phase, particularly for young women, who must struggle with a second phase of separation–individuation from their mothers. Most theorists conclude that separation and differentiation is further complicated for young women because, as they attempt to articulate differences from their mothers, their bodies betray them by taking on more physical likeness. Cross (1993) pointed to the feminine body, to partially hidden genitalia, and socialization of passivity, as central to girls' alienation from their bodies. This creates a schism between mind and body in which young women with eating disorders may relate to their bodies as foreign and "other," something that must be controlled. In Cross's view,

> partially internal genitalia, menstruation, relatively abrupt changes in body contours at puberty, and pregnancy all contribute to an ambiguous, paradoxical, and discontinuous experience of the body for women. Women's efforts to control, understand, and generally negotiate these body vicissitudes have a significant impact on their object relations and psychopathology, as well as lending them special sources of wisdom and psychological strength. (p. 42)

Our results that age was the single best predictor of bulimia in our sample is consistent with clinical reports (Cross, 1993; Chasseguet-Smirgel, 1995; Laufer, 1996) that mark the onset of bulimia and other eating disorders during adolescence, when struggles for autonomy, conflicts over budding sexuality, and uncontrollable changes in the feminine body are at their height. We cannot conclusively determine from our analyses that bulimia was first manifest during puberty in our sample, but data support the contention that the bulimic patients in this hospital setting were clearly struggling with autonomy, as evidenced by the average pathological score on the MOA. Bulimic women, although they did not differ significantly from the control group, did produce an average of 1.5 pathological scores per protocol, suggesting that these women are frequently unable to maintain adequate autonomous self- and other representations and that when diffusions of boundaries occur they are experienced as malevolent impingements.

Most psychoanalytic theories assume that powerful dependency needs and the equally powerful fear of being engulfed or controlled by the object of desire have central importance in the development of eating disorders. In keeping with this, most researchers who have explored the dependency–eating disorder link have found higher levels of oral and interpersonal dependency in self-report and projective data (for an extant review of the literature, see Bornstein, 1996). Given this, the most striking result to emerge from our analysis was that bulimic women actually produced fewer oral-dependent responses on the Rorschach. Because previous studies have demonstrated that anorexic and bulimic patients score between two and three times higher on measures of dependency than control groups (e.g., Bornstein & Greenberg, 1991), it is important to consider why this study did not yield a similar pattern. Because the treatment environment of the Austen Riggs Center involves intensive psychoanalytic psychotherapy, it is possible that the mobilization of transference to the therapist and the institution creates a regressive, dependent experience that is reflected in all the patients' testing during this initial phase of treatment. Although this sample of bulimic patients manifested extremely high levels of oral-dependent imagery (on average 5.5 ROD scores per protocol), their scores were actually lower than the control group's (6 ROD scores per protocol), as indicated by the ROD score's negative beta weight in the regression model. This inverse finding raises the possibility that, although bulimic patients appear to experience intense dependency needs and wishes, they may be more ambivalent than other females in accepting their longings.

This formulation is supported by the finding that bulimic women produced more responses involving a fusion of dependent and aggressive themes. Bulimic women in our study manifested a significantly greater number of Rorschach percepts involving a fusion of dependent and aggressive themes and more secondary process aggressive affects than did patients without eating disorders. The expression of hostile dependency is consistent with more recent findings that some patients "perceive, structure, and organize their world around oral themes, but whose 'orality' is manifest not as excessive, receptive dependency, but rather closed, mistrustful independence" (Duberstein & Talbot, 1993, p. 298).

The high degree of hostile–dependent themes appear to have been lived out in their interactions with people in the hospital: Bulimic patients were less isolative, but they actually spent less time socializing with staff and peers. One is left with the impression that these women were unable to be alone in their rooms but avoided direct social contacts. When they did engage directly with nursing staff, their interactions were more volatile and hostile than those of their female counterparts. Although bulimic patients' engagement in more hostile interactions with nursing staff may be attributable in part to the patients' youth, it seems equally plausible that bulimic patients gratify their dependent longings through verbally combative interactions—a type of warmth through friction that may obscure their desire for contact and protect them from fears of merger.

Psychoanalytic theories have proposed a distinctive link between the development of eating disorders and the failures of young women to create self–other ego boundaries that are separate from mother and family. The widely held view that bulimic women struggle most seriously with the sense of control, mastery, and ownership over their bodies (Chasseguet-Smirgel, 1995; Cross, 1993) was partially supported by the current findings. Contrary to previous findings, bulimic patients did not manifest more pathological object representations. The most parsimonious explanation is that both groups struggle to maintain adequately functioning boundaries and that the level of psychic disturbance creates a serious struggle for autonomous psychic functioning. In reviewing the results we found that 36 (56%) of the 64 clinical controls and 31 (55%) of the 56 bulimic patients produced at least one pathological score on the MOA, indicating that the majority of these women have a clinically significant disturbance in the cohesiveness of body boundaries and that this disturbance is not specific to the formation of eating disorders.

Bulimic patients did not produce more primary process aggression responses, and they appeared to be more conscious of their hostility and frustration. This may be an important difference between anorexic and bulimic women. Bruch (1973) and a host of other theorists noted that anorexic patients experience deficits in "interoceptive awareness" and are less able than other females to cognitively process bodily sensations, including affective experiences (such as aggression). Given the mounting evidence that bulimic women experience and express hostility more readily than control groups, perhaps one of the psychological factors that discriminates those with bulimia from those with anorexia is their ego capacity to recognize anger as an internal process. Some confirmation for this hypothesis is found in our results indicating that bulimic patients manifest more secondary process aggression scores than the control group, suggesting that these women were conscious of at least some feelings of hostility. In clinical encounters bulimic patients frequently ward off frustration and anger toward the therapist only to leave the session to engage in the ritual of devouring and then purging food.

Although we had no firm expectations regarding how bulimic patients might differ from clinical controls in their defensive functioning, it was surprising that no differences were found in splitting, idealization, or devaluation. Given the relatively high incidence of aggressive and oral aggressive contents in bulimic female protocols, one might expect that devaluation of others would be a preferred defense to justify why others are to be avoided and warded off. Because no significant differences emerged, we can tentatively assume that the level of primitive defensive functioning is equivalent and that focal conflicts centering on dependent longings and persecutory fears lead bulimic patients to behave in more counterdependent ways.

Our findings are far from definitive, but they do provide some intriguing data from which to speculate about the gender-specific nature of eating disorders. Two gender-specific formulations apply to the findings and may help highlight the broader social influences that affect the expression of bulimia in female patients.

Steiner-Adair (1986) postulated that bulimic and anorexic women are quite aware of their frustration and hostility and that they use their bodies as a medium for making a political statement about the intolerable position they are placed in by society and their families. Drawing on psychoanalytic feminist theory, she made a compelling case to explain why any direct expression of anger is antithetical to societal norms for femininity. First, women are expected to be affiliative and agreeable, whereas young boys and men are rewarded for more aggressive and competitive strivings. She pointed to the paradox of individuation for young girls and women, "By adolescence, today's girls have simultaneously been socialized to devalue the importance of relationships, and value independence and autonomy, toward which males are socialized" (p. 99). This general cultural expectation may create a schism for young women that inhibits their direct expressions of anger. Minuchin et al. (1978) observed that bulimic and anorexic females adopted a peacekeeping role in their highly enmeshed families that simultaneously made any direct expression of anger toward family members taboo and made any move toward greater independence from the family deeply conflictual. From this social perspective one can postulate that bulimic patients may feel deeply conflicted about directly stirring controversy in their family by claiming some independence and may express frustration and hostility through their eating disorder.

Although many females may not interpret their bulimic symptoms as an expression of frustration and hostility, all 10 of those treated by J. Christopher Fowler readily discovered the link between their anger and the intense urge to binge and purge. These women were not solely focused on escaping from their mothers—some were furious with their fathers, whose narcissistic investment in their prized family made these young women feel their individuality had been subverted to serve the father's desire. One young woman expressed her derision and hatred for her father directly in a psychotherapy hour by stating, "I'm not ready to give up my bulimia yet . . . he hasn't paid enough for the pain he caused my mother and sister." This direct statement of deliberate purpose to her symptom was in part a rationalization, but it was also a statement of political purpose. This woman was determined to represent, through her symptomatic behavior, her family's suffering at the hands of the father. It is interesting that she adopted a demure and caretaking role in family meetings, hiding all signs of her anger at her father. When asked about the schism between her feelings in the psychotherapy hours and her actions in the family meetings, she stated,

> I could confront him, scream at him, tell him he's a jerk, but my mother is the one that has to drive home with him. I can't do that to her. But I can get back at him . . . it drives him crazy that he can't control my eating.

A second bulimic patient initially presented as aloof and highly self-contained—her drug use, bingeing and purging, and preoccupation with obtaining more drugs and food occupied nearly all her waking life. Early in treatment she revealed how her secretive, ritualistic behaviors were expressions of her anger. She quite spontaneously spoke of her need to keep her anger at her mother, father, and older brother a secret because "I was the glue that kept the peace . . . everyone fought about everything and everyone confided in me. I was the go-between with my parents." In addition to her peacekeeping mission she harbored a fantasy that if she were to express her anger directly at anyone in the family she would immediately be exiled. Although this fantasy served various intrapsychic functions, there was a reality to her fears—in the past, arguments among members of her extended family resulted in chronic impasses that led to the exile of weaker members of the clan. Added to this external reality the patient, who was the youngest and only daughter, was assigned the role of mediator in her immediate family's quarrels.

Both clinical examples highlight the intersection of intrapsychic conflict over expressing hostility and shed light on the complicated roles that these bulimic young women hold in their families. From a family systems perspective it is quite understandable why these two young women developed severe conflicts over dependency, autonomy, and aggression.

For all our formulations and empirical evidence, it is still not possible to determine the true nature of bulimia. It is clear that genetics play some role in determining susceptibility, but many factors determine who will develop the disorder. The precise role of gender is unclear, but there is little doubt that bodily changes of puberty and the psychological challenges of adolescence, with its increasing internal and external pressures to conform to societal standards of beauty while simultaneously staking a claim of a separate identity from parents, can be overwhelming for young women. For those who have the additional burden of trauma and inadequate emotional supports that weaken or subvert already inadequate ego structures, pathological eating may be an effort to quiet restless stirrings of dependency, hostility, and fears of abandonment and merger with powerful others. From the perspective of the self, bulimia may be an effort to exert massive control over a body and emotions that feel both alien and out of control. We conclude with a passage from Cross (1993), a woman whose effort to draw together the causal pathways to this vexing disorder has resulted in impressive clarity and compassion:

All women must come to terms with the esoteric—hidden, changeable, and unruly—aspects of their reproductive anatomy and function; in so doing, they (ideally) develop a sense of ownership over the body, despite its intrusion or inhabitation by the "other." However, instead of *embracing* the paradoxes the body presents, these particular patients try to *erase* all contradictions and ambiguities. Ownership of the body is distorted into ruthless tyranny over and mortification of the body. (p. 63)

References

American Psychiatric Association. (1980). *Diagnostic and statistical manual of mental disorders* (3rd ed.). Washington, DC: Author.
American Psychiatric Association. (1987). *Diagnostic and statistical manual of mental disorders* (3rd ed., rev.). Washington, DC: Author.
American Psychiatric Association. (1994). *Diagnostic and statistical manual of mental disorders* (4th ed.). Washington, DC: Author.
Becker, B., Bell, M., & Billington, R. (1987). Object relations ego-deficits in bulimic college women. *Journal of Consulting and Clinical Psychology, 43,* 92–95.
Bell, R. M. (1985). *Holy anorexia.* Chicago: University of Chicago Press.
Benjamin, L. (1977). Structural analysis of a family in therapy. *Journal of Consulting and Clinical Psychology, 45,* 391–406.
Berg, J. L., Packer, A., & Nunno, V. J. (1993). A Rorschach analysis: Parallel disturbance in thought and in self/object representation. *Journal of Personality Assessment, 61,* 311–323.
Blatt, S. J., & Berman, W. (1984). A methodology for the use of the Rorschach in clinical research. *Journal of Personality Assessment, 48,* 226–239.
Bornstein, R. F. (1993). *The dependent personality.* New York: Guilford.
Bornstein, R. F. (1996). Construct validity of the Rorschach Oral Dependency Scale: 1967–1995. *Psychological Assessment, 8,* 200–205.
Bornstein, R. F., & Greenberg, R. P. (1991). Dependency and eating disorders in female psychiatric inpatients. *Journal of Nervous and Mental Disorders, 179,* 148–152.
Bruch, H. (1966). Anorexia nervosa and its differential diagnosis. *Journal of Nervous and Mental Disorders, 141,* 555–566.

Bruch, H. (1973). *Obesity, anorexia nervosa and the person within.* New York: Basic Books.

Bruch, H. (1988). Conversations with anorexics. In D. Czyewski & M. A. Suhr (Eds.), *Conversations with anorexics.* New York: Basic Books.

Brumberg, J. J. (1988). *Fasting girls: The emergence of anorexia nervosa as a modern disease.* Cambridge, MA: Harvard University Press.

Bulik, C. M., Wade, T. D., & Kendler, K. S. (2001). Characteristics of monozygotic twins discordant for bulimia nervosa. *International Journal of Eating Disorders, 29,* 1–10.

Chasseguet-Smirgel, J. (1995). Auto-sadism, eating disorders, and femininity: Reflections based on case studies of adult women who experienced eating disorders as adolescents. In M. A. Hanley (Ed.), *Essential papers on masochism* (pp. 453–470). New York: New York University Press.

Cochrane, C. E., Brewerton, T. D., Wilson, D. B., & Hodges, E. L. (1993). Alexithymia in eating disorders. *International Journal of Eating Disorders, 14,* 219–222.

Coonerty, S. (1986). An exploration of separation–individuation themes in borderline personality disorder. *Journal of Personality Assessment, 50,* 501–511.

Cross, L. W. (1993). Body and self in feminine development: Implications for eating disorders and delicate self-mutilation. *Bulletin of the Menninger Clinic, 57,* 41–68.

Davis, L. J., & Offord, K. P. (1997). Logistic regression. *Journal of Personality Assessment, 68,* 497–507.

DeGroot, J. M., & Rodin, G. (1994). Eating disorders, female psychology, and the self. *Journal of the American Academy of Psychoanalysis, 22,* 299–317.

DeGroot, J. M., Rodin, G., & Olmstead, M. P. (1995). Alexithymia, depression, and treatment outcome in bulimia nervosa. *Comprehensive Psychiatry, 36,* 53–60.

Duberstein, P. R., & Talbot, N. L. (1993). Rorschach oral imagery, attachment style, and interpersonal relatedness. *Journal of Personality Assessment, 61,* 294–310.

Dykens, E. M., & Gerrard, M. (1986). Psychological profiles of purging bulimics, repeat dieters, and controls. *Journal of Consulting & Clinical Psychology, 54,* 283–288.

Exner, J. E. (1993). *The Rorschach: A comprehensive system. Volume 1* (3rd ed.). New York: Wiley.

Fisher, S., & Cleveland, S. E. (1958). *Body image and personality.* New York: Van Nostrand.

Fonagy, P., & Target, M. (2000). Playing with reality: The persistence of dual psychic reality in borderline patients. *International Journal of Psychoanalysis, 81,* 853–873.

Fowler, C., Hilsenroth, M. J., & Handler, L. (1996). A multi-method assessment of dependency using the Early Memories Test. *Journal of Personality Assessment, 67,* 399–413.

Friedlander, M. R., & Siegel, S. M. (1990). Separation–individuation difficulties and cognitive behavioral indicators of eating disorders among college women. *Journal of Counseling Psychology, 37,* 74–78.

Garfinkel, P. E., & Garner, D. M. (1982). *Anorexia nervosa: A multidimensional perspective.* New York: Brunner/Mazel.

Gerard, H. B., Kupper, D. A., & Nguyen, L. (1993). The causal link between depression and bulimia: Counterposing two theories of development. In J. M. Masling & R. F. Bornstein (Eds.), *Psychoanalytic perspectives on psychopathology* (pp. 225–251). Washington, DC: American Psychological Association.

Gray, J. J. (1969). The effect of productivity on primary process and creativity. *Journal of Projective Techniques and Personality Assessment, 33,* 213–218.

Gull, W. W. (1873). "Apepsia hysterica: Anorexia hysterica." *Transcripts of the Clinical Society of London, 7,* 22–28.

Herkov, M. J., Greer, R. A., Blau, B. I., McGuire, J. M., & Eaker, D. (1994). Bulimia: An empirical analysis of psychodynamic theory. *Psychological Reports, 75,* 51–56.

Hilsenroth, M. J., Hibbard, S. R., Nash, M. R., & Handler, L. (1993). A Rorschach study on narcissism, defense, and aggression in borderline, narcissistic and cluster c personality disorders. *Journal of Personality Assessment, 60,* 346–361.

Holt, R. (1977). A method for assessing primary process manifestations and their controls in Rorschach responses. In M. Rickers-Ovsiankina (Ed.), *Rorschach psychology* (pp. 375–420). New York: Krieger.

Jacobson, R., & Robins, C. J. (1989). Social dependency and social support in bulimic and non-bulimic women. *International Journal of Eating Disorders, 8,* 665–670.

Jeammet, P., & Chabert, C. (1998). A psychoanalytic approach to eating disorders: The role of dependency. In A. H. Esamn (Ed.), *Adolescent psychiatry: Developmental and clinical studies* (Vol. 22, *Annals of the American Society for Adolescent Psychiatry,* pp. 59–84). Hillsdale, NJ: Analytic Press.

Kernberg, O. F. (1992). *Aggression in personality disorders and perversions.* New Haven, CT: Yale University Press.

Krueger, D. W. (1988). Body self, psychological self, and bulimia: Developmental and clinical considerations. In H. J. Schwartz (Ed.), *Bulimia: Psychoanalytic treatment and theory* (pp. 55–72). Madison, CT: International Universities Press.

Lasegue, C. (1964). "De l'anorexie hysterique." In M. R. Kaufman & M. Heiman (Eds.), *Evolution of Psychosomatic Concepts: Anorexia Nervosa* (pp. 141–155). New York: International Universities Press. (Original work published 1873)

Laufer, M. E. (1996). The role of passivity in the relationship to the body during adolescence. *The Psychoanalytic Study of the Child, 51,* 348–364.

Lerner, P. (1991). *Psychoanalytic theory and the Rorschach.* Hillsdale, NJ: Analytic Press.

Lerner, P., & Lerner, H. (1980). Rorschach assessment of primitive defenses in borderline personality structure. In J. Kwawer, H. Lerner, P. Lerner, & A. Sugarman (Eds.), *Borderline phenomena and the Rorschach test* (pp. 257–274). New York: International Universities Press.

Masling, J., Rabie, L., & Blondheim, S. H. (1967). Obesity, level of aspiration, and Rorschach and TAT measures of oral dependence. *Journal of Consulting Psychology, 31,* 233–239.

Minuchin, S. B., Rosman, B., & Baker, L. (1978). *Psychosomatic families: Anorexia nervosa in context.* Cambridge, MA: Harvard University Press.

Morton, R. (1694). *Phthisiologia: Or a treatise of consumptions.* London: Smith & Walford.

Muller, J. P. (1996). *Beyond the psychoanalytic dyad: Developmental semiotic in Freud, Pierce and Lacan.* New York: Routledge.

Parmer, J. C. (1991). Bulimia and object relations: MMPI and Rorschach variables. *Journal of Personality Assessment, 56,* 266–276.

Patton, C. J. (1992). Fear of abandonment and binge eating: A subliminal psychodynamic activation investigation. *Journal of Nervous and Mental Disease, 180,* 484–489.

Pendleton, L., Tisdale, M. J., & Marler, M. (1991). Personality pathology in bulimics versus controls. *Comprehensive Psychiatry, 32,* 516–520.

Pilkonis, P., Heape, C., Ruddy, J., & Serrao, P. (1991). Validity in the diagnosis of personality disorders: The use of the LEAD standard. *Psychological Assessment, 3,* 46–54.

Russ, S. W. (1988). Primary process thinking on the Rorschach, divergent thinking and coping in children. *Journal of Personality Assessment, 52,* 539–548.

Ryan, R., Avery, R., & Grolnick, W. (1985). A Rorschach assessment of children's mutuality of autonomy. *Journal of Personality Assessment, 49,* 6–12.

Schwartz, H. J. (1988). Bulimia: Psychoanalytic perspectives. In H. J. Schwartz (Ed.), *Bulimia: Psychoanalytic treatment and theory* (pp. 31–53). Madison, CT: International Universities Press.

Smith, J. E., Hillard, M. C., & Roll, S. (1991). Rorschach evaluation of adolescent bulimics. *Adolescence, 26,* 687–696.

Sours, J. A. (1980). *Starving to death in a sea of objects.* New York: Jason Aronson.

Spitzer, R. (1983). Psychiatric diagnosis: Are clinicians still necessary? *Comprehensive Psychiatry, 24,* 399–411.

Steiner-Adair, C. (1986). The body politic: Normal female adolescent development and the development of eating disorders. *Journal of the American Academy of Psychoanalysis, 14,* 95–114.

Strauss, J., & Ryan, R. M. (1987). Autonomy disturbances in subtypes of anorexia nervosa. *Journal of Abnormal Psychology, 96,* 254–258.

Stuart, G. W., Laraia, M. T., Ballenger, J. C., & Lydiard, R. B. (1990). Early family experiences of women with bulimia and depression. *Archives of Psychiatric Nursing, 4,* 43–52.

Sugarman, A., & Kurash, C. (1981). The body as a transitional object in bulimia. *International Journal of Eating Disorders, 1,* 365–372.

Tabin, C. J., & Tabin, J. K. (1988). Bulimia and anorexia: Understanding their gender specificity and their complex of symptoms. In H. J. Schwartz (Ed.), *Bulimia: Psychoanalytic treatment and theory* (pp. 173–225). Madison, CT: International Universities Press.

Taylor, G. J., Parker, J. D. A., Bagby, M., & Bourke, M. P. (1996). Relationships between alexithymia and psychological characteristics associated with eating disorders. *Journal of Psychosomatic Research, 41,* 561–568.

Tisdale, M. J., Pendleton, L., & Marler, M. (1990). MCMI characteristics of *DSM–III–R* bulimics. *Journal of Personality Assessment, 55,* 477–483.

Tuber, S. (1989). Children's Rorschach object representations: Findings for a non-clinical sample. *Psychological Assessment, 1,* 146–149.

Urist, J. (1977). The Rorschach test and the assessment of object relations. *Journal of Personality Assessment, 41,* 3–9.

Urist, J., & Schill, M. (1982). Validity of the Rorschach Mutuality of Autonomy Scale. *Journal of Personality Assessment, 46,* 451–454.

Walters, E. E., & Kinder, K. S. (1995). Anorexia nervosa and anorexic-like syndromes in a population-based female twin sample. *American Journal of Psychiatry, 152,* 64–71.

Wechsler, D. (1958). *The measurement and appraisal of adult intelligence* (4th ed.). Baltimore: Wilkins & Wilkins.

Weiner, I. B. (1991). Editor's note: Interscorer agreement in Rorschach research. *Journal of Personality Assessment, 56,* 1.

Weisberg, L. J., Norman, D. K., & Herzog, D. B. (1987). Personality functioning in normal weight bulimia. *International Journal of Eating Disorders, 6,* 615–632.

Wonderlich, S., Ukestad, L., & Peracki, R. (1994). Perceptions of nonshared childhood environments in bulimia nervosa. *Journal of the American Academy of Child and Adolescent Psychiatry, 33,* 740–747.

Zakin, D. F. (1989). Eating disturbance, emotional separation, and body image. *International Journal of Eating Disorders, 8,* 411–416.

Zerbe, K. J. (1993). Whose body is it anyway? Understanding and treating psychosomatic aspects of eating disorders. *Bulletin of the Menninger Clinic, 57,* 161–177.

5

Unconscious Response to "Mommy and I Are One": Does Gender Matter?

Staffan Sohlberg and Billy Jansson

According to van Dam (cited in Carlberg, 1989), "girls and boys are dissimilar before puberty, but not after" (p. 185). van Dam's assertion was meant to convey a joking protest against poor readiness among psychoanalytic theorists in accommodating developmental hypotheses to social and cultural change. The quote serves well also to introduce the puzzling "now-you-see-it, now-you-don't" quality of gender-related effects in our own experi-

These studies were supported by the Magnus Bergvall Foundation and by Grant F24/95 from the Swedish Research Council for the Humanities and Social Sciences. We thank Per Tell for assistance with the gender-related identification analyses; all experimenters who collected data; and Andreas Birgegard, Lars Bäckman, and Katja Claesson for valuable input in the planning of the attachment false memory study.

mental work with adults. In this chapter we describe a series of experiments in which we used subliminal stimulation with "Mommy and I are one" (MIO), and we end the chapter with comments on whether our data demand change in theory or confirm that things are just the way we were once taught they are.

We begin, however by asking another question entirely: What can a therapist do to help schizophrenic patients? Assuming that the patients' problems are rooted in a developmental arrest in the symbiotic phase (Mahler, Pine, & Bergman, 1975), do they need a renewed symbiosis with the therapist-object from which to resume the process of separation–individuation (Limentani, Searles, & Sechehaye, cited in Weinberger & Silverman, 1990), or should the therapist instead discourage any tendency toward a symbiotic relationship and emphasize boundaries, separateness, and individuality (Des Lauriers, Knowlton, & Lidz, cited in Weinberger & Silverman, 1990)?

To Lloyd Silverman, this issue seemed vitally important but impossible to decide through the kind of clinical debate familiar to generations of psychoanalysts (Silverman, Lachman, & Milich, 1982). Both sides, he held, would be able to marshal case studies that appear to support their views, with few hard-and-fast rules to help them separate the useful evidence from the not-so-useful evidence. Silverman's solution was to turn to experimental studies, in which unconscious, temporary, and illusory fulfillment of a symbiotic merger fantasy could be attained through subliminal stimulation technology. Silverman showed schizophrenic patients the words "Mommy and I are one" for a few ms by means of a tachistoscope, sometimes accompanied by a picture of a man and a woman merged at shoulder level. He expected changes in symptoms to reveal what the encouragement of a symbiotic merger fantasy might really mean to these patients and, indirectly, what a therapist encouraging such fantasies might expect to happen (Silverman et al., 1982).

In opting for an experimental, double-blind method Silverman chose one of the most powerful approaches ever adopted by psychoanalytically oriented scientists. In the company of experimenters such as Bornstein, Erdelyi, Masling, and Shevrin, Silverman and Weinberger and their collaborators produced findings that, unlike much psychoanalytic writing, were capable of impressing more individuals than those already won for the cause (e.g., Bornstein, 1990b, 1992, 1999; Bornstein, Leone, & Galley, 1987; Bornstein & Masling, 1984; Erdelyi, 1992; Masling, 1992; Masling, Bornstein, Poynton, Reed, & Katkin, 1991; Shevrin, 1992; Snodgrass, Shevrin, & Kopka, 1993). Authors who subscribed to the popular but erroneous (Fisher & Greenberg, 1996; Westen, 1998) notion that the "entire psychoanalytic framework . . . is itself largely unvalidated" nonetheless asserted that "this area of research adds further weight to the proposal that the direct manipulation of nonconscious processes may potentially exert a therapeutic influence in cases of psychopathology" (Williams, Watts, MacLeod, & Mathews, 1997, p. 275).

Silverman and his collaborators eventually concluded that if schizophrenic patients were "relatively differentiated" that is, they did not on testing ascribe identical characteristics to a picture of a person intended as a self-referent and another intended as a mother-object—their symptoms diminished following stimulation. If, however, there were few or no signs of differentiation, subliminal stimulation with MIO had little influence (Weinberger & Silverman, 1990).

In retrospect it is easy to see how Silverman's work could have developed in two different ways from these observations. One way would have been to view the existence of two subgroups of patients with different responses as but a special instance of the general case normally presumed by psychoanalysts: Peoples' response to any event is determined by the meaning they see in it, and this meaning will be highly individual, if not unique. If Silverman had taken this road he might have done the kind of work done by another pioneer in experimental psychodynamics: Howard Shevrin, whose group went to great lengths in tailoring procedures and stimuli to individual research participants (Balay & Shevrin, 1988; Shevrin et al., 1992).

This was not what Silverman did, however. Rather, on the basis of a series of studies with varying groups of participants, he gradually extended his understanding of how MIO influenced research participants, to say finally that there is a ubiquitous wish for symbiotic merger that can be temporarily satisfied through the kind of experimental manipulation he devised. This wish, by no means restricted to schizophrenic patients, is a remnant of the normal symbiotic phase during infancy but is kept unconscious through defense activity because of its inconsistency with the adult's self-image as a separated and differentiated individual.

Silverman et al. (1982) noted that positive consequences of MIO stimulation require that the person be "relatively differentiated" (see also Siegel & Weinberger, 1998). He also noted a few instances in which such stimulation appeared to have negative consequences (although not, it appears, in schizophrenics; see Silverman et al., 1982, pp. 130–131).

Nevertheless, it is patently clear that the main message communicated by Silverman and his coworkers had exactly the opposite thrust. Put succinctly, MIO stimulation is a panacea that not only improves therapeutic relationships and reduces psychiatric symptoms but also improves academic performance (e.g., Greenberg, cited in Slipp, 2000). The main threat to this explanation of the findings was thought to be not individually different meanings in MIO but a "general, positive, affective tone of the message 'mommy and I are one'" (Weinberger & Silverman, 1990, p. 322). Protests from some of Silverman and his colleagues' fellow psychodynamically oriented experimentalists who theoretically focused on individual differences in response to MIO did little to put the brakes on this campaign (Balay & Shevrin, 1988; Bornstein & Masling, 1984). The same was true for experimental data suggesting both gender-related effects and effects linked to individual differences in patients' relationships with their mothers (Greenberg & Slipp, cited in Slipp, 2000).

MIO Effects Vary in a Predictable Way

The thesis underpinning our work is that if we are truly to understand what is surely one of the most intriguing findings in modern psychology, a way must be found to reconcile the MIO-as-panacea literature with the theoretically well-founded criticisms of this idea (Balay & Shevrin, 1988; Bornstein & Masling, 1984) as well as with the reservations Silverman himself sometimes expressed. Sohlberg, Samuelberg, Sidén, and Thörn (1998) accomplished such a reconciliation by noting that the improvements in implicit (unconscious) mood observed by Weinberger, Kelner, and McClelland (1997) might not be a foregone conclusion. Rather, some of our own experiments have indicated that the likelihood for improvements in implicit mood would be increased if researchers (a) use male participants and (b) stimulate these participants only a few times. This is exactly what Weinberger et al. (1997) did. The problem, then, was not in their findings but in assuming that the results were valid for an unselected population and with any number of stimulations. Although Sohlberg, Samuelberg, et al. (1998) emphasized the highly speculative nature of their interpretation, they suggested that MIO stimulation can be assumed to improve mood only with people who are highly differentiated from their mothers (more likely for males) but who simultaneously have a sense of connectedness.

Since that time, our work has developed to focus theoretically on attachment, interpersonal theory, and affect theory; we view these as modern-day approaches that owe much of their power to ideas developed within the original psychoanalytic schools of thought (Sohlberg, Birgegard, Czartoryski, Ovefelt, & Strömbom, 2000; cf. Westen, 1998; Westen & Gabbard, 1999). We now also use technology borrowed from the cognitive psychologist's toolbox, for example, the modified Stroop (Birgegard & Sohlberg, 1999; Sohlberg, Arvidsson, & Birgegard, 1997) and word selection tasks (Sohlberg, Samuelberg, et al., 1998).

Our working assumption is that MIO stimulation activates an unconscious associative network for the self-with-mother relationship, that is, a relational associative network. Although it has very early roots, this network has undergone many revisions from the day it began to evolve to the day participants report to a laboratory to receive their stimulations (cf. Lachman & Beebe, 1989). Described by concepts such as internal working models in attachment theory, and important people and their internalized representations in Benjamin's (1996) interpersonal theory, such networks have long been studied more loosely under the rubric of self–object relations and representations in psychoanalysis.

In a scholarly review, Baldwin (1992) suggested *relational schema* as the most broadly useful term for such phenomena. A relational schema contains an image of the self, an image of the other, and regularities in patterns of interpersonal relatedness. Activation of a relational schema involves effects on self-concept, expectancies, motivation, and emotion, as well as procedural memory associated with whatever interpersonal script or goal motivation is contained in the interaction (Baldwin, 1992). Baldwin explicitly noted that these schemas can include "possible relationships ... including idealized relationships existing only in fantasy, for example, the contention by Silverman ... and others that people often seek to experience the feelings of ultimate reunion with the good mother of infancy" (p. 470).

Although we agree with Baldwin's (1992) approach on most counts, in the final analysis we prefer the term *associative relationship network* over his suggested *relational schema* (Sohlberg, Birgegard, et al., 2000). The schema concept originally referred to a rather narrow and sharply defined structure and sits uneasily with the extensive set of interrelated phenomena Baldwin (1992) discussed. More congenial to psychoanalytically inspired open constructs, an associative network is "any network of elements connected together that can influence one another's states" (Sutherland, 1995, p. 38). Moreover, if activation of a relational schema more or less invariably implies a change in self-concept, expectancies, motivation, and emotion, as well as procedural memory associated with whatever interpersonal script or goal motivation is contained in the interaction, it might be useful to direct attention to the entire package of response. Associative relationship network is a concept that does precisely that. It is heuristic because it prevents a narrowing of research attention to only some of the ways in which internal working models, important people and their internalized representations, self–object relations, and relational schemas govern behavior. Indeed, Baldwin (1999, p. 196) later cited Carlston and Smith to suggest that a relational schema can be seen as a "chunk of associative network."

Should Researchers Care About Gender When Studying MIO?

Although we and our colleagues routinely study differences in response due to participant gender as one aspect of individuality, and comment on these results when relevant (Sohlberg, Arvidsson, & Birgegard, 1997; Sohlberg, Birgegard, et al., 2000; Sohlberg,

Samuelberg, et al., 1998), participant gender has never been the focal point of our studies. Our initial theoretical–intuitive sense that gender should matter received a rebuttal from Hardaway (1990), whose meta-analysis revealed no gender differences in response to MIO that could not more parsimoniously be accounted for by chance.

However, meta-analyses do not provide all the answers, either. Because gender is a fundamental human category (see, e.g., Freud, 1930/1958; Maccoby, 1988), perhaps our initial acceptance of Hardaway's (1990) results was a mistake. Because analysis by gender has not always proven illuminating to the aims of our work, perhaps it was not a mistake. In this chapter we review and highlight some of those earlier findings in an attempt to understand more about the conditions in which analysis by gender does prove illuminating. We also describe two experiments not previously reported, with an eye specifically on gender-related effects. Silverman and Weinberger (1988), while generally emphasizing MIO as a panacea and a ubiquitous wish for symbiotic oneness, discussed observations implying that gender matters; so did Slipp (2000). For Tabin and Tabin (1987), the question was not whether gender matters but whether this is better explained by a pre-Oedipal symbiosis interpretation or an early version of Oedipal experience.

The term *gender* as used here refers to the experimenter's classification of participants as either male or female on the basis of their names and approximately 30 minutes of interaction in the laboratory. The term does not logically imply anything concerning participants' identity, self-concept, or sexual preferences. Although we assume that there is a high correlation between experimenters' classification and participants' identity, self-concept, and sexual preferences, there is likely to be some slack that will introduce error when speculating about, for instance, sexual–relational implications of the MIO stimulus to the men and women who participated in our experiments.

Because we look for trends across a series of experiments, and because previous literature is equivocal in regard to whether gender matters for MIO response, we are equally happy here defining the meaning of results associated with p values of .99 as we are when $p = .01$. If we looked only at the latter outcomes we would bias conclusions toward Type II errors; if we looked only at the former outcomes we would bias conclusions toward Type I errors (Cohen, 1969, 1994; Kirk, 1996; Rosenthal, Rosnow, & Rubin, 2000; Rosenthal & Rubin, 1982). Estimates of percentage differences in effect provide a common ground across experiments and analyses, as does Cohen's effect size d in the sense that, although merely conventions, the small (.20), medium (.50), and large (.80) estimates do not depend on sample size the way p levels do. Because this study is not a meta-analysis, we will nevertheless comment on single results, using such expressions as, "There was little evidence for an effect at d = .19, p = .13," or "Although not significant at p = .33, there was a marked gender difference, with d = .03 for men but .46 for women." The one underlying principle is that we distinguish between conclusions that apply to the sample only and conclusions that, using the $p < .05$ convention, can be generalized to the population. Note that each time we used regression statistics to analyze effects of MIO in conjunction with a moderator variable we excluded bivariate outlier participants. Participants were defined a priori as outliers if they were atypical enough in their condition to produce standardized prediction residuals smaller than Z = −2.5 or greater than 2.5. There were usually one or two such participants in each experiment, sometimes in only one condition, at other times in both. Note finally that all experiments had between-groups designs in which a small number of stimulations (most often four or eight) were given to separate experimental and control groups. In all experiments we used Silverman's classic control stimulus "people are walking" (PAW; Silverman et al., 1982).[1]

---

[1]Critics of Silverman and his supporters have debated the possibility that large differences in structure and meaning between this stimulus and MIO might substantially reduce the possibilities of meaningfully interpreting experimental results (e.g., Balay & Shevrin, 1988; Fudin, 1986; Weinberger, 1986, 1989). Space limitations preclude a comprehensive review of even our own data that bear on this issue. However, Birgegard and Sohlberg (1999) suggested that solutions proposed in the literature (e.g., anagrams) may mean a cure worse than the disease. Bornstein's (1990a) meta-analysis revealed larger effects of subliminal presentation of the stimuli than of supraliminal presentation, inconsistent with an argument that MIO effects are due to single words or fragments of word only (the partial-cues hypothesis). Citing a study by Hansen, Masling (1992) asserted that sentences up to six words long can be detected (uncon-

Previous Studies

Identification With Mother

The first series of experiments relied heavily on measuring participants' identification with their mothers to make their response to MIO predictable (Sohlberg, Billinghurst, & Nylén, 1998). Inspired by Silverman's attempt to assess differentiation by having participants rate a picture of a person intended as a self-referent and another intended as a mother-object, Birgitta Jenssen and Staffan Sohlberg developed a task that instructed participants to rate themselves and their mothers on 40 adjectives (e.g., *humorous, diplomatic, pessimistic*). Highly descriptive words were given 5 points, and words that did not fit well were scored 1; intermediate points were given to semidescriptive words. After rating themselves, participants put aside the form and resumed ratings on another form, now with the instruction to think about their mothers. Correlating a participant's two rated profiles produced a 1.00 to −1.00 scale:

---

sciously) and understood at exposure speeds as brief as 0.7 ms. Weinberger et al. (1997) recorded a significant linear trend implying more positive implicit mood after MIO than after PAW but less after "Mommy is gone." In Hardaway's (1990) meta-analysis effects of MIO compared to PAW and similar control stimuli were twice as large as those of other "oneness" stimuli (e.g., "my prof and I are one"). They were three times as large as those of other "Mommy and I" stimuli (e.g., "Mommy and I are alike"). Very much the same orders of magnitude were observed in a large ($N = 122$) experiment in which effects of MIO (compared to PAW) versus the effects of "One are and Mommy I" and "Mommy ndi era rn oae" were examined (Sohlberg & Birgegard, 2001, Experiment 4). In our view, a hypothesis that participants in properly conducted MIO experiments respond to the syntax-dependent meaning in the entire five-word phrase is supported by at least as much evidence as the opposite possibility. However, it is well to remember that some experimental paradigms in unconscious perception may limit processing to word parts (Abrams & Greenwald, 2000). Even in MIO-type experiments some similarity of effect may sometimes result from stimuli that are substantially different in syntax-dependent meaning but similar in structure and in the presence of single words (MIO vs. "Mommy and I are dissimilar"; Sohlberg & Birgegard, 2001, Experiment 2). Conditions that increase the likelihood of syntax-dependent effects may include sufficient time for unconscious stimulus processing after the actual exposures and sensitive dependent measures, for example, measures that pick specific associative themes.

1.00 indicated perfect profile similarity, 0 indicated no similarity at all, and −1.00 indicated mirror-image profiles. In practice, we learned that scores most often range from approximately .90 down to −.40.

Higher scores are associated with more positive responses when this measure is used in MIO experiments (Sohlberg, Arvidsson, & Birgegård, 1997; Sohlberg, Billinghurst, & Nylén, 1998). The higher the similarity scores, the more likely it is that participants respond with positive childhood memories after MIO stimulation, which is how implicit mood is most often measured using a task developed by Weinberger (1992; Weinberger et al., 1997).

Theoretically, we had several reasons to avoid calling our task a measure of symbiosis versus differentiation. Instead, we tentatively described it as reflecting aspects of identification with the mother (Sohlberg, Stahlheuer, & Tell, 1997). Scores were assumed to express the degree of similarity between conscious–cognitive aspects of self- and object representations. In their entirety such representations can be defined to include both conscious and unconscious and cognitive and affective components (Bornstein, 1993). We emphasized first getting robust, replicable results in an area as esoteric and controversial as this before going into the finer details of how best to conceptualize these results. Nevertheless, tests that could reveal whether the data were clearly inconsistent with the concepts we applied to them were completed from the outset. Relevant to the present purposes, and as one would expect for a measure of identification with the mother, female participants in the first series of experiments had higher scores than male participants (Sohlberg, Billinghurst, & Nylén, 1998). Further supporting validity—at least, given stereotypical patterns of gender-specific identification—a nonexperimental study in clinical psychology revealed that levels of Beck Depression Inventory dysphoria were more strongly related to identification with mother in females but to identification with father in males (Sohlberg, Stahlheuer, & Tell, 1997).

Observations such as these could clearly lead to expectations that the implications of identification with mother for response to MIO is different in men and women. The first series of experiments indicated that this is not so. A higher score for identification with mother was associated with a more positive response, irrespective of whether this score was delivered by a man (n = 57) or a woman (n = 100; Sohlberg, Billinghurst, & Nylén, 1998).

In a more extensive analysis of the data for the present purposes we found, first, a 6% difference between genders in the size of the effect: Identification with mother explained 10% more of the variance in the experimental group than in the neutral control group when analysis was restricted to women, but 16% when analysis was restricted to men. Bracketing the question of the reliability and size of this effect, the difference logically supports the conclusion that although higher identification with mother does generally forecast positive response to MIO, as stated in our original article (Sohlberg, Billinghurst, & Nylén, 1998), women are somewhat less predictable than men. Consistent with such a conjecture, our new reanalyses also demonstrated that the 6% difference occurred at dissimilar overall levels of predictability. When we collapsed data across stimulation conditions to obtain a main effect of identification with mother, this variable predicted 2.4% of the variance in mood among women (p = .1276) but 19.8% among men (p = .0005). Thus, less predictable responses to MIO among women appeared to be an aspect of less general predictability when using an identification-with-mother measure.

Consistent with this implication, and perhaps testifying to greater fluidity of identification patterns in modern women, Sohlberg, Tell, and Stahlheuer (2001) found in an as-yet-unpublished study that Sohlberg, Stahlheuer, and Tell's (1997) gender-specific Beck Depression Inventory-versus-identification results replicated among men but not among women. The earlier results could be reproduced for women too, Sohlberg, Tell, et al. (2001) found post hoc, but only if the analysis was restricted to participants in stereotypically female areas of study rather than stereotypically male areas. Among female students of subjects such as music and the arts, levels of dysphoria were more strongly related to identification with mother than to identification with father. Among female students of physics, computer science, math, and some other related areas of study, the reverse was true (Sohlberg, Tell, et al., 2001). Woelfel (cited in Kiesler, 1996, p. 76) found that boys and girls most often named same-sex significant others when asked about people influencing their attitudes toward studies and choice of occupation. However, girls more often than boys tended to include both parents.

We believe these data support two conclusions. First, MIO stimulation affects psychological structures that, in absolute terms, are relevant for both men and women. Second, MIO stimulation affects psychological structures that, in relative terms, are slightly more relevant for men. The generality of this conclusion is restricted by the moderator measure used. Other moderators might reveal that women's responses to MIO are more predictable than men's, but we do not yet know what this moderator would be. It is important to note, however, that the failure to generally replicate the mother identification results for women (Sohlberg, Tell, et al., 2001) implies that the meaning of MIO might actually be more variable for them than for men, hence the greater difficulty in predicting their response. Under this interpretation the greater difficulty might be true in general, not just with the particular moderators that have been tried.

Effects of Gender Per Se

What about the straightforward implications of gender, without considering individual-difference variables such as identification with mother? Further post hoc analyses of this data set revealed a marginally significant analysis of variance interaction ($p = .0630$). When we computed separate effect sizes by gender we found a positive small-to-moderate effect ($d = .39$) among men but a small negative effect ($d = -.23$) among women.

These results, although limited, support the notion that the MIO response is not identical in men and women. Specifically, at least unless one controls for various potential moderators, the likelihood of a positive response is greater in men. These post hoc observations provided the background for a later attempt, as described earlier, to understand the differences between such findings and those of Weinberger et al. (1997). They also led Sohlberg, Samuelberg, et al. (1998) to study an exclusively female sample. Although two more independent variables were controlled along with gender in a concerted effort to demonstrate negative effects of MIO, making interpretation of causality equivocal, both experiments in Sohlberg, Samuelberg, et al.'s study produced negative effects that were significantly different from the positive estimates found in Hardaway's (1990) meta-analysis.

Modified Stroop Task

In further work, Sohlberg, Arvidsson, and Birgegard (1997) used the modified Stroop task to access more closely the unconscious associative networks they assumed were responsible for the observed mood effects. Controlling for performance on neutral words such as *tree*, the authors timed participants as they color named symbiosis-related words such as *unity*. The small number of male participants severely restricts conclusions, but in the present context it is notable that men (n = 10) and women (n = 28) responded in opposite directions, interaction $F(1, 34)$ = 2.864, p = .0997. Whereas women demonstrated the classic Stroop interference effect, suggesting that MIO stimulation caused preoccupation with symbiosis words (d = .56), men showed the paradoxical Stroop facilitation effect (d = −.65; e.g., Lundh, Wikström, & Westerlund, 2001). This could mean that MIO stimulation made the male participants unconsciously defend against symbiosis words. Deprived of personal meaning, the symbiosis words appeared to the male participants as nothing more than blots of ink that could be quickly color named. Alternatively, men associated to MIO along different lines than women, also making the symbiosis words appear as mere blots of ink, but without the connotation of defense. We return to these possibilities later but note now that these results imply qualitatively different effects of MIO in men and women.

Using a Story Task: Experiment 1

Sohlberg, Birgegard, et al. (2000) noted that once again small sample size precluded firm conclusions when results were divided by gender. Still, identification with mother predicted responses on a story task in a similar way among men and women. After MIO stimulation participants were asked to imagine writing a short story. They were then given a list of topics as well as suggestions regarding possible traits and wishes of the main character in the story, including sayings that might apply to this character. Comprising also items showing a *neutral* response, these lists had been constructed to permit computation of scores for *symbiotic oneness* and *defensive autonomy*, with items inspired by clinical experience, Bornstein and Masling (1984), attachment theory (Bowlby, 1988), and Weinberger's "Oneness Motive Scoring System" (Weinberger, Stefanou, Scroppo, McLeod, & McClelland, 1993). Sohlberg, Birgegard, et al. expected the degree of identification with mother to predict whether MIO stimulation would prompt participants to select more symbiotic oneness items or more defensive autonomy items. If identification with mother was high, then MIO should activate a set of associations with mainly positive affective connotations, increasing the likelihood that symbiotic oneness items would be selected. If, on the other hand, identification with mother was low, then MIO should activate a set of associations with mainly negative affective connotations, increasing the likelihood that defensive autonomy items would be selected. This prediction was borne out by the data and at reasonably similar levels of effect across participant gender, although one should keep in mind the caveat about sample size.

New Experiments

Using the Story Task a Second Time: Experiment 2

We had an opportunity to again analyze gender-related effects in our first attempt to replicate Sohlberg, Birgegard, et al.'s (2000) story task study. We designed an experiment that was in part an exact replication of their study. Forty university students were rewarded with an open movie ticket in exchange for participation. Because gender effects were not the focus when we planned this study, we merely matched the number of men and women to that in the previous experiment, disregarding the small number of men this entailed (8 in the MIO group and 7 in the PAW control group; there were 13 women in the MIO group and 12 women in the PAW group). Procedures were the same as those in Sohlberg, Birgegard, et al.'s study. An experimenter blind to the stimulus shown to each participant obtained consent in writing and then instructed the participant to look into a tachistoscope. Having ascertained that the participant was seated so that four small, dim, orienting lights were visible, the experimenter then administered eight 5-ms exposures of the MIO or PAW stimulus. Immediately afterward the participant completed a 5-min self-paced story task. After this, participants were asked to report what they had seen during exposures (typically "nothing" or "there was some kind of dim light") and were then asked to look into the tachistoscope again. New exposures using increasing stimulus duration were now administered, and participants reported what they saw each time. Using Silverman's criteria (Silverman, 1984; Weinberger & Silverman, 1990), we defined participants' level of conscious awareness using the stimulus duration at which they reported seeing anything structured (e.g., "a line").[2] In this experiment this first occurred at 13 ms, as compared to the 5 ms used during the experiment proper. As is usually the case in our laboratory, typical values were much higher (MIO: $M = 147$ ms, $SD = 208.6$ ms; PAW: $M = 107$ ms, $SD = 70.9$ ms), $t(38) = 0.79$, $p = .435$. Using Mann–Whitney to control two univariate outliers in MIO, the difference between conditions was still far from significant, $p = .454$.

Participants returned 7 days later to take the identification-with-mother test and, last, a novel memory task. The latter simply consisted of trying to re-create the selections on the story task originally made in the laboratory. We reasoned that because MIO stimulation affects mood, and emotion affects memory, experimental participants should show a different pattern of response from controls when trying to re-create their original performance. We hypothesized that any kind of response revealing more intense

---

[2]Claesson (1997) noted that because this happens long before they report stimulus content even with innocuous control stimuli such as PAW or "I can read," this procedure is immune against the kind of criticisms leveled at the taboo-word studies of the 1950s. With respect to modern debate, our criterion for the threshold between conscious and unconscious awareness seems most similar to Cheesman and Merikle's (1986) "subjective threshold"; however, Sohlberg, Billinghurst, and Nylén (1998) carried out a discrimination study inspired by Masling et al.'s (1991) study. The results implied that exposure conditions in Sohlberg, Billinghurst, and Nylén's laboratory are actually closer to Cheesman and Merikle's "objective threshold" than to their subjective threshold. Although some level of stimulus energy is required for perception to work, data suggest that powerful subliminal effects are more likely with stimuli that are comfortably below the level of conscious awareness (Birgegard & Sohlberg, 1999).

emotional involvement would predict better performance. Thus, participants who favored symbiotic oneness or defensive autonomy items over neutral items were expected to perform better on the memory task 7 days later.

Story task subscale correlations. Results showed that, as in Sohlberg, Birgegard, et al.'s (2000) experiment, there was a strong negative correlation between selection of symbiotic oneness items and selection of defensive autonomy items ($rs = -.82$ vs. $-.88$ in Sohlberg, Birgegard, et al., 2000). Because participants were free to select neutral items also, this result was not forced by logic but indicates that symbiotic oneness and defensive autonomy worked as alternative response options, just as we had intended. Because of the strong correlation, we restrict analysis here only to symbiotic oneness.

MIO, identification, and symbiotic oneness. There were fewer participants this time with high scores for identification with mother, resulting in a significantly lower overall level than in Sohlberg, Birgegard, et al.'s (2000) experiment ($Ms = .25$ vs. $.40$), $F(1, 76) = 5.41$, $p = .0227$. Although our efforts at replicating procedures in detail were thus apparently not sufficient to prevent some systematic difference between experiments, we nevertheless proceeded with analyses as before. A Stimulus + Identification + Stimulus × Identification regression analysis revealed that MIO participants selected somewhat fewer symbiotic oneness items (a decrease of 0.536 points; total score range 0–6). This was a nonsignificant result ($p = .3106$) but logically consistent with the relative absence of participants high on identification with mother in this sample. Furthermore, there was an independent, trend-significant increase in symbiotic oneness selections with high levels of identification with mother, $t(35) = 1.807$, $p = .0797$. Last, there was a significant interaction, $t(35) = -2.053$, $p = .0478$. Using the equation and test case participants at high versus low levels of identification ($Z = 2$ vs. $Z = -2$), a high score for identification corresponded to 1.3 symbiotic oneness items in MIO but 4.0 in PAW. Conversely, a low score for identification corresponded to 3.0 symbiotic oneness items in MIO but 1.4 in PAW. Thus, this was a crossing, significant interaction, just as in Experiment 1 (Sohlberg, Birgegard, et al., 2000), but opposite in direction.

Gender. A qualitative comparison of gender differences supports the conclusion from Experiment 1. Although Sohlberg, Birgegard, et al. (2000) noted that the analysis was "of doubtful value" because of the small number of men involved, the data from their experiment suggest that identification with mother predicted performance in a similar fashion across gender. The new results, although tentative because of the small samples, nevertheless suggest the same conclusion. Higher scores were associated with the selection of fewer symbiotic items in both men and women and at highly similar effect sizes.

When we disregarded identification with mother and estimated the negative main effect of MIO with Cohen's d, the effect was $-.31$. Splitting results by gender changed little here (men: $d = -.26$, women: $d = -.33$), interaction $F(1, 36) = 0.049$, $p = .8268$. Thus, the results to this point imply not only that the sample data conformed to expectations based on previous research regarding the main effect of MIO but also that the link between prediction and outcome was the reverse of that seen in Experiment 1. Gender did not matter much. Simply put, it seemed that if MIO at all generally affects participants' selections on the story task, it makes them avoid symbiotic oneness themes, and this is equally true in men and women. Gender did not help explain the unexpected result with respect to how identification moderated MIO effects either.

Memory. On the memory task participants were able to re-create approximately 75% of the selections they originally made in our laboratory a week previously. There was no main effect of stimulus ($d = .11$), $F(1, 38) = 0.12$, $p = .7309$. When gender was added to the model there was no effect among men ($d = -.12$) but a small effect among women ($d = .26$). Thus, women in this sample recalled their original selections slightly better if they had been stimulated with MIO than if they were in the neutral control group. With small effect sizes and small samples, this interaction, of course, was not significant, $F(1, 36) = 0.325$, $p = .5721$. Thus, it seemed that if there is at all a story task memory effect of MIO a week later, it will more likely be observed in women.

Memory, emotion, and gender. In the final step of the analyses we looked at the possibility that MIO would affect memory through its presumed association with emotion. Emotion was computed as a sum of symbiotic oneness + defensive autonomy items, and the sum indexed how often participants favored these items over the neutral ones. As a preparatory step, direct comparison revealed that MIO was associated with a small increase ($d = .33$) in emotion, $F(1, 38) = 1.026$, $p = .1588$, one-tailed.

When we added gender to the model we found that this result depended entirely on the women. No effects were significant (interaction and other $ps > .44$), but effect sizes revealed a small-to-medium ($d = .47$) increase in women and almost no effect at all ($d = .01$) among men. Thus, women in this sample responded with more emotion in the laboratory and were better a week later at remembering the selections they had made on our story task.

We then entered Stimulus, Emotion, and the Stimulus × Emotion interaction as independent variables in a regression analysis, using memory performance as the dependent variable. The data showed no significant main effects of Stimulus, $t(37) = -0.079$, $p = .9378$, or Emotion, $t(37) = 0.434$, $p = .6667$. The Stimulus × Emotion interaction, however, was significant, $t(37) = 2.164$, $p = .0372$. When we applied the equation to test cases at high versus low levels of Emotion ($Z = 2$ vs. $Z = -2$), we found a crossing interaction in which an MIO participant who responded with much emotion remembered more than equally emotional counterparts in PAW (91% > 76%), but an MIO participant who responded with little emotion remembered less than equally low responsive peers in PAW (58% < 73%).

The $d = .33$ increase in Emotion scores in MIO was logically consistent with our assumption that MIO involves emotion; however, the crossing pattern when predicting memory from the Stimulus × Emotion interaction clearly was not. If Emotion were the true causal variable, then an ordinal interaction would be the most likely result. Even MIO participants with unusually low scores on the Emotion variable would still perform at least on par with typical control group participants. Instead, they performed less well ($Z = -2$ test case: 58% vs. 73%). Either defense was involved, or some aspect other than emotion was really more influential in causing the Stimulus × Emotion interaction. Using the symbiotic oneness and defensive autonomy variables separately was only marginally helpful. We obtained clear and significant results only when we counted symbiotic oneness and defensive autonomy together as indicators of a latent variable with power both to improve and worsen memory.

Symbiotic oneness and defensive autonomy items by design concern relationships directly or indirectly (Sohlberg, Birgegard, et al., 2000); however, not all neutral items do. It may be that regardless of whether participants select symbiotic oneness or defensive autonomy items MIO stimulation imbues these relationship items with a more vivid, personal meaning. This meaning, in turn, affects memory. For some, it improves memory. For others, memory is worsened in a manner consistent with the repression construct (Brenner, 1957; Freud, 1930/1958; Wolman, 1968).

We subjected these conjectures to renewed consideration given that virtually all the emotion increase in MIO previously found was due to the women ($d = .47$ vs. $d = .01$ for men). With the same caveats as before, the whole-sample crossing interaction was nevertheless replicated in minute detail in both genders.

Thus, the sample data suggested a two-variable effect: First, women on average responded with more emotion or relational associations after MIO, which helped them remember more. Second, participants of both genders remembered more if they originally were in MIO and selected many emotion–relation items on the story task but remembered less if they originally were in MIO and selected few such items.

Interpreting experiment 2. Summarizing the present experiment then, there was a small decrease in symbiotic oneness after MIO, not significant but logically consistent with the relative absence of high scorers on identification with mother in the sample. Gender mattered little for this outcome. MIO did not generally affect memory, but there was some nonsignificant indication that gender mattered here. Furthermore, there was a small increase in Emotion–Relation after MIO, due entirely to female participants. Finally, Identification with mother interacted with Stimulus to influence significantly story task performance, and Emotion interacted with Stimulus to influence significantly memory. These effects were nearly identical across genders. Thus, several aspects of the sample data were somewhat related to gender, but there were no significant, generalizable results involving this variable.

These data clearly suggest that MIO stimulation affects psychological structures that are more similar than different across genders. To the extent that there is a difference, Experiment 2 suggests that future research investigate memory and emotional or relational associations after MIO. In general, however, all these observations pale in comparison with significantly lower levels of identification with mother in this experiment than in the former one (Sohlberg, Birgegard, et al., 2000), and a pattern of interaction between Identification and Stimulus on story task performance that was significant but reversed, compared to the results of Experiment 1 (Sohlberg, Birgegard, et al., 2000). This occurred even though we designed the present study as an exact replication of the previous one, even recruiting participants from the same university departments. One variable we could not control for practical reasons was the gender of the experimenter; we next address this variable.

One cannot logically rule out that participants rated themselves, their mothers, or both, differently when completing the mother identification task at the request of a man than when complying with the request of a woman. Alternatively, of those approached, fewer people at high levels of identification with mother may have elected to take part in the study when approached by a man than when approached by a woman. Both explanations are speculative, but the former one is less likely true. There was a small albeit nonsignificant decrease in symbiotic oneness after MIO in this experiment, but not in Experiment 1. That result is logical if in Experiment 2 we studied a slightly different population, but not if we studied the same population as in Experiment 1 that only superficially appeared to be different because of temporary experimenter effects.

Also, the reversed relationship between identification with mother and symbiotic oneness after MIO was a dramatic effect that demanded explanation. Participants completed the story task in the immediate presence of the experimenter. It is possible that completing this task has a different meaning in the presence of a man than in the presence of a woman. Besides the obvious fact that our participants were aware of experimenters' genders and could be affected by that knowledge, recent evidence for effects related to experimenter gender extends to striking demonstrations with respect also to nonpsychological variables. Jacob (1998) found that extremely small and nondetectable amounts of a putative pheromone were sufficient to affect mood and psychophysiological measures in young women. In both of Jacob's experiments, however, this occurred only in the presence of a male experimenter, not with female experimenters.

Using the Story Task a Third Time: Experiment 3

Our preference for the last experiment in this series ($N = 50$) was once again to focus on the unconscious associative networks whose activation we assume explains MIO effects and to do it using a male experimenter rather than a female one. We previously noted that future studies might benefit from the hypothesis that the tachistoscopically delivered stimulus is a prime that influences how participants respond to the laboratory context as a whole (Sohlberg, Claesson, & Birgegard, 2001). It does not seem farfetched to assume that experimenter gender might be more important than most other variables in that context in a fundamentally social- and gender-attentive species such as ours (Baumeister & Leary, 1995; Guisinger & Blatt, 1994; Maccoby, 1988). Thus, describing the main character of our story task as "wishing for a long, close relationship," a response to a request from a woman might mean something different than doing it in response to a request from a man, at least if the selection were immediately preceded by subliminal stimulations with MIO. Although they believed experimenter gender to be more important in studies of hypotheses relating to Oedipal competition, Weinberger and Silverman (1990) identified the role of experimenter gender as a general knowledge gap in Subliminal Psychodynamic Activation and an area for future research.

We reasoned that if our change of experimenter was indeed responsible for the change in results, then data in the new Experiment 3, in which the same male experimenter took part, should look more like those in Experiment 2 than those in Experiment 1. Specifically, this applied to mother identification levels closer to .25 than to .40 and to a decrease in selection of symbiotic oneness items at high levels of identification (as in Experiment 2) rather than an increase (as in Experiment 1; Sohlberg, Birgegard, et al., 2000).

Second, we complemented the story task with a new attachment false memory measure. We assumed that Bartholomew's (1990) model of adult attachment might clarify the effects of MIO. We included 18 words we believed relevant to attachment experiences as described by Bartholomew (1990) in a study list (e.g., *together, considerate, free, indifferent, condemning, deserted*), along with 6 words with positive or negative valence but unrelated to attachment issues (e.g., *intelligent, clumsy*). If MIO activates attachment-related unconscious associative networks, then this activation might influence the kinds of words to which a participant attends. If effects can later be found on new words that are only associatively related to the studied words, then the existence of a network (schema) may be inferred (Baldwin, 1999). Therefore, after a distraction task, participants were given another word list comprising 48 words, on which 24 were new and only associatively related to the previously studied words (18 for attachment, e.g., *community, reliable, independent, cold, criticizing, unloved*), again along with 6 words with positive or negative valence but unrelated to attachment issues (e.g., *humorous, unprofessional*). Correcting for response bias (total number of times participants say they have seen words that were actually not shown before), we computed false-memory scores for each of the 18 new attachment words and then used principal-components analysis to create three components for use as dependent variables.

Because this was an exploratory attempt at transporting the false-memory technique from cognitive psychology to MIO research, we restricted predictions to a difference between MIO and PAW and interactions between identification with mother and MIO–PAW on performance. The former outcome would support an inference about activation of unconscious associative networks, in a manner satisfying Baldwin's (1999) criteria for the demonstration of a schema. The latter outcome would be consistent with our previous results and general expectations. We formulated no directional hypotheses. Research on person memory supports both schema-congruent and -incongruent memory, and results may depend on task demands (Rojahn & Pettigrew, 1992). In the first case, activation or priming directs attention toward material thematically or otherwise related to the activated schema. Attention leads to learning, and learning leads to improved memory. With lists of words to study after priming, and lists of words to assess at a later point, participants will falsely recognize words they did not study, if these words are thematically related to those they were primed to focus attention on earlier.

In the second case, priming also leads to attention first being directed toward specific categories of words but, given sufficient time for processing, remembered best are words that deviate from expectation, that is, ones that stick out.

Procedure. At recruitment, participants were given an envelope with the identification measure and two other instruments unrelated to the present study to complete at home. At our laboratory they were seated in front of a tachistoscope as in previous experiments. After four exposures they were given written instructions to "take a look" at the word study list for purposes of a later exercise. The experimenter then allowed the participants 10 s to inspect the 24 words before he removed the list. Participants then received written instructions to remember as many three-digit numbers as possible for later recall. They were further instructed to turn the page after 60 s and then begin writing as many numbers as they could remember for another 30 s. This task was designed to limit participants' possibilities for conscious rehearsal of the attachment words they had seen for 10 s. Finally, they received new instructions in writing to respond to each word now presented by the experimenter, saying "yes" if they believed they had seen the word before and "no" if they felt they had not. The experimenter then presented the participants with a 48-word booklet. There was 1 word per page, and each word was shown for 5 s. Half of these words were those studied before, and half were new but thematically related to the previously shown words. We noted how many times participants said "yes" to the new words. To control for general response bias, we derived final scores by dividing by total number of "yes" answers. Thus, for instance, a participant who responded "yes" to the word *intimate* but "no" to all other new words would earn a score of 1.00 for *intimate* (1/1 = 1). A participant who responded "yes" to *intimate* and to 9 new words in all would earn a score of .11 for *intimate* (1/9 = .11).

Immediately after completing this task, participants were administered the story task, as in Experiments 1 and 2. Finally, thresholds for conscious awareness were established as before, with data showing that the first reports of a line or something equivalent occurred at 30 ms, that is, 6 × the 5 ms used during the experiment proper (MIO: $M = 100$, $SD = 89.2$; PAW: $M = 109$, $SD = 72.9$), $t(48) = 0.405$, $p = .687$).

Story task subscale correlations. Once again symbiotic oneness and defensive autonomy worked as alternative responses (rs = −.85 vs. −.82 in Experiment 2 and −.88 in Sohlberg, Birgegard, et al., 2000). Therefore, here too we restricted further analysis to symbiotic oneness.

Identification. The mean level of identification with mother was .27, similar to the .25 recorded in Experiment 2 but markedly lower than that in Experiment 1.

Effects on symbiotic oneness. We regressed symbiotic oneness scores onto a Stimulus + Identification + Stimulus × Identification model. The interaction results replicated those of Experiment 2 rather than those of Experiment 1, $t(46) = -1.590$, $p = .0594$, one-tailed. Thus, participants at higher levels ($Z = 2$) of identification were less likely to select symbiotic oneness items after MIO than after PAW (3.1 vs. 6.5). Conversely, participants at lower levels ($Z = -2$) of identification were more likely to select symbiotic oneness items after MIO than after PAW (3.3 vs. 2.7). There was also a significant main effect of MIO per se, $t(46) = -2.258$, $p = .0288$. The negative direction of effect here also replicated Experiment 2 rather than Experiment 1, a logical finding given the lower levels of identification we obtained in Experiments 2 and 3 versus Experiment 1, in which there was negligible evidence of a main effect. Finally, although not germane to the present purposes, there was a significant effect of identification. Independent of the other effects, selection of symbiotic oneness items was more likely for participants at high levels of identification, $t(46) = 2.152$, $p = .0368$. This outcome, too, replicated the results of Experiment 2.

With the slightly greater number of men in this experiment compared to the number of men in previous experiments with the story task we could repeat the analysis split by gender (women, $n = 27$; men, $n = 23$). As in previous experiments, this revealed some small differences in the context of great similarities. Thus, the direction of effect was the same across gender for all effects, with the magnitude appreciably different only for the main effect of MIO. In women, MIO lowered the selection of symbiotic oneness items by 0.746 of a point, but in men by 2.097 points (score range, 0–8). Direct comparison revealed that this difference corresponded to a small-to-moderate negative effect ($d = -.42$) in women but a large effect ($d = -.83$) in men. Given the small samples, the moderating effect of gender still was far from significant (interaction $p = .45$).

Effects on the attachment false memory task. A principal-components analysis on the 18 attachment false memory words revealed several components with eigenvalues >1. A scree test suggested a break after three components accounting for 13%, 12%, and 12% of the variance. Therefore, we forced the creation of three components and regressed them separately onto the same independent variables, as before. All effects on Components 1 and 2 were unreliable ($ps > .22$). However, MIO significantly lowered participants' scores on Component 3, $t(46) = -3.116$, $p = .0032$. When we computed d for the direct MIO-versus-PAW contrast, the significant result corresponded to a large $-.92$ decrease. Using $\geq.40$ loadings as a guide to interpretation, we noted that Component 3 loaded positively on *cold, worthless,* and *furious* but negatively on *useless, independent,* and *self-governed.* With a caveat regarding the negative loading *useless* had, on this component it seemed possibly related to both ambivalent and avoidant attachment. However, there was little evidence that identification with mother influenced the effect of MIO here or that identification with mother was important per se ($ps > .43$).

Nonetheless, we found an effect when we split the results by gender: MIO lowered women's scores by half a point but lowered men's scores by twice as much (-0.551 vs. -1.065, $ps = .1189$ vs. $.0024$). Also, the Stimulus × Identification interaction was significant in men, interaction $t(19) = -3.432$, $p = .0030$, but not in women ($p = .2498$). Specifically, men high in identification with mother had lower scores on the third component if given MIO rather than PAW. Those low in identification had higher scores on the third component. Thus, the simple main effect of MIO was stronger in men, and although identification with mother did not matter much among women, it affected the way men responded to MIO.[3]

To interpret the latter finding we analyzed how identification with mother moderated the effects of MIO on the individual words

---

[3]Although this is not germane to the present purposes, once the effects of MIO and the Stimulus × Identification interaction were accounted for, Identification per se was also significantly associated with the third component score in men, $t(19) = 3.678$, $p = .0017$.

contained in the third component.[4] We based our interpretation on a rank of the interaction *p* levels and found little evidence for an effect on *useless* (.6333). More important for the outcome among men seems to be that, for those highly identified with their mothers, MIO caused a decrease in false memories of *worthless* (.0098) and, to some small extent, *cold* (.2796), but an increase in false memories of *independent* (.0635) and *self-governed* (.1123). Men who did not identify with their mothers experienced the reverse outcome.

Interpreting experiment 3. In summary, male participants who were given MIO rather than PAW selected fewer items indicating symbiotic oneness. To some small extent this was especially true for those at higher levels of identification with mother. Furthermore, male participants given MIO tended falsely to believe they had seen words such as *independent* and *self-governed*. They were less prone than their control group peers to believe mistakenly that they had seen words such as *worthless* and *cold*. To a significant extent the false memory findings were especially true for men at higher levels of identification with mother. This experiment satisfied Baldwin's (1999) criteria for schema activation and thus strengthened our hypothesis that MIO activates associative relational networks, although more so in men than in women. Furthermore, we again noted individually different responses connected with mother identification.

Elucidating the exact meaning of the false-memory data remains a task for the future, but the findings open exciting possibilities for further research. Assumptions about schema-congruent versus -incongruent memory influence whether the data support or question our previous interpretation that unconscious defense lies behind a reduction in symbiotic oneness and an increase in defensive autonomy (Sohlberg, Birgegard, et al., 2000). Assumptions about how successful a defense can be are also important. Patton (1992) made young women with disturbed eating attitudes eat more crackers by stimulating them subliminally with "Mama is leaving me." She also noted that the reason they did not show more neg-

---

[4]We did not test *furious*. Very few participants believed at all that they had seen this word.

ative mood than controls may have been that the defense of eating was successful. In Experiment 3 we observed a reduction in symbiotic oneness and an increase in defensive autonomy alongside a decrease in false memories related to *worthless* and *cold*. Assuming schema-incongruent memory—that is, assuming that MIO really caused participants to associate along the lines suggested by words such as *worthless* and *cold*, although it appeared otherwise —the data suggest that the reduction in symbiotic oneness and increase in defensive autonomy we saw was indeed a defense, but one that failed.

Because we allowed participants only 10 s to look at the 24-word study list, and followed that with a distraction task to make conscious rehearsal of the words impossible, schema-congruent memory might be more likely in Experiment 3 however. Assuming such memory, the data indicate that the reduction in symbiotic oneness and increase in defensive autonomy was a successful defense, along the lines suggested by Patton's (1992) analysis. We noted earlier that in Sohlberg, Arvidsson, and Birgegard's (1997) modified Stroop study trend, significantly more rapid color naming of symbiosis words in men after MIO might have been a defense; deprived of personal meaning, the Stroop words appeared as nothing more than blots of ink that could be color-named quickly. Cramer (1998) demonstrated that both men and women responded with identification as a defense when given false test feedback indicating that they had an opposite-sex gender identity. To some male participants, activation of associations to MIO could serve as singularly powerful "false test feedback" that threatens their gender identity. According to Cramer's findings, they would seek to defend against this provocation by increased efforts to identify with other males. In our experiment, however, men had precious little chance to do so, except by relying on gender stereotypes (Baldwin, 1992) with respect to the minimally interacting male experimenter. They therefore selected story task items relating more to phrases such as "do-it-yourself" and "self-confident" than to "community is safety" and "trusting."

Alternatively, more rapid color naming in the Stroop study simply showed that men tended to ignore the meaning in the symbiosis word because they made associations along the concepts of autonomy and exploration. In a similar fashion, the present data perhaps do not indicate defense activation. If associative networks activated by MIO always concern issues around both attachment and exploration, dependency, and independence (Lachman & Beebe, 1989; Sohlberg, Samuelberg, et al., 1998), then the presence of a male experimenter may be all it takes to make positive responders shift their stories toward autonomy and exploration (Experiments 2 and 3). A female experimenter may be more likely to induce an emphasis on intimacy and relatedness (Experiment 1).

For the time being, however, we note that an average positive effect of MIO (Hardaway, 1990) is logically consistent with unconscious associations along the variables suggested by a decrease of *worthless* and *cold* and an increase of *independent* and *self-governed*, not the reverse. Because the effect we saw was twice as strong in men, such an interpretation is also consistent with the higher likelihood of positive mood after MIO in men, as seen in several of our experiments.

Conclusion

The results of these experiments support the inference that subliminal MIO stimulation affects behavior because it activates individually different unconscious associative networks of an affective–cognitive nature (cf. the schema account of Siegel & Weinberger, 1998, and the fantasy conceptualization emphasized by Weinberger et al., 1997, and Weinberger & McLeod, 1989). Implicit mood was affected in several experiments, and there were effects on a modified Stroop task, an attachment false memory task, and a story task. In most cases these effects were related to an individual-difference variable: level of identification with mother. We defined this variable as degree of similarity between conscious and cognitive representations of mother and self.

Gender Matters

Some small but recurring findings imply that participant gender should not be disregarded when theorizing about these unconscious associative networks or when planning MIO studies. As noted earlier, the contrasting mother identification results for women in two nonexperimental studies imply that the meaning of MIO might actually be more variable for women than for men (Sohlberg, Stahlheuer, & Tell, 1997; Sohlberg, Tell, et al., 2001). This interpretation not only accounts for the greater difficulty in predicting women's responses in the present studies but also implies that the greater difficulty might be true in general, not only with the particular moderators we tried.

Why, then, might the meaning of MIO be more variable for the young women we studied than for young men? Cramer (2000) listed three ways in which adolescent identity development might be more complicated in females. First, early separation from the mother in males but not females necessitates loosening the ties from both parents in adolescence for girls. Second, whereas males are thought by some theorists to develop personal identity first and resolve issues around intimacy later, females work simultaneously on both of these issues. Third, current Western culture to a greater extent encourages females, compared to males, to model the adult self on both parents. Thus, females are given more options but also greater complexity with which to deal. Unconscious associations activated by MIO in a group of females might simply include a greater variety of affect, wishes, and fears than in a group of males.

With regard to possible clinical implications of our findings, Westen (1999) noted the similarity between activation of transference and the experimental priming of a network of associations that leads to a pattern of inference, interpretation, or expectation consistent with activated cognitive content. That analysis can usefully be reversed to note also the possibility that our experiments successfully model some aspects of transference. We previously suggested that strongly deviant pretherapy responses to MIO stimulation might help therapists anticipate qualitatively or quantitatively unusual patient responses to the therapeutic relationship. Therapeutic neutrality versus empathy in the regulation of interpersonal distance may be a particularly delicate issue in such cases (Sohlberg, Samuelberg, et al., 1998). Sohlberg, Samuelberg, et al. (1998) further wrote that as "indicated by the gender-specific response to MIO in our previous preliminary observations and the present study, possible male–female differences in the interpretation of therapist attitudes and actions in this area may need special attention" (p. 109).

We now believe we have a stronger case for regarding gender-related differences in MIO responses as established. The somewhat less predictable and somewhat less strong response to MIO seen in women in the present experiments could imply a somewhat less predictable and somewhat less strong response to any situation in therapy in which a therapist activates the patient's unconscious associative "self-with-mother" network.[5]

When do therapists activate patients' unconscious associative self-with-mother networks? Citing work by Kiesler, psychotherapy theorists Safran and Muran (2000) suggested that for patients to be rapidly and thoroughly embedded in a relational matrix, in which transference and countertransference are but names for the inevitable influence of old relationship schemas on new relationships, therapists may need to resemble their patients' attachment figures in some respects. Greenberg (cited in Safran & Muran, 2000, p. 66) believed that "therapists may have to be sufficiently like old objects for their patients in order for core relational themes to emerge in the therapeutic relationship and be worked through in a new way." If these conjectures are true, then experimental MIO results generally have the greatest relevance for female therapists. Attitudes and behavior vary widely across genders, time, and situation, but only a caricature social constructionist would dispute that female therapists on average are more like mothers than are male therapists. It also goes without saying that from the viewpoint of experimentalists systematic programs of "Daddy and I are one" studies are now needed. Such studies could benefit from complementing stimuli directly or indirectly related to Mahlerian theory with stimuli based on theory on how adults structure their relationship memories. Attachment theory offers such a perspective (Bartholomew, 1990). Also, by using stimuli such as "Daddy lets

---

[5]This applies to the average response only, not the response of individual women. The person inspiring Silverman to choose the words "Mommy and I are one" was a female patient in psychotherapy with Silverman's colleague and wife, D. K. Silverman (Hardaway, 1990). We do not doubt that the response of individual women to MIO can be as strong as the response of any man. Given the transference perspective we alluded to earlier, it is interesting also to speculate whether this patient was commenting only on her relationship with her mother or also on her relationship with her therapist.

me be who I am," "Daddy loves me," "Daddy protects me," "Daddy controls me," "Daddy blames me," "Daddy hates me," "Daddy rejects me," and "Daddy lets me be," researchers could benefit from using Benjamin's well-validated circumplex interpersonal model (Benjamin, 1974, 1996, 2000; Pincus, Gurtman, & Ruiz, 1998). Even those who consciously disavow all links between the present and the past might respond strongly to reminders of fundamental attachment figures, when these reminders are administered subliminally and set in the empirically firmly established contexts of love and hate, enmeshment and differentiation.

Gender Matters, But Sometimes Not Very Much

That said, it must be emphasized that all our findings indicate that participant gender does not matter to the degree that it will always have a statistically significant ($p < .05$) effect in experiments of the size often conducted in experimental, personality, or clinical psychology. Also, the finding most clearly implicating a possible qualitative difference in MIO response between genders was obtained in the modified Stroop study, the smallest of the experiments. Thus, chance is a self-evident competing explanation.

Because both the size and direction of gender-related effects may be tied to the specific moderator and dependent variables used, meta-analyses may well find no consistent effect that cannot more parsimoniously be accounted for by chance (Hardaway, 1990). Bornstein (1990a) reported tentative meta-analytic data implying a generally larger difference between sub- and supraliminal stimulation effects in males than in females. The difference, however, was very small. We regard gender effects as probable not because of replicated, strong findings but because, barring one or two small exceptions, differences between men and women kept coming back across experiments logically carrying the same message: MIO effects are weaker and less predictable in women.

It must be noted, too, that it is possible that temporal and cultural change can increase or diminish differences between the genders. We have suggested several times already that the meaning of MIO might be more variable for present-day young women than for present-day young men. If meanings of MIO were more equally variable in men and women in the 1960s and onward, then Hardaway's (1990) conclusion may have been entirely correct based on the data he had available. We arrived at a slightly different conclusion because we worked with new data.

Gender Matters, But Whose Gender?

We were able to look more systematically at participant gender than at experimenter gender. We cannot rule out that the radical change of results seen from the first story task experiment (Sohlberg, Birgegard, et al., 2000) to the two new experiments we report in this chapter resulted from our change from a female to a male experimenter. To be sure, gender was only one aspect of the many ways in which the persons involved differed. In contrast to many other differences, however, this one has the advantage of being both theoretically interesting and easily varied in experimentation. Further studies on this issue are warranted.

In conclusion, we note a considerable amount of evidence indicating that the effects of unconscious activation of a self-with-mother associative network are largely similar in men and women. However, some evidence relates MIO effects to participant gender, and speculation about experimenter gender can be entertained also. Regardless of whether van Dam's (cited in Carlberg, 1989) joking complaint about psychoanalytic developmental theorists being slow to accommodate to new data is still relevant, the experiments we report here suggest that girls and boys are somewhat dissimilar even after puberty.

References

Abrams, R. L., & Greenwald, A. G. (2000). Parts outweigh the whole (word) in unconscious analysis of meaning. *Psychological Science, 11,* 118–124.

Balay, J., & Shevrin, H. (1988). The subliminal psychodynamic activation method: A critical review. *American Psychologist, 43,* 161–174.

Baldwin, M. (1992). Relational schemas and the processing of social information. *Psychological Bulletin, 112,* 461–484.

Baldwin, M. W. (1999). Activation and accessibility paradigms in relational schemas research. In D. Cervone & Y. Shoda (Eds.), *Coherence in personality* (pp. 127–154). New York: Guilford.

Bartholomew, K. (1990). Avoidance of intimacy: An attachment perspective. *Journal of Social and Personal Relationships, 7,* 147–178.

Baumeister, R. F., & Leary, M. R. (1995). The need to belong: Desire for interpersonal attachments as a fundamental human motivation. *Psychological Bulletin, 117,* 497–529.

Benjamin, L. (1974). Structural analysis of social behavior. *Psychological Review, 81,* 392–425.

Benjamin, L. S. (1996). *Interpersonal diagnosis and treatment of personality disorder* (2nd ed.). New York: Guilford.

Benjamin, L. S. (2000). Scientific discipline can enhance clinical effectiveness. In S. Soldz & L. McCullough (Eds.), *Reconciling empirical knowledge and clinical experience: The art and science of psychotherapy* (pp. 197–219). Washington, DC: American Psychological Association.

Birgegard, A., & Sohlberg, S. (1999). New methodological advice for research in subliminal psychodynamic activation. *Perceptual & Motor Skills, 88,* 747–755.

Bornstein, R. F. (1990a). Critical importance of stimulus awareness for the production of subliminal psychodynamic activation effects: A meta-analytic review. *Journal of Clinical Psychology, 46,* 201–210.

Bornstein, R. F. (1990b). Subliminal mere exposure and psychodynamic activation effects: Implications for the psychoanalytic theory of conscious and unconscious mental processes. In J. Masling (Ed.), *Empirical studies of psychoanalytic theories* (pp. 55–88). Hillsdale, NJ: Analytic Press.

Bornstein, R. F. (1992). Critical importance of stimulus unawareness for the production of subliminal psychodynamic activation effects: An attributional model. *Journal of Nervous and Mental Disease, 180,* 69–76.

Bornstein, R. F. (1993). Parental representations and psychopathology: A critical review of the empirical literature. In J. M. Masling & R. F. Bornstein (Eds.), *Psychoanalytic perspectives on psychopathology* (pp. 1–42). Washington, DC: American Psychological Association.

Bornstein, R. F. (1999). Source amnesia, misattribution, and the power of unconscious perceptions and memories. *Psychoanalytic Psychology, 16,* 155–178.

Bornstein, R. F., Leone, D. R., & Galley, D. J. (1987). The generalizability of subliminal mere exposure effects: Influence of stimuli perceived without awareness on social behavior. *Journal of Personality and Social Psychology, 53,* 1070–1079.

Bornstein, R. F., & Masling, J. M. (1984). Subliminal psychodynamic stimulation: Implications for psychoanalytic theory and therapy. *International Forum for Psychoanalysis, 1,* 187–204.

Bowlby, J. (1988). Developmental psychiatry comes of age. *American Journal of Psychiatry, 145,* 1–10.

Brenner, C. (1957). *An elementary textbook of psychoanalysis* (2nd ed.). New York: International Universities Press.

Carlberg, G. (1989). *Dynamisk utvecklingspsykologi* [Dynamic developmental psychology]. Stockholm: Natur och Kultur.

Cheesman, J., & Merikle, P. M. (1986). Distinguishing conscious from unconscious perceptual processes. *Canadian Journal of Psychology, 44,* 343–367.

Claesson, K. (1997). *Measures of awareness and accuracy of participant report.* Unpublished manuscript, Department of Psychology, Uppsala University, Sweden.

Cohen, J. (1969). *Statistical power analysis for the behavioral sciences.* New York: Academic Press.

Cohen, J. (1994). The earth is round ($p < .05$). *American Psychologist, 49,* 997–1003.

Cramer, P. (1998). Threat to gender representation: Identity and identification. *Journal of Personality, 66,* 336–357.

Cramer, P. (2000). Development of identity: Gender makes a difference. *Journal of Research in Personality, 34,* 42–72.

Erdelyi, M. H. (1992). Psychodynamics and the unconscious. *American Psychologist, 47,* 784–787.

Fisher, S., & Greenberg, R. P. (1996). *Freud scientifically reappraised: Testing the theory and the therapy.* New York: Wiley.

Freud, S. (1958). *Drömtydning* [The interpretation of dreams]. Stockholm: Bonniers. (Original work published 1930)

Fudin, R. (1986). Subliminal psychodynamic activation: Mommy and I are not yet one. *Perceptual & Motor Skills, 63,* 1159–1179.

Guisinger, S., & Blatt, S. J. (1994). Individuality and relatedness: Evolution of a fundamental dialectic. *American Psychologist, 49,* 104–111.

Hardaway, R. A. (1990). Subliminally activated symbiotic fantasies: Facts and artifacts. *Psychological Bulletin, 107,* 177–195.

Jacob, S. (1998). *Steroids as human chemosignals: How isolated putative pheromones affect behavior, physiology and brain metabolism.* Unpublished doctoral dissertation, University of Chicago.

Kiesler, D. J. (1996). *Contemporary interpersonal theory and research: Personality, psychopathology, and psychotherapy.* New York: Wiley.

Kirk, R. E. (1996). Practical significance: A concept whose time has come. *Educational and Psychological Measurement, 56,* 746–759.

Lachman, F. M., & Beebe, B. (1989). Oneness fantasies revisited. *Psychoanalytic Psychology, 6,* 137–149.

Lundh, L.-G., Wikström, J., & Westerlund, J. (2001). Cognitive bias, emotion, and somatic complaints in a normal sample. *Cognition & Emotion, 15,* 249–277.

Maccoby, E. E. (1988). Gender as a social category. *Developmental Psychology, 24,* 755–765.

Mahler, M. S., Pine, F., & Bergman, A. (1975). *The psychological birth of the human infant: Symbiosis and individuation.* London: Hutchinson.

Masling, J. M. (1992). What does it all mean? In R. F. Bornstein & T. S. Pittman (Eds.), *Perception without awareness: Cognitive, clinical, and social perspectives* (pp. 259–276). New York: Guilford.

Masling, J., Bornstein, R. F., Poynton, F. G., Reed, S., & Katkin, E. S. (1991). Perception without awareness and electrodermal responding: A strong test of subliminal psychodynamic activation effects. *Journal of Mind and Behavior, 12*, 33–48.

Patton, C. J. (1992). Fear of abandonment and binge eating: A subliminal psychodynamic activation investigation. *Journal of Nervous and Mental Disease, 180*, 484–490.

Pincus, A. L., Gurtman, M. B., & Ruiz, M. A. (1998). Structural analysis of social behavior (SASB): Circumplex analyses and structural relations with the interpersonal circle and the five-factor model of personality. *Journal of Personality and Social Psychology, 74*, 1629–1645.

Rojahn, K., & Pettigrew, T. F. (1992). Memory for schema-relevant information: A meta-analytic solution. *British Journal of Social Psychology, 31*, 81–109.

Rosenthal, R., Rosnow, R. L., & Rubin, D. B. (2000). Contrasts and effect sizes in behavioral research: A correlational approach. Cambridge, England: Cambridge University Press.

Rosenthal, R., & Rubin, D. B. (1982). A simple, general purpose display of magnitude of experimental effect. *Journal of Educational Psychology, 74*, 166–169.

Safran, J. D., & Muran, J. C. (2000). *Negotiating the therapeutic alliance: A relational treatment guide.* New York: Guilford.

Shevrin, H. (1992). Subliminal perception, memory, and consciousness: Cognitive and dynamic perspectives. In R. F. Bornstein & T. S. Pittman (Eds.), *Perception without awareness: Cognitive, clinical and social perspectives* (pp. 123–142). New York: Guilford.

Shevrin, H., Williams, W. J., Marshall, R. E., Hertel, R. K., Bond, J. A., & Brakel, L. A. (1992). Event-related potential indicators of the dynamic unconscious. *Consciousness and Cognition, 1*, 340–366.

Siegel, P., & Weinberger, J. (1998). Capturing the MOMMY AND I ARE ONE merger fantasy: The oneness motive. In J. M. Masling & R. F. Bornstein (Eds.), *Empirical perspectives on the psychoanalytic unconscious* (pp. 71–97). Washington, DC: American Psychological Association.

Silverman, L. H. (1984). *Further comments on subliminal psychodynamic activation studies.* Unpublished manuscript, Department of Psychology, New York University.

Silverman, L. H., Lachman, F. M., & Milich, R. H. (1982). *The search for oneness.* New York: International Universities Press.

Silverman, L. H., & Weinberger, J. (1988). Reply to O'Dowd and to Tabin and Tabin: Historical priority and alternative interpretations. *American Psychologist, 43*, 198–199.

Slipp, S. (2000). Subliminal stimulation research and its implications for psychoanalytic theory and treatment. *Journal of the American Academy of Psychoanalysis, 28,* 305–320.

Snodgrass, M., Shevrin, H., & Kopka, M. (1993). The mediation of intentional judgments by unconscious perceptions: The influence of task strategy, task preference, word meaning, and motivation. *Consciousness and Cognition, 2,* 169–193.

Sohlberg, S., Arvidsson, M., & Birgegard, A. (1997). Stroop and mood/memory measures in the study of unconscious "oneness." *Perceptual & Motor Skills, 85,* 81–82.

Sohlberg, S., Billinghurst, A., & Nylén, S. (1998). Moderation of mood change after subliminal symbiotic stimulation: Four experiments contributing to the further demystification of Silverman's "Mommy and I are one" findings. *Journal of Research in Personality, 32,* 33–54.

Sohlberg, S., & Birgegard, A. (2001). *Enduring subliminal activation effects.* Unpublished manuscript, Department of Psychology, Uppsala University, Sweden.

Sohlberg, S., Birgegard, A., Czartoryski, W., Ovefelt, K., & Strömbom, Y. (2000). Symbiotic oneness and defensive autonomy: Yet another experiment demystifying Silverman's findings using "Mommy and I are one." *Journal of Research in Personality, 34,* 108–126.

Sohlberg, S., Claesson, K., & Birgegard, A. (2001). *Memories of mother, complementarity, and shame: Hypotheses about unconscious associative networks activated by "Mommy and I are one."* Manuscript submitted for publication.

Sohlberg, S., Samuelberg, P., Sidén, Y., & Thörn, C. (1998). Caveat medicus —Let the subliminal healer beware. Two experiments suggesting conditions when the effects of Silverman's "Mommy and I are one" phrase are negative. *Psychoanalytic Psychology, 15,* 93–114.

Sohlberg, S., Stahlheuer, P., & Tell, P. (1997). Depression, gender and identification. *British Journal of Clinical Psychology, 36,* 453–455.

Sohlberg, S., Tell, P., & Stahlheuer, P. (2001). [Gender-specific identification in relation to dysphoria]. Unpublished raw data.

Sutherland, S. (1995). *The Macmillan dictionary of psychology* (2nd ed.). Basingstoke, England: Macmillan Press.

Tabin, J. K., & Tabin, C. J. (1987). An alternative interpretation of oneness. *American Psychologist, 42,* 954–955.

Weinberger, J. (1986). Comment on Robert Fudin's paper "Subliminal Psychodynamic Activation: Mommy and I Are Not Yet One." *Perceptual & Motor Skills, 63,* 1232–1234.

Weinberger, J. (1989). Response to Balay & Shevrin: Constructive critique or misguided attack? *American Psychologist, 44,* 1417–1419.

Weinberger, J. (1992). Validating and demystifying subliminal psychodynamic activation. In R. F. Bornstein & T. S. Pittman (Eds.), *Perception without awareness* (pp. 170–190). New York: Guilford.

Weinberger, J., Kelner, S., & McClelland, D. (1997). The effects of subliminal symbiotic stimulation on free-response and self-report mood. *Journal of Nervous and Mental Disease, 185,* 599–605.

Weinberger, J., & McLeod, C. (1989, August). *The need to belong: A psychoanalytically-based affiliative motive in the McClelland–Atkinson tradition.* Paper presented at the 97th Annual Convention of the American Psychological Association, New Orleans, LA.

Weinberger, J., & Silverman, L. H. (1990). Testability and empirical verification of psychoanalytic dynamic propositions through subliminal psychodynamic activation. *Psychoanalytic Psychology, 7*(Suppl.), 299–339.

Weinberger, J., Stefanou, S., Scroppo, J., McLeod, C., & McClelland, D. (1993). *Oneness motive scoring system.* Unpublished manuscript, Derner Institute, Adelphi University.

Westen, D. (1998). The scientific legacy of Siegmund Freud: Toward a psychodynamically informed psychological science. *Psychological Bulletin, 124,* 333–371.

Westen, D. (1999). Psychodynamic theory and technique in relation to research on cognition and emotion: Mutual implications. In T. Dalgleish & M. Power (Eds.), *Handbook of cognition and emotion* (pp. 727–746). New York: Wiley.

Westen, D., & Gabbard, G. O. (1999). Psychoanalytic approaches to personality. In L. A. Pervin & O. P. John (Eds.), *Handbook of personality: Theory and research* (pp. 57–101). New York: Guilford.

Williams, J. M. G., Watts, F. N., MacLeod, C., & Mathews, A. (1997). *Cognitive psychology and emotional disorders.* Chichester, England: Wiley.

Wolman, B. B. (1968). *The unconscious mind: The Meaning of Freudian psychology.* Englewood Cliffs, NJ: Prentice-Hall.

Emotions, Defenses, and Gender

Leslie R. Brody, Serra Muderrisoglu, and
Ora Nakash-Eisikovits

In this chapter we explore gender differences in emotions, defenses, and in the relationship between the two, drawing on our
own research as well as on the work of other gender theorists and
researchers. We also investigate the ways in which gender differences in self-esteem, anxiety, and depression in a nonclinical sample may be mediated as well as moderated by gender differences
in defenses and emotions.

Not much is known about how particular defenses, such as denial, are systematically related to the acknowledgment of particular
emotions, such as shame or anger. Even less is known about gender differences in the patterns of these relationships. What is
known is that women tend to report defenses and dysphoric emotions that are associated with an inward focus on the self more
than men, whereas men report defenses and dysphoric emotions

associated with an outward focus on others more than women. Women report more internalizing dysphoric emotions (such as shame, guilt, hurt, fear, and anxiety) than men, and more internalizing defenses, such as turning against the self. In contrast, men report more externalizing dysphoric emotions (such as contempt) than women, and more externalizing defenses, such as turning against the other (Brody, 1999; Cramer, 1991). Although these patterns appear to be well established, especially among middle-class European Americans (see Brody, 1999), little is known about gender differences in the patterns of relationships between emotional functioning and the use of specific defenses.

In a related vein, several theorists have suggested that the internalizing problems (such as depression, anxiety disorders, or low self-esteem) that characterize women more than men are due to an inability to regulate internalizing emotions, such as shame, whereas the externalizing disorders (such as aggression) that characterize men are due to an inability to regulate externalizing emotions, such as anger (see Gross, 1998; Major, Barr, Zubek, & Babey, 1999; Nolen-Hoeksema & Rusting, 1999). If we consider defense use to be an emotion regulation strategy, then investigating the patterns of relationships among emotional experiences, defense use, and various aspects of adjustment may clarify this issue.

Gender and Development

Psychoanalytic thinking has historically had an ambivalent relationship with the notion of gender and its impact on psychic life and personality functioning. Drive-based psychoanalytic theorists tended to generalize about intrapsychic and interpersonal development based on the male psyche and only later adjusted their theories to explain female development while leaving many of the basic theoretical assumptions intact (see Horney, 1967). Freud (1926/1959) believed that the primary source of anxiety for men was castration, whereas the predominant source of anxiety for women was loss of love. Because castration anxiety was more remote from interpersonal relationships than fear of losing love, Freud thought that male development provided a more impersonal foundation for the development of the superego, leading to a more rigid and enhanced sense of morality for men than for women (Freud, 1925/1964). (One implication of this theory is the idea that men would be more defensive about violating moral standards than would women.) In one of the most important critiques of Freud's psychology of women, Schafer (1974) suggested that Freud's ideas were significantly flawed because of the influence of traditional 19th-century patriarchal and evolutionary values that dominated his conceptualization. Schafer (1974) emphasized the importance of masculine value-laden social forces, pre-Oedipal stages in development, and the role of the maternal figure in affecting women's development.

A comprehensive psychoanalytic theory about the role that gender plays in intrapsychic development was largely missing until the work of Nancy Chodorow (1978) and other feminist object-relations theorists (see Benjamin, 1988; Fast, 1984). Among other things, Chodorow posited that parent–child relationships are inherently shaped by gender and that the qualities of these gendered relationships are internalized and organized as intrapsychic aspects of development that differ for the two sexes. Specifically, the fact that mothers, who are women, serve as the primary caretakers for their children has a disparate effect on the development of boys and girls. Same-sex identification is fundamental to mother–daughter relationships, and cross-sex de-identification is fundamental to mother–son relationships. Interacting primarily with a same-sex caretaker with whom they identify enables girls to develop a heightened capacity for empathy and intimacy and a self-definition inherently oriented toward someone outside of the self, toward connecting with an "other." However, this identification also results in a restricted sense of autonomy and agency.

Boys, on the other hand, are required to differentiate from the feminine role model provided by their mothers in order to develop a distinct gender-role identity. Developing a masculine identity involves distancing oneself from intimacy, particularly because fathers are often unavailable as intimate same-sex identificatory role models. Recent theorists such as Pollack (1995) and Bergman (1995) have hypothesized that feelings of vulnerability, loss, and shame in men's lives result as a partial consequence of cultural emphases on premature separation from mothers. These feelings of vulnerability are theorized to be defended against through the expression of anger and aggression (Pollack, 1995), as well as a dread and avoidance of intimate relationships that may potentially replicate the early pattern of premature separation they experienced (Bergman, 1995). Mother–son separation is thus viewed by these theorists as a developmental trauma that contributes to men's future difficulties in intimacy, empathy, and commitment. In its emphases on disconnection, male development inculcates the pursuit of individual rather than communal goals and encourages the expression of emotions that are adaptive for agency.

Gender theorists thus stress how girls' development gives primacy to communion, or relationships with others, whereas boys' development gives primacy to agency, or the pursuit of individual ambitions. We use gender differences in communion and agency as a framework within which to understand and explain gender differences in emotions and defense use. *Communion* and *agency* were terms originally used by Bakan (1966) to denote the tendency to focus on connections with others (which has been found to be more characteristic of women) versus the tendency to focus on the separateness of the self (which has been found to be more characteristic of men). The importance and complexity of these ideas were recognized as early as 1958 by the philosopher Hanna Arendt, who claimed that access to "who" we are (our "qualities, gifts, talents and shortcomings" [p. 179]) could be gained only through speech and action, through human contact. She viewed autonomy not as a fixed property of the self but rather as a potential that needs others in order to develop. Although she was not a feminist philosopher, Arendt's emphasis on how relationships with others contribute to the development of an autonomous self can be viewed as a precursor to future feminist scholarship (Arendt, 1958; see also Bilsky, 1997).

Communion and agency have been viewed as broad styles of personality organization, or self-schemas that may relate to gender differences in many aspects of cognitive, emotional, and interpersonal functioning (see Cross & Madson, 1997). For example, Cross and Madson (1997) supported the idea that men and women often differ in their use of communal versus agentic strategies to preserve self-esteem. Women have been found to enhance self-esteem by protecting and strengthening their relationships with others, whereas men have been found to enhance self-esteem by overestimating the uniqueness of their own abilities and belittling their partners.

In an extensive theoretical review, Helgeson and Fritz (1999) argued that unmitigated communion—a tendency to focus on others to the exclusion of the self—characterizes women more than men and is related to psychological distress and depression. Men are more likely to score highly on unmitigated agency, a focus on the self and separation to the exclusion of the other. This is associated with low self-esteem, psychological distress, and poor health. Tendencies toward unmitigated communion in women and toward unmitigated agency in men can potentially lead to nonmutually empathic relationships in both sexes, which, in and of themselves, are related to distress in men (see Nolen-Hoeksema & Rusting, 1999) as well as to heightened depression, anxiety, and lowered self-esteem in women (Lee & Robbins, 1998; Sperberg & Stabb, 1998).

Communion, Agency, and Emotional Expression

We draw on the concepts of communion and agency to understand why and in what contexts women report more internalizing negative emotions (such as shame and hurt) than men do, and how and why gender differences in defense styles relate to these negative emotions. Markus and Kitayama (1991) marshaled evidence for the idea that internalizing, or interpersonally engaging emotions, such as shame and hurt, are adaptive for communion because these emotions function to preserve or repair relationships. In contrast, externalizing, or interpersonally disengaging emotions, such as anger or pride, are adaptive for agency because they further individual goals and disrupt interpersonal bonds.

Data indicate that women report internalizing emotions that are adaptive for communion (e.g., shame, warmth, fear, vulnerability) at greater intensities than men, whereas men express some externalizing emotions that are adaptive for agency (e.g., loneliness, pride, and contempt) at greater intensities than women (Brody, 1999; Markus & Kitayama, 1991). When women and men are asked about which emotions they choose to express, women report not disclosing emotions that may risk damaging their relationships, whereas men report not disclosing feelings that threaten their sense of control (Rosenfeld, 1979). However, data that run counter to these ideas indicate that women express more verbal anger than men, even though anger is an externalizing emotion thought to be more adaptive for agency and interpersonal disengagement (Brody, 1997). Moreover, some studies also have shown that men express more guilt—an emotion thought to be adaptive for communion and interpersonal engagement—than women (Brody, 1999).

The theoretical work of Helen Block Lewis (1971) suggests that gender differences in shame and guilt, with women hypothesized to express more intense shame and men more intense guilt, may stem not only from the communal function of these two emotions but also from their origins in communal versus agentic styles of personality organization. According to Lewis, women's shame-prone tendencies stem primarily from their disposition to inter-nalize feelings of hostility and anxiety, reflecting a lack of differ-entiation between self and other (which is also manifested in a field-dependent cognitive style). Men, on the other hand, are the-orized to be guilt prone, partly as a consequence of social pressures that encourage strong ego boundaries, a field-independent cogni-tive style, and competitiveness. These qualities can place men in a position of hurting others, which in turn causes feelings of guilt. To reduce feelings of guilt men use externalizing defense mecha-nisms and isolation of emotion. In partial support of these ideas, Ferguson and Crowley's data (1997) indicate that men's guilt is more related to their defensive style—including attributing less blame to others—than is their shame, whereas women's shame is more related to their defensive style—including their likelihood to punish themselves—than is their guilt.

Context Specificity of Gender Differences in Emotion

It is important to bear in mind that gender differences in emotional functioning are context specific and are especially dependent on the kinds of situations that precipitate the emotion (Brody, 1999). For example, men express more anger when achievement is frustrated, whereas women express more anger when interpersonal trust is violated or betrayed (Stapley & Haviland, 1989). Men express more jealousy when their partners are sexually involved with someone else; women express more jealousy when their partners are emotionally involved with someone else (see Brody, 1999). If women's sense of self is more highly related to their relationships with others than is men's, then women's dysphoric emotions should be more intense than men's when a loss of an intimate relationship is threatened. Moreover, the types of defenses women report using should be those that are internalizing and function to preserve social relationships. In contrast, men should report more dysphoric emotions than women when their autonomy is threatened. Men should also report using externalizing defenses that function to preserve a sense of self based on separateness from others.

On the basis of the literature, our first research prediction was that men and women would report differential negative emotions in response to two different kinds of interpersonal stress: rejection by a partner and demands for more intimacy from a partner. Men should express more dysphoric emotions than women when partners demand intimacy from them, because their self-construals of separateness would be threatened. Women should express more dysphoric emotions than men when partners act in rejecting ways toward them, because their self-construals of communion would be threatened. Consistent with Lewis's (1971) theory, we also predicted that men would report more guilt in response to both interpersonal rejection and demands for intimacy, whereas women would report more shame in response to both kinds of situations. We also explored how gender differences in emotional expression were related to gender differences in patterns of defense use, which we turn to next.

Defense Mechanisms, Agency, and Communion

The classical psychoanalytic view of defense mechanisms generally asserts that they are unconscious processes that serve to avert or modulate unwanted conflicts, impulses, or feelings. Acknowledging the presence of these unwanted processes could result in the disruption of ego functions (Cramer, 1998b). Bion's (1962) and Winnicott's (1965) work represents the beginning of a shift from an emphasis on an intrapsychic to an interpersonal understanding of the function of defense mechanisms. In this vein, defenses are viewed as emerging in a two-person interpersonal context and not simply as a response to intrapsychic conflicts. Newer psychoanalytic conceptualizations view defense mechanisms as part of a set of "relational and cognitive patterns that develop in the context of close relationships with important others" (Cooper, 1998, p. 949). The purpose of defense mechanisms from this standpoint is not only to protect the individual from the awareness of unacceptable thoughts or wishes but also to protect against the actual or psychic loss of a relationship with another person (the relationship being internalized as an integral part of the self; Cooper, 1998; Modell, 1975, 1984). Following from both more traditional and newer conceptualizations of defense mechanisms, men and women's differing self-construals of communion and agency may lead them to feel vulnerable in different situations, leading to the use of defenses in those situations. Women may use defenses in situations in which relationships are threatened; men may use defenses in situations in which an autonomous sense of self is threatened. Moreover, women and men may use different defenses because these defenses differentially facilitate communal or agentic goals. The expression of internalizing defenses, such as turning against the self and withdrawal, may be adaptive for preserving social relationships. Externalizing defenses, such as projection and turning against the other, may be adaptive for asserting separateness from others.

The research literature demonstrates patterns that are consistent with these ideas. Internalizing defenses are used more frequently by women than by men, whereas the reverse is true of externalizing defenses (Cramer, 1991). Moreover, men are more likely to use coping strategies involving self-control, as consistent with an agentic self-definition, and women are more likely to use coping strategies involving seeking support from others, as consistent with a communal self-definition (Folkman, Lazarus, Pimley, & Novacek, 1987). As with defense mechanisms, coping styles are theorized to modulate conflict, and they function to protect the self but involve more conscious processes than do defenses (Cramer, 1998a).

Cramer and Blatt (1990) researched two developmental personality lines characterized by consistent emotional and defensive patterns that parallel agency and communion. The *anaclitic line* involves the development of stable, mutually satisfying interpersonal relationships, similar to communion, whereas the *introjective line* involves the development of a stable, realistic, and positive self-identity, similar to agency. Individuals with an anaclitic personality configuration tend to incorporate the use of avoidance defenses such as denial, repression, and displacement to maintain interpersonal relationships while neglecting the development of the self, whereas those with more introjective configurations use externalizing defenses such as projection, which protect and preserve the self, while neglecting to form satisfying interpersonal relationships (Cramer & Blatt, 1990). Cramer and Blatt reported that the majority of anaclitic individuals are females and the majority of introjectives are males.

Defense Mechanisms and Emotions

How defense mechanisms relate to the quality of emotions that are experienced and expressed is an extremely complex issue. First, it is important to distinguish between emotional *experiences* and emotional *expressions* in relation to defense use. Emotional experiences are often not observable to others, whereas emotional expressions are, and this private–public distinction may lead to the use of defenses for different purposes. For example, defenses may be used to ward off emotional experiences because such experiences violate one's self-concept. In contrast, defenses may be used to ward off the public expression of specific emotions because these emotions may be socially unacceptable or undesirable. Because the way one is viewed in the eyes of others may become internalized as one's self-concept, it is possible that defenses simultaneously protect one's public as well as one's private images, distorting both expressions and experiences.

Further complicating the relationship between defense use and emotional functioning is that expressed emotions may themselves serve as defenses. Waelder's (1930/1976) principle of multiple function allows for a complex relationship between defense and that which is defended, in that the same behavior, emotion, or idea can be simultaneously an expression of, and a defense against, a particular wish, feeling, thought, or need. For example, expressing anger may be a defense against a conflict involving vulnerability, or anger may itself be partly the emotion on which the conflict centers, or both.

One also needs to consider that defenses may differ from each other in the way they relate to emotional expressivity. Plutchik (1998) theorized that defenses are derivatives of emotional experiences, with repression deriving from intense anxiety, displacement from anger, and compensation from sadness. Other researchers have viewed defenses along a maturity continuum. Mature defenses are more adaptive for functioning and well-being and include humor, sublimation, and suppression, whereas immature defenses are less adaptive for functioning and well-being and include denial, acting out, reaction formation, projection, and turning against the other (Vaillant, 1971, 1977). Mature defenses can be hypothesized to involve a conscious acknowledgment of difficult emotions with little distortion. Emotions are viewed as originating in and belonging to the person's internal world (Kernberg, 1980, 1984). For example, humor and suppression both involve an awareness of a feeling, such as anger, perhaps accompanied by more conscious decisions to minimize the feeling or put it aside. In contrast, immature defenses, such as projection or reaction formation, involve a distortion of a feeling such as anger, so that awareness of the feeling may never surface. Such defenses confuse internal conflicts with external reality (Kernberg, 1980, 1984). These ideas lead to the predictions that more mature defenses should be more positively associated with the acknowledgment of dysphoric emotions appropriate to a given situation than should immature defenses, whereas immature defenses should be more negatively associated with the acknowledgment of dysphoric emotions appropriate to a given situation than should mature defenses.

Somewhat different predictions about the relationships between defenses and emotions emerge from a functionalist perspective (see Brody, 1999). Because defenses and emotions are both functional and adaptive for the maintenance of self-esteem and self-construals, then similar categories (externalizing versus internalizing) of defenses and emotions should be called into play in the same situation. For example, if a situation involves relationship rejection, and women's communal sense of self is threatened, then they should report internalizing emotions as well as internalizing types of defenses in response to such situations. Both the emotions and the defenses would minimize damage to the relationship and possibly repair it. The same could be hypothesized of men using externalizing emotions and externalizing defenses: Both are functional for the maintenance of an autonomous sense of self. These hypotheses lead to the predictions that internalizing emotions and defenses should be positively related; that externalizing emotions and defenses should be positively related; but that internalizing emotions and externalizing defenses, as well as externalizing emotions and internalizing defenses, should be negatively related.

Yet another set of predictions emerges when emotions and defenses are viewed from the perspective of how socially acceptable they are for each sex. Cultural display rules are prescriptive stereotypes that dictate how, when, and where each sex can express emotions. These display rules have powerful effects on both interpersonal and intrapsychic functioning, because violating them can have negative social and intrapsychic consequences, such as social rejection, teasing, and feelings of failure. For men, display rules prescribe minimizing the expression of internalizing feelings, especially those connoting vulnerability, such as shame, hurt, and sadness. Research has shown that men who display vulnerable emotions are perceived more negatively than men who display bravado (Zillmann, Weaver, Mundorf, & Aust, 1986). For women, cultural display rules prescribe minimizing the expression of externalizing or agentic feelings, such as aggression, or pride in the face of a rival's failure (Brody, 1999). Women who display aggression are often punished in the form of social rejection. These cultural standards are undoubtedly internalized and may lead to the use of defenses when the unacceptable feelings are experienced. For example, if men experience vulnerability, they may (a) either unconsciously or consciously replace vulnerability with more acceptable externalizing feelings or (b) use other

defense mechanisms, such as denial, to ward off their vulnerability. For women, similar processes would take place if aggression or contempt should arise. One prediction that arises from
this reasoning is that for men the ability to acknowledge socially
unacceptable internalizing feelings, such as sadness or hurt, will
be more negatively related to the use of defenses than they will
be for women, whereas for women the ability to acknowledge
externalizing feelings, such as contempt or anger, will be more
negatively related to using defenses than they will be for men.

It is important to note that defensive behaviors themselves,
and not just emotional expressions, are subject to cultural display
rules. For example, it is more socially acceptable for a man than
for a woman to act out aggression. Because both defensive behaviors and emotions are subject to the same display rules, it is likely
that women will report both higher levels of internalizing defenses
and internalizing emotions than men, whereas men will report
both higher levels of externalizing defenses and emotions than
women.

We have been arguing on the one hand that the types of emotions acknowledged and the types of defenses used will be positively related for internalizing defenses and emotions and that externalizing emotions and defenses will have a similar relationship.
This argument emerges from several different perspectives, including the ideas that (a) the reported emotions themselves are a type
of defense, (b) defenses and emotions are subject to similar display
rules, and (c) defenses and emotions are both functional for maintaining communal and agentic self-construals. On the other hand,
we have also argued that a pattern of gender differences should
emerge such that, for men more than for women, all types of defense use will be negatively related to the acknowledgement of
internalizing emotions. In contrast, for women more than for men,
all types of defense use will be negatively related to the acknowledgment of externalizing emotions. Finally, we have argued that
more mature defenses, such as sublimation, humor, and suppression, should involve less distortion of appropriate dysphoric emotions than immature defenses, such as denial, acting out, and
reaction formation. Mature defenses should show positive relationships with the acknowledgment of appropriate dysphoric
emotions and negative relationships with the acknowledgment of

inappropriate dysphoric emotions; whereas the reverse should be true of immature defenses.

There is scant empirical research on the relationship between emotions and defenses that would clarify the accuracy of our predictions. A recent study by Offer, Lavie, Gothelf, and Apter (2000) indicated that self-reports of anger were related to self-reports of projection, displacement, and regression, whereas self-reports of anxiety were related to displacement, reaction formation, and undoing. Some of the results support at least some of our predictions: For example, externalizing defenses (projection and displacement) were found to be associated with an externalizing emotion (anger); whereas internalizing defenses (reaction formation and undoing) were found to be associated with an internalizing emotion (anxiety). However, displacement was also found to be associated with anxiety, a finding we would not have predicted. Because Offer et al. did not explore emotions as a function of situational context, and did not specifically focus on gender, their results are only partially relevant to our ideas. They did not clarify how gender differences were measured, but reported finding no gender differences in the patterns of relationships among anger, anxiety, and defenses.

In our research we focused on the conscious acknowledgment of emotions in specific situations and, by systematically considering the ways in which emotional experiences and general defense style were related to each other, we hoped to develop a clearer understanding of gender differences in these patterns of relationships. We also hoped to better understand the ways in which emotions themselves may be a form of defensiveness or may precipitate other defensive strategies.

Defenses, Emotions, and Adjustment

How do emotions and defenses relate to gender differences in self-esteem, depression, and anxiety? A recent meta-analysis of gender differences in self-esteem revealed that women generally report lower self-esteem than men, although the magnitude and the direction of gender effects differ depending on age, social class, and ethnicity of participants as well as the method of assessing self-esteem (Major et al., 1999). Similarly, women generally show higher rates of depression and mood disorders than men, with the results becoming especially pronounced in early adolescence (Nolen-Hoeksema & Rusting, 1999). Psychoanalytic theories to explain these gender differences have ranged from penis envy (Freud, 1925/1964) to explanations involving women's lower social status and power (Horney, 1967). Although the explanations for these gender differences are undoubtedly complex, and span multiple interacting intrapsychic, cultural, and possibly even biological factors, our focus here is on the role of intrapsychic processes, specifically the role of emotions and defenses.

Do women generally suffer from lower self-esteem, higher depression, and higher anxiety than men partly because they use different defenses and emotion regulation strategies than men do? Research has pinpointed three possible types of defense–emotion regulation difficulties that may mediate, or underlie, these gender differences in adjustment. First, some research has noted a relationship between the use of denial and reports of depression (Offer et al., 2000). Margo, Greenberg, Fisher, and Dewan (1993) showed that as the level of depression increases, not only denial, but also optimistic defenses that protect self-esteem—such as principalization (intellectualization, rationalization, isolation of affect) and reversal (negation, repression, suppression, and reaction formation)—are used significantly less. Some of these defenses may be used less by women than by men.

Second, researchers have shown that depression is associated with either the suppression of anger, the expression of anger, or both, leading researchers to theorize that it is the frequent experience of anger and failure to regulate it that may be related to depression (see Brody, 1999; Sperberg & Stabb, 1998). It may be that gender differences in depression are related to corresponding gender differences in anger regulation strategies, with women's relatively high depression related to a relatively high suppression of anger.

Third, Nolen-Hoeksema and her colleagues (Nolen-Hoeksema, 1987, 1990, 1998; Nolen-Hoeksema, Larson, & Grayson, 1999) have persuasively argued that males are more likely to respond to depressive mood states with active, instrumental defensive and coping strategies, whereas women are more likely to react to depressive states by ruminating over their problems. *Ruminating* involves a tendency to experience feelings or repeated thoughts about a specific object or situation for an extended period of time. A ruminative style of responding to depression amplifies the dysphoric effects of the depressed mood, making negative interpretations of events and memories more accessible and more influential. In addition, rumination inhibits engagement in everyday behaviors that could have facilitated a sense of control over and improvement in mood. Thus women's propensity to ruminate over negative emotion may offer an important explanatory paradigm for their heightened and sustained experience and expression of depression and related emotions.

Nolen-Hoeksema's work suggests that defenses or coping strategies that help distance negative or upsetting thoughts, emotions, or events may create lower subjective experiences of distress and that these strategies are more apt to be used by men than by women. For example, Parkes (1990) reported that men in her sample evidenced significantly more suppression characterized by restraint, withdrawal, and ignoring the problem than women and that higher levels of suppression were associated with lower levels of distress.

In accordance with previous research, we predicted that both the expression of anger and other externalizing emotions, as well as the expression of externalizing defenses, especially defenses that distance emotion, such as sublimation and suppression, would be higher in men than in women. We also predicted that gender differences in using these types of emotions and defenses would mediate any gender differences in self-esteem, anxiety, and depression. However, we also thought it was possible that gender would interact with emotional expression and defense use in predicting adjustment—in other words, gender might be a moderator variable. For example, perhaps low self-esteem would be evident only among men, and not women, who expressed high levels of internalizing emotions. Such a possibility is suggested by several researchers who have found that individuals who use defense strategies atypical for their sex differ in adjustment levels from those who do not use atypical defenses, sometimes with poorer adjustment (Cramer & Blatt, 1990) and sometimes in complex and different ways for each sex that are not easily interpretable (see Frank, McLaughlin, & Crusco, 1984).

Description of the Study

In a nonclinical sample of college students we investigated gender differences in reported emotional responses to hypothetical scenarios in which partners were either rejecting or demanding of intimacy. We also explored gender differences in reported patterns of defense use and the relationships between defense use and types of emotions expressed. Finally, we analyzed how gender differences in self-esteem, depression, and anxiety might be mediated by gender differences in emotions and defenses or might moderate emotions and defenses to predict adjustment.

Our measures of emotions, defense use, and distress were all based on self-reports, although we attempted to assess participants' reported emotional reactions to particular situations rather than in general. However, the use of self-report measures raises the caution so convincingly described by Shedler, Mayman, and Manis (1993) that some people may present the illusion of being psychologically healthy simply because they deny distress on self-report measures. In our data, this caution is particularly warranted as we explore relationships among reports of defenses such as denial and reports of distress. For example, if we find that use of denial predicts psychological health, does that mean that denial is an adaptive defense, or does that mean that people who use denial give the illusion of being healthy because they are apt to deny distress along with their other negative emotional experiences? We attempt to grapple with these questions as we present our results, and we place special emphasis on results that demonstrate complex interactions among our variables, allowing us to clarify differing patterns in the relationships among self-reported adjustment, emotions, and defenses for men and women.

The sample was composed of 118 undergraduate students (57 women and 61 men) who were enrolled in a psychology course at a major east coast university. The mean age of the women was 18.75 years ($SD = 0.99$), and for men it was 19.00 years ($SD = 1.28$). Ninety percent of the sample was American, and 10% was from several other countries in Asia, South America, Europe, and the Middle East. Sixty-six percent of the sample was European American, 9.3% was Asian American, 7.6% was Hispanic American, and 6.8% was African American.

We explored reported emotions to eight hypothetical stories: five concerning rejection by partners and three concerning partners needing care and intimacy. These stories were labeled *Romantic Relationships Vignettes* (Muderrisoglu, 1999) and had previously been used to assess participants' attachment styles. An example of a rejection story was as follows: "Chris had made plans to introduce you to his/her family. Recently Chris has appeared less interested in arranging that get-together." An example of a story depicting partners needing intimacy was the following: "Chris is going through a rough period of time and has been needing your comfort and asking to see you more often."

Participants were asked to rate the intensity of 24 emotions they would potentially feel in the stories using a 5-point scale (1 = *not at all* to 5 = *extremely*). We selected 12 emotions for analysis in this study: 6 dysphoric, internalizing emotions, including hurt, shame, disappointment, nervousness, sadness, and guilt, and 6 externalizing emotions, including anger, annoyance, contempt, disgust, boredom, and surprise. For some analyses we averaged the intensity of these 2 sets of 6 emotions separately for rejection and partner-needs stories, generating four scores: internalizing emotions to rejection stories (alpha reliability = .77), internalizing emotions to partner demands for intimacy stories (alpha reliability = .78) and, correspondingly, externalizing emotions to rejection stories (alpha reliability = .77) and externalizing emotions to partner needs stories (alpha reliability = .74).

We conceptualized defenses as unconscious processes that aim to avoid or distort some aspect of intolerable affect in order to sustain self-esteem or to maintain relationships. To explore general defense use, participants completed the Defense Style Questionnaire (DSQ; Bond, Gradner, Christian, & Sigal 1983), a self-report measure that assesses participants' conscious awareness of the types of defensive behaviors they use. It can be argued that using a self-report measure violates the conceptualization of defenses as unconscious processes. However, it has been theorized that the actual behaviors through which defense mechanisms manifest themselves may be more accessible to conscious awareness than the functions they serve, thus allowing for the validity of self-report measures of defensive behaviors (Bond et al., 1983).

We used a modified 64-item version of the DSQ, including 17 of the original 25 defense mechanisms that we thought were most conceptually relevant for relationship stresses, including suppression, sublimation, humor, reaction formation, undoing, inhibition, withdrawal, idealization, projection, passive aggression, acting out, omnipotence/devaluation, isolation, splitting, regression, denial, and affiliation. Our selection of the DSQ was based partly on the broad range of defenses it assessed, and our selection of particular defenses was based on the work of several highly influential psychoanalytic writers, including Anna Freud and Otto Fenichel, as compiled by Vaillant (see Vaillant, 1977, p. 79).

Sample items for each defense are presented in Table 6.1. Each item is rated on a 9-point scale ranging from *strongly disagree* to *strongly agree*. Each defense score is calculated by taking the mean of the corresponding items for the defense measured. On the basis of Bond et al.'s (1983) suggestion, we performed a principal-components factor analysis to explore the best fitting factor solution, as opposed to using the factor solutions obtained in previous studies. A principal-components analysis with a varimax rotation revealed four conceptually meaningful factors with eigenvalues >1 that explained 51.5% of the total variance. Defenses were considered part of a factor if their loading was greater than .45. The first factor, labeled *Impulsive Action-Oriented Defenses*, included acting out, omnipotence–devaluation, passive aggression, projection, splitting, and lowered use of sublimation. This factor comprises immature defenses that involve high levels of distortion of internal and external reality. The second factor, labeled *Internalizing Defenses*, included inhibition, isolation, withdrawal, and denial. The defenses in this factor involve shifting from engagement with the outside world to a more internal focus and, in so doing, limiting and constricting potential opportunities to confront or repair interpersonal conflicts directly. The third factor, labeled *Social Preservation Defenses*, included affiliation, idealization, reaction formation, and undoing and involves defenses that aim to maintain interpersonal connections, sometimes by transforming intolerable ideas and emotions into more tolerable ones. The fourth factor, labeled *Distancing Defenses*, includes humor, suppression, and lowered use of regression, which share an acknowledgment of conflictual emotions or ideas with only subtle changes in their form of expression.

Table 6.1

Sample Items From the Defense Style Questionnaire

Type of defense	Sample item
Suppression	I'm able to keep a problem out of my mind until I have time to deal with it.
Sublimation	I work out my anxiety through doing something constructive and creative like painting or woodwork.
Humor	I'm usually able to see the funny side of an otherwise painful predicament.
Reaction formation	I try to be nice to people I don't like.
Undoing	After I fight for my rights, I tend to apologize for my assertiveness.
Inhibition	I'm very shy about standing up for my rights with people.
Withdrawal	I withdraw from people when I feel hurt.
Idealization	There is someone I know who can do anything and who is absolutely fair and just.
Projection	Most of what happens to me is not my responsibility.
Passive aggression	If my boss bugged me, I might make a mistake in my work or work more slowly so as to get back at him or her.
Acting out	I often act impulsively when something is bothering me.
Omnipotence/devaluation	I am superior to most people I know.
Isolation	Often I find that I don't feel anything when the situation would seem to warrant strong emotions.
Splitting	As far as I'm concerned, people are either good or bad.
Regression	I fall apart under stress.
Denial	People say I'm like an ostrich with my head buried in the sand. In other words, I tend to ignore unpleasant facts as if they don't exist.
Affiliation	When I feel bad, I try to be with someone.

We also explored levels of general defensiveness using the sub-scales of Denial of Distress and Repressive Defensiveness from the Weinberger Adjustment Inventory (WAI; Weinberger & Schwartz, 1990). Denial of Distress (11 items, $\alpha = .75-.78$) measures the extent to which individuals do not acknowledge normative experiences of distress. Sample items (scored in reverse) include "I feel a little down when I don't do as well as I thought I would" and "If people I like do things without asking me to join them, I feel a little left out." The Repressive Defensiveness scale (11 items, $\alpha = .79$) measures the extent to which individuals describe themselves as al-ways considerate of others, responsible, and in control of their so-cially undesirable impulses. Sample items (scored in reverse) include "There have been times when I said I would do one thing but did something else" and "Once in awhile, I don't do something someone asked me to do."

To explore psychological adjustment, we used three subscales from the Distress scale of the WAI (Weinberger & Schwartz, 1990): Anxiety, Depression, and Self-Esteem. Each item is rated on a 5-point scale (1 = *not at all true of me* to 5 = *very true of me*).

Results

Gender differences in reported emotions. Using the agency–communion framework we had predicted that (a) men would ex-press more negative emotions than women in response to partners' intimacy demands and (b) women would express more negative emotions than men in response to partners' rejection. On the basis of previous literature on emotional expression, we also predicted that (c) men would express more guilt than women to both partner rejection and partner intimacy scenarios and that women would express more shame than men to both types of scenarios.

We performed two sets of repeated measures multivariate anal-yses of variance (MANOVAs), consisting of gender as a between-groups variable, type of situation (rejection vs. intimacy demands) as a repeated measure, and types of emotion as the multiple out-come measure in the analysis. One MANOVA focused on the six internalizing emotions (hurt, shame, disappointment, sadness, guilt, and nervousness); the second focused on the six externalizing emotions (anger, annoyance, contempt, disgust, boredom, and surprise).

The MANOVA for internalizing emotions indicated that the multivariate main effect of gender was significant, multivariate $F(6, 111) = 3.47$, $p < .01$. Specific emotions that showed significant gender differences were guilt, univariate $F(1, 116) = 4.40$, $p < .04$, with women expressing less guilt than men (women: $M = 0.18$, $SD = 0.32$; men: $M = 0.34$, $SD = 0.48$), and sadness, univariate $F(1, 116) = 3.70$, $p < .06$, with women expressing more sadness than men (women: $M = 0.97$, $SD = 0.72$; men: $M = 0.73$, $SD = 0.65$). The multivariate main effect of situation was highly significant, multivariate $F(6, 111) = 75.63$, $p < .001$, with every emotion except nervousness showing a significant univariate F and with means indicating that both men and women reported more intense emotions (except for nervousness) when partners rejected them than when partners demanded intimacy. The multivariate Gender × Situation interaction was also significant, $F(6, 111) = 3.14$, $p < .01$; with significant univariate interactions for hurt, $F(1, 116) = 5.28$, $p < .02$; and sadness, $F(1, 116) = 9.75$, $p < .002$. In accordance with our hypotheses, these interactions revealed that men reported more hurt and sadness than did women when partners demanded intimacy but reported less hurt and sadness than women when partners rejected them (see Table 6.2).

The MANOVA in which externalizing emotions were the outcome variables revealed no main effects of gender. Although the

Table 6.2

Means and Standard Deviations for Emotions in Different Situations

| | Men ($n = 61$) | | | | Women ($n = 57$) | | | |
| | Partner rejection | | Partner demand | | Partner rejection | | Partner demand | |
Emotion	M	SD	M	SD	M	SD	M	SD
Sadness	1.28	1.10	0.19	0.40	1.84	1.30	0.11	0.40
Hurt	2.23	1.30	0.10	0.30	2.66	1.10	0.03	0.20
Anger	1.63	1.00	0.14	0.40	1.92	1.00	0.07	0.30

multivariate Gender × Situation interaction was not significant, $F(6, 111) = 1.68$, $p = .13$, a univariate Gender × Situation interaction for anger tended to be significant, $F(1, 116) = 3.52$, $p = .06$. This interaction revealed a tendency for men to be less angry than women in response to rejection scenarios but more angry than women in response to scenarios involving a partner's demands for intimacy. Finally, the main effect of situation was again highly significant, $F(6, 111) = 66.15$, $p < .001$, with all emotions showing significant univariate F values, indicating that both men and women reported more intense emotions in response to rejection than in response to a partner's needs for intimacy.

Gender differences in defense use. We had predicted that expressing externalizing emotions, especially anger, and externalizing defenses, would be higher in men than in women. We have already discussed gender differences in anger, which were context specific to either rejection or partners' needs situations, and we have more to say later about how the expression of anger related to adjustment variables. As displayed in Table 6.3, a one-way MANOVA for gender using the four DSQ defense styles as outcome measures showed that men tended to report distancing de-

Table 6.3

Means and Standard Deviations for Defenses

	Men (n = 61)		Women (n = 57)	
Defense	M	SD	M	SD
DSQ Acting out	.08	1.00	−.09	.90
DSQ Internalizing	−.04	1.00	.04	.90
DSQ Social Preservation	−.13	1.00	.14	.90
DSQ Distancing	.19	1.00	−.21	.90
WAI Denial of Distress	24.39	5.30	21.37	4.90
WAI Repressive Defensiveness	24.34	5.70	27.36	7.60

Note. DSQ = Defense Style Questionnaire; WAI = Weinberger Adjustment Inventory.

fenses (suppression, humor, and less regression) significantly more than women, multivariate $F(4, 113) = 2.15$, $p < .08$, univariate $F(1, 116) = 5.11$, $p < .03$. A separate MANOVA based on the two WAI defense scales also indicated multivariate main effects of gender, $F(2, 115) = 11.86$, $p < .001$, with men denying normative experiences of distress significantly more than women (Denial of Distress scale on the WAI: univariate $F[1, 166] = 10.23$, $p < .002$); women reported significantly higher amounts of always doing the right thing and never giving in to temptations (Repressive Defensiveness scale on the WAI: univariate $F[1, 116] = 6.02$, $p < .02$). These findings suggest that for men, defenses may be related to experiencing negative emotions or distress, whereas for women defenses may be triggered by feelings, wishes, and behaviors that do not conform to strict cultural standards for interpersonal and moral behaviors.

Relationships between DSQ defenses and WAI defenses. As displayed in Table 6.4, denial of distress on the WAI was related significantly positively to distancing defenses for both sexes and negatively to internalizing defenses. Other correlations indicated that the more acting-out defenses that were reported on the DSQ, the less Repressive Defensiveness was reported on the WAI (significant for women, a trend for men). It seems that for both sexes, but especially for women, wishes to conform to social standards relate to lowered tendencies to report acting-out defenses. This relationship may be due to the socially undesirability of externalizing behaviors and defenses, especially for women.

Relationships between emotions and defenses. We had predicted that (a) the types of emotions expressed and the types of defenses reported would be positively related, that is, that internalizing defenses and internalizing emotions would be positively related, as would externalizing emotions and externalizing defenses, whereas externalizing defenses and internalizing emotions would be negatively related, as would internalizing defenses and externalizing emotions; (b) among men, more frequent reports of defenses would be negatively related to internalizing emotions, whereas among women, more frequent reports of defenses would be negatively related to externalizing emotions; and (c) that mature defenses would be positively related to reports of appropriate dysphoric emotions and negatively related to reports of inappropriate dysphoric emotions, whereas immature defenses would be nega-

Table 6.4

Pearson Correlations Between Defense Style Questionnaire Defenses and Weinberger Adjustment Inventory (WAI) Defenses for Each Gender

Defense	Acting out		Internalization		Social preservation		Distancing	
	Men	Women	Men	Women	Men	Women	Men	Women
WAI Denial of Distress	.03	−.04	−.16	−.32**	−.04	.07	.41***	.42***
WAI Repressive Defensiveness	−.23*	−.39**	−.05	.07	.19	.21	.19	.03

*$p < .10$. **$p < .05$. ***$p < .01$.

tively related to reports of appropriate dysphoric emotions and positively related to the reports of inappropriate dysphoric emotions.

Pearson correlations between specific defenses on the DSQ and WAI and internalizing and externalizing emotions are displayed in Table 6.5. These correlations revealed that for both men and women, externalizing and internalizing emotions were related to increased reports of acting-out defenses, such as "I often am driven to act impulsively." Neither internalizing nor externalizing emotions was related to the use of other defenses on the DSQ. This finding only partially supports our hypotheses. The data suggest that acting-out defenses are precipitated by intense levels of emotion or that intense levels of emotion themselves are defenses that accompany the use of acting-out defenses. Alternatively, acting out may be a less efficient defense strategy for regulating emotions than are other types of defenses.

Other results revealed that men's internalizing emotions to partners' demands for intimacy, such as hurt and sadness, were sig-

Table 6.5

Pearson Correlations Between Defenses and Emotions for Each Gender

	DSQ Acting-out defenses		WAI repressive defensiveness	
Emotion	Men	Women	Men	Women
Internalizing emotions to partners' demands	.29**	.25	−.26**	.06
Internalizing emotions to partners' rejection	.24	.04	−.04	.06
Externalizing emotions to partners' demands	.30**	.27**	−.19	−.01
Externalizing emotions to partners' rejection	.37***	.19	−.20	.02

Note. DSQ = Defensive Style Questionnaire; WAI = Weinberger Adjustment Inventory.
**$p < .05$. ***$p < .01$.

nificantly negatively related to their reports of repressive defensiveness on the WAI ($r = -.26$). This relationship was near 0 for women ($r = .06$). A Fisher's z test for the differences between the women's and men's correlations indicated that the correlations were significantly different (Fisher's $z = 1.73$, $p < .05$, one-tailed). These results are consistent with the idea that men who use defenses to conform to social and moral conventions acknowledge less intense feelings of vulnerability than do other men and that the acknowledgment of vulnerability is not related to social conformity in women.

A somewhat different relationship emerges when emotions are categorized into those that are appropriate (or realistic) when partners are rejecting versus those that are inappropriate or unrealistic. We considered appropriate internalizing emotions in response to rejection to be those that did not imply a negative judgment about the role of the self in the rejection and included disappointment, sadness, and hurt, whereas inappropriate internalizing emotions were those that did imply a negative judgment about the role of the self in the rejection and included guilt, shame, and nervousness. Appropriate externalizing emotions were those that did not imply a demeaning attitude toward the other, including anger, annoyance, and surprise, whereas inappropriate externalizing emotions were those that did imply a demeaning attitude toward the other, including contempt, disgust, and boredom. We derived scores for each of these four categories (appropriate and inappropriate internalizing and externalizing emotions) by calculating means across the three emotions in each category. Consistent with our previous results for sadness, gender differences for appropriate internalizing emotions were significant, $t(116) = 2.31$, $p < .03$, with women reporting more appropriate internalizing emotions than men (women: $M = 2.31$, $SD = 0.99$; men: $M = 1.88$, $SD = 1.01$), but gender differences for the other three categories of emotions were not significant.

We then correlated the four types of emotions with (a) mature defenses (sublimation, suppression, humor, undoing, withdrawal, and affiliation), (b) immature defenses (acting out, idealization, omnipotence–devaluation, passivity–aggression, projection, reaction formation, inhibition, denial, and splitting), (c) the four DSQ defenses, and (d) the two WAI defenses. (We did not calculate appropriate and inappropriate emotions for the stories concerning partners' needs for intimacy, because it wasn't clear that any of our dysphoric emotions was an appropriate or realistic reaction to these scenarios.)

The results are displayed in Table 6.6 and indicate that for the entire sample reports of inappropriate externalizing emotions tended to be positively correlated with the use of immature defenses. For men only, using immature defenses was significantly related not only to reports of inappropriate externalizing emotions but also to reports of appropriate externalizing emotions and inappropriate internalizing emotions and was also positively, although not significantly, related to appropriate internalizing emotions. In contrast, and contrary to our predictions, for women, mature defenses were negatively related to reports of appropriate internalizing and appropriate externalizing defenses. Fisher's z tests analyzing the differences between men's and women's correlations revealed that the only significant difference was in the relationship between immature defenses and appropriate external-

Table 6.6

Pearson Correlations Between Appropriate and Inappropriate Emotions and Defenses for Each Gender

Type of emotion	Mature defenses		Immature defenses	
	Men	Women	Men	Women
Appropriate internalizing emotions	−.02	−.27**	.21	−.02
Appropriate externalizing emotions	−.07	−.27**	.30**	−.05
Inappropriate internalizing emotions	−.07	.09	.30**	.03
Inappropriate externalizing emotions	−.06	−.14	.30**	.23*

*$p < .10$. **$p < .05$.

izing emotions (Fischer's $z = 1.90$, $p < .05$), which was significant for men and not for women.

It is worth noting that reaction formation, true to its definition, was significantly negatively related to the expression of inappropriate externalizing emotions ($r = -.19$, $p < .05$) as well as to the expression of appropriate externalizing emotions ($r = -.23$, $p < .02$). This was in contrast to the other immature defenses, which were each positively related to the expression of externalizing emotions. These patterns tended to emerge similarly for both genders.

Emotions and psychological adjustment. Table 6.7 shows the means and standard deviations for self-esteem, depression, and anxiety for each gender. We found that the women in our sample reported significantly lower self-esteem and higher levels of anxiety than the men did. Levels of depression did not differ for men and women. These three variables (self-esteem, anxiety, and depression) were highly and significantly correlated with each other in both sexes (the lowest correlation between any pair was for anxiety and depression in men: $r = .50$, whereas the highest was between depression and self-esteem in men: $r = .69$). However, because of conceptual differences among the three variables, we analyzed them separately in relation to defenses and emotions.

Interactions among gender, emotions, and defenses. First, to test the moderation hypothesis, we explored whether there was a significant interaction between defenses and gender in predicting

Table 6.7

Means and Standard Deviations for Adjustment Measures

Measure	Men		Women	
	M	*SD*	*M*	*SD*
Anxiety	25.51	4.95	27.77	5.72
Depression	19.91	6.20	20.67	5.81
Self-esteem[a]	14.66	5.21	16.74	5.39

[a]Reverse scored.

the adjustment variables. We conducted six regression analyses in which the outcome variables were the adjustment measures (self-esteem, anxiety, or depression). For three of these analyses the four DSQ factors were predictors, and for the other three the two WAI defenses were predictors. The first block of predictors entered comprised the four DSQ factors or the two WAI defenses. The second block of predictors consisted of dummy variables that coded the interaction between gender and each of the defenses. We interpreted interactions, when significant, by performing regressions separately for each gender looking at the relationships between outcome variables and predictors.

A significant main effect revealed that higher denial of distress was related to higher self-esteem in both sexes (B = 0.65, $p < .03$). Significant interactions revealed that, for self-esteem, gender significantly interacted with internalization defenses such as withdrawal (B = -0.74, $p < .01$). For women, higher internalization defenses were related to lower self-esteem (B = 0.46, $p < .001$), whereas for men there was no significant relationship between internalization defenses and self-esteem (B = 0.14, $p < .25$). That higher levels of internalizing defenses predict lower self-esteem in women is consistent with previous work showing that rumination (an internalizing coping strategy) is maladaptive for women (Nolen-Hoeksema, 1998).

For both sexes, those who reported lower distancing defenses reported higher anxiety (B = 0.43, $p < .05$). The interaction of gender with three defenses also predicted anxiety: DSQ internalization defenses (B = 0.52, $p < .05$), DSQ social preservation defenses (B = 0.94, $p < .004$), and WAI denial of distress (B = 0.62, $p < .05$). For women, higher internalization defenses and lower denial of distress predicted higher anxiety, but this was less true of men (women: B = 0.36, $p < .001$ for internalization; B = 0.63, $p < .001$ for denial of distress; men: B = 0.19, $p = .09$ for internalization; B = 0.37, $p < .01$ for denial of distress). Here again, an internalizing style for women predicted worse adjustment—in this case, higher levels of anxiety. In contrast, for men, DSQ social preservation defenses predicted higher anxiety (B = 0.26, $p < .005$), which was not true of women (B = 0.16, ns). The relationship between social preservation defenses and heightened anxiety for men is consistent with Cramer and Blatt's (1990) finding that men who use stereo-typically feminine defenses have worse adjustment.

The Gender × Defense interactions did not predict depression, which was predicted by main effects of type of defense. In both sexes, higher internalization defenses were related to higher depression (B = 0.70, $p < .02$), and higher denial of distress was related to lower depression (B = -0.50, $p < .08$). These results are consistent with other research on the defenses that predict depression, especially higher denial predicting lower depression (see Nolen-Hoeksema, 1990).

Next we performed a parallel set of regressions, using internalizing and externalizing emotions to partners' rejection and partners' needs as predictors, along with dummy variables for the interactions between gender and each type of emotion. The outcome variables were self-esteem, depression, or anxiety. These regressions revealed a main effect of higher externalizing emotions in response to partners' rejection predicting higher self-esteem (B = 0.81, $p < .08$). A significant interaction between gender and internalizing emotions when partners made demands also predicted self-esteem (B = 1.23, $p < .02$). Men who reported more internalizing emotions, such as shame and sadness, when partners made demands reported lower self-esteem (B = 0.80, $p < .001$), whereas women did not (B = 0.03, ns). Anxiety and depression were also predicted by interactions between gender and externalizing emotions when partners made demands (B = 0.96, $p < .06$, for anxiety; B = 1.32, $p < .001$, for depression). Men who reported more externalizing emotions reported lower anxiety (B = -0.59, $p < .01$) and lower depression (B = 0.69, $p < .01$), whereas women did not show this relationship (B = 0.07, ns, for anxiety, and 0.13, ns, for depression). That internalizing emotions predicted lower self-esteem and that externalizing emotions predicted lower anxiety and depression in men are again consistent with Cramer and Blatt's (1990) finding that men who have a gender-inappropriate emotional style have worse adaptation than do men who have a gender-appropriate style.

Finally, we performed a set of three regressions using appropriate–inappropriate emotions, gender, and the interactions between gender and these four types of emotions as predictors of depression, self-esteem, and anxiety. For depression, neither main effects of the emotions nor interactions were significant. For anxiety, gender significantly interacted with inappropriate internalizing emotions to rejection (B = 0.98, p < .05). Simple regressions revealed that, for men, expressing inappropriate internalizing emotions, such as shame, guilt, and nervousness, was related to higher anxiety (B = 0.33, p < .01), but not for women (B = −0.06, ns). For self-esteem, gender tended to interact with appropriate externalizing emotions. Simple regressions revealed that, for women, self-esteem tended to be higher when the expression of appropriate externalizing emotions was higher (B = 0.21, p = .11), whereas for men there was no relationship (B = 0.02, ns).

Mediating Hypotheses

Our final question was whether the differing emotions and defense styles reported by the two sexes mediated the gender differences in psychological adjustment. We had originally predicted that gender differences in externalizing emotions (especially anger) and in externalizing defenses (especially distancing) would mediate any gender differences in adjustment, including self-esteem, anxiety, and depression. However, because our data did not show main effects of gender differences in anger, we instead considered potential mediators to be the variables that had shown gender differences: namely, distancing defenses on the DSQ, repressive defensiveness and denial of distress on the WAI, and the average intensities of sadness and guilt attributed to all of the stories.[1] To assess whether these gender differences in feelings and defenses mediated the relationship between gender and defenses, we conducted mediational analyses using multiple regressions in accordance with the recommendations of Kenny, Kashy, and Bolger (1998).

Four steps are required to show mediation. First, an initial variable (gender) must be correlated with an outcome variable (self-

---

[1] Although the use of appropriate internalizing emotions has also shown gender differences, this difference was largely accounted for by the gender difference in sadness. Because sadness was already being tested as mediating variable, it was not necessary to do a separate analysis to test the degree to which appropriate internalizing emotions served as mediators.

esteem and anxiety). (Because depression did not show gender differences in this sample, we could not examine the variables that mediated gender differences in depressive functioning.) Second, the initial variable (gender) must be significantly correlated with the potential mediators (types of defenses or emotions). In this case, gender was correlated with distancing defenses, denial of distress, repressive defensiveness, and sadness and guilt reported to stories. Third, the mediator should be related to the outcome variable when controlling for the initial variable. When defenses were analyzed as mediators of self-esteem and anxiety, distancing defenses and denial of distress still significantly predicted self-esteem and anxiety after gender was controlled (self-esteem: distancing defenses, $B = -0.35$, $p < .001$, and denial of distress, $B = 0.46$, $p < .01$; anxiety: distancing defenses, $B = 0.50$, $p < .001$, and denial of distress, $B = 0.51$, $p < .001$). Repressive defensiveness also tended to predict anxiety significantly after gender was controlled ($B = -0.17$, $p = .06$), although now it did not predict self-esteem ($B = 0.13$, ns).

These first three steps demonstrate partial mediation. A fourth step is necessary for demonstrating complete mediation in that the relationship between the initial variable (gender) and the outcome variables (self-esteem or anxiety) should be reduced to near 0 when the mediator's influence is controlled. When the defenses of distancing or denial of defenses are each controlled, gender's relationship to self-esteem and anxiety becomes nonsignificant (when distancing is controlled as a predictor of self-esteem: $B = 0.12$, ns, as a predictor of anxiety: $B = -0.11$, ns; when denial of distress is controlled: for self-esteem, $B = -0.06$, ns, and for anxiety, $B = 0.06$, ns. In contrast, gender continues to predict both self-esteem ($B = 0.22$, $p < .02$) and anxiety ($B = 0.25$, $p < .008$) when repressive defensiveness is controlled. Thus, gender differences in anxiety and self-esteem seem to be fully mediated by gender differences in the defenses of distancing and denial of distress. Gender differences in anxiety are only partially mediated by repressive defensiveness, whereas repressive defensiveness does not mediate gender differences in self-esteem.

When sadness and guilt are entered into similar types of mediational analyses they appear to be partial mediators of gender differences in anxiety and self-esteem. Guilt and sadness both continue to predict anxiety and self-esteem when gender is controlled (anxiety: guilt after gender, B = 0.18, p = .05, and sadness after gender, B = 0.17, p = .06; self-esteem: guilt after gender, B = 0.21, p < .02, and sadness after gender, B = 0.18, p < .05). However, gender also continues to predict anxiety and self-esteem when sadness and guilt are controlled (anxiety: gender after guilt, B = 0.24, p < .01, and gender after sadness, B = 0.17, p = .06; self-esteem: gender after guilt, B = 0.23, p < .01, and sadness after guilt: B = 0.18, p < .05).

Discussion

Tables 6.8 and 6.9 summarize the major findings of our study. Perhaps most important, the data show that men report more negative internalizing emotions, such as shame and hurt, in response to partners' needs than do women, whereas women report more negative internalizing emotions in response to partners' rejection than do men. We have argued that these data are consistent with feminist object-relations theories of development, such as Chodorow's (1978), that stress the importance of agency to men's self-construals and the importance of communion to women's self-construals. If we theorize that emotions such as shame and hurt are functional and defensive processes that serve to restore or repair a relationship with another to protect the self, then gender differences in these emotions indicate the kinds of situations in which men's and women's self-esteem are differentially threatened. Women are more apt to view rejection by partners as a threat to their communal sense of self and therefore react with dysphoric emotions; men are more apt to view partners' demands for intimacy as a threat to their separate sense of self and therefore react with dysphoric emotions.

We also found that men reported less sadness and more guilt than women in situations involving both rejection and partners' needs. Less sadness is consistent with cultural display rules for men that discourage the expression of personal vulnerability. Another of our findings—that men who conformed more highly to social and moral conventions acknowledged less intense feelings of vulnerability than other men—supports this interpretation. Gender differences in guilt perhaps result from men having a more

Table 6.8

Summary of Key Results for Reported Emotions and Defense Use

Both genders	Men	Women
	Reported emotions	
	□ Report more negative internalizing affects (e.g., shame and hurt) in response to partners' needs than women. □ Report less sadness and more guilt than women across situations of rejection and partners' needs for intimacy.	□ Report more negative internalizing affects in response to partners' rejection than men. □ Tend to report more anger than men in response to rejection and less anger than men in response to partners' needs.
	Defense use	
	□ Report more externalizing defenses (e.g., distancing and denial of distress) than women.	□ Report more defensiveness about violations of social and moral standards than men.
	Relationships between defense use and emotional expression	
□ Use of immature defenses was related to greater reports of externalizing and internalizing emotions. (Only use of reaction formation was negatively related to reports of emotions.)	□ For men more than women, immature defenses relate positively to expressing appropriate externalizing emotions (e.g., anger). □ High repressive defensiveness is related to low internalizing emotions in situations involving partners' needs for intimacy.	□ Mature defenses relate negatively to reporting appropriate internalizing and externalizing defenses.

Table 6.9

Summary of Key Results for Relationships Among Adjustment, Reported Emotions, and Defenses

Both sexes	Men	Women
Defenses and adjustment: Women report higher anxiety and lower self-esteem than men		
□ Lower anxiety is related to higher reports of distancing defenses. □ Higher depression is related to higher reports of internalization and higher denial of distress. □ Higher denial of distress is related to higher self-esteem.	□ Higher social preservation defenses are related to higher anxiety.	□ Higher internalization defenses are related to higher anxiety and lower self-esteem.
Emotions and adjustment		
□ Higher externalizing emotions (e.g., anger) in response to partners' rejection are related to higher self-esteem.	□ Higher internalizing emotions (e.g., shame, sadness, or nervousness) are related to lower self-esteem and higher anxiety. □ Higher externalizing emotions to partners' needs are related to lower anxiety and depression.	□ For women, self-esteem tends to be higher when the expression of appropriate externalizing emotions is higher.
Defenses and emotions as mediators		
□ Gender differences in the use of distancing and denial of distress mediate gender differences in anxiety and self-esteem. □ Gender differences in reported sadness and guilt partially mediate gender differences in anxiety and self-esteem. □ Gender differences in repressive defensiveness partially mediate gender differences in anxiety.		

active and agentic stance than women, which may lead them to feel more responsible when things go wrong in relationships, in accordance with Lewis's (1971) theory. A male agentic sense of self was also indicated by our findings that men used more external- izing defenses than did women, including distancing, and that they were less defensive about violations of social and moral stan- dards than were women. Externalizing defenses are also consistent with cultural display rules that encourage an outward-directed emotional stance.

That men used less repressive defensiveness than women, which measured a concern for upholding social and moral standards, seems to contradict Freud's idea that men have a more rigid and enhanced sense of morality than women. The results are more con- sistent with newer theoretical ideas that moral standards can take both impersonal and interpersonal forms and that women's mo- rality may be based more on interpersonal connections to others than is men's (Gilligan, 1982). Women's communal self-construals may make them more defensive than men about violating social or group norms.

Defenses, emotions, and adjustment. In general, for both gen- ders, reports of internalizing defenses, such as inhibition and with- drawal, were associated with increased depression, and less denial of distress was also associated with poorer adjustment. Conversely, the heightened expression of externalizing emotions in the face of a partner's rejection (such as anger and contempt) was associated with higher self-esteem, and reports of more externalizing de- fenses, such as distancing, were associated with better adjustment. Our data, along with those of other research, support the idea that the expression of anger (especially when it is appropriately labeled and verbally expressed) is adaptive, perhaps because it is func- tional for changing relationships in a desired direction (see Brody, 1999).

Several of our results may be a function of self-presentation bi- ases, as Shedler et al. (1993) cautioned, in particular the relation- ship between denial of distress and better adjustment. At least some of the participants who reported both denial and better ad- justment may suffer from what Shedler et al. termed *illusory mental health*, which is accompanied by potentially maladaptive increased autonomic reactivity. We do not have the kinds of data available that would help us to sort out this issue, and it is possible that the relationship between higher denial of distress and better adjustment is spurious. However, other results of our study are not so easily dismissed as being due to illusory mental health. For example, the findings that participants who reported using internalizing defenses such as withdrawal and inhibition also reported more depression, and that externalizing emotions such as anger are related to heightened self-esteem, do not seem to reflect response biases in an obvious way. Moreover, the distancing defenses that men reported using more than women, including humor and suppression, are not among those that are differentially socially acceptable for the two sexes, making it unlikely that a self-presentation bias is the reason that men reported the use of these defenses more than women did.

Our results add to the growing body of literature indicating that men report distancing defenses (as well as the more suspect defense of denial) more than women and that such defenses are more adaptive for lower distress (Nolen-Hoeksema, 1998; Nolen-Hoeksema et al., 1999; Parkes, 1990). Our data extend this literature by showing that such gender differences significantly mediate gender differences in self-esteem and anxiety. These data suggest that if women used distancing defenses more often, they would report lower levels of anxiety and higher self-esteem than they currently do, and gender reports of distress and self-esteem might be equalized. Defenses were more powerful mediators of adjustment than were reported feelings, in that not only did distancing and denial of distress fully mediate gender differences in self-esteem and anxiety, but also repressive defensiveness partially mediated gender differences in anxiety. In contrast, reports of sadness and guilt only partially mediated gender differences in self-esteem and anxiety.

Why should distancing defenses be adaptive for adjustment? These defenses involve a conscious awareness of experienced feelings that are distorted only subtly when expressed. Our conceptualization is that the distancing factor, including defenses such as humor, enables the expression of feelings in ways that continue to convey their meaning. Suppression, another defense in the distancing factor, allows for feelings to be set aside until an appropriate forum is available for their expression, and the lowered use of regression involves expressing feelings in developmentally appropriate ways. Much research indicates that expressing painful feelings, even long after the initial event eliciting the affect has occurred, is related to positive health consequences and is adaptive for interpersonal relationships (Pennebaker, 1989, 1993). By expressing and not inhibiting feelings, especially through the use of language, people can more readily understand and find meaning in their experiences, thus assimilating them. Moreover, people can receive support and legitimacy for their experiences, and social support itself has many positive health consequences (see Brody, 1999).

The general pattern of our data also revealed that women who used fewer internalizing defenses relative to other women, such as withdrawal, isolation, and inhibition, as well as women who denied distress, had higher self-esteem, lower anxiety, or both. These results differ somewhat from previous literature that has shown that using defenses typical of the opposite sex is related to poorer adjustment (Cramer & Blatt, 1990). Especially for women, heightened use of gender-role appropriate defenses seems to be maladaptive, as is consistent with Helgeson and Fritz's (1999) work on unmitigated communion. Also consistent with this argument is the finding that women who reported gender-role atypical patterns of emotion, such as anger, in response to partners' rejection tended to report higher self-esteem.

It is not surprising that the use of internalizing defenses and coping processes, such as inhibition, may be related to poorer adjustment. Previous research has indicated that inhibition influences health negatively by producing short-term increases in autonomic activity that may accumulate over time, leading to long-term stress-related disease, including impaired cardiovascular and immune functioning (Hughes, Uhlmann, & Pennebaker, 1994; Pennebaker, 1993; Pennebaker, Kiecolt-Glaser, & Glaser, 1988). For example, research participants who have been instructed to inhibit the expression of emotions such as disgust show evidence of greater sympathetic nervous system activation, including increased skin conductance, when compared with control groups who are given no inhibition instructions (Gross, 1998; Gross & Levenson, 1993).

An interesting feature in our data is that the pattern of relationships among internalizing defenses, higher anxiety, and lower self-esteem did not hold true for men. (It is worth remembering that men reported using internalizing defenses at levels equal to those reported by women.) For men, the general pattern of the data revealed that internalizing defenses such as withdrawal or inhibition did predict depression but did not predict self-esteem and anxiety. It is possible that the negative consequences of using internalizing defenses in men is tempered by their relatively higher expression of externalizing emotions, such as anger, in some situations. In fact, Pearson correlations indicated that, for the two genders, the relationship between reports of internalizing defenses and of externalizing emotions were in opposite directions, although neither correlation was significant. For men, internalizing defenses related positively to expressing externalizing emotions in response to a partner's rejection ($r = .13$), whereas for women, they related negatively ($r = -.10$). It may also be that for women, using internalizing defenses is especially problematic because it prevents women from having satisfying social relationships that are so integral to a communal sense of self.

Rather than being predicted by the use of internalizing defenses, men's anxiety and self-esteem were predicted by the quality of their emotional reactions to interpersonal stress. Reports of internalizing emotions, such as shame and sadness, were related to lower self-esteem, anxiety, or both, whereas reports of relatively higher externalizing emotions in response to partners' demands, including anger and contempt, were related to lower anxiety and depression. These findings support research showing that cross-gender defenses and emotional styles in men are associated with poorer adjustment (Cramer & Blatt, 1990) and extends this work to include the controversial idea that the expression of vulnerable feelings in men is associated with poorer adjustment. Here again, Shedler et al.'s (1993) cautions about self-report data are worth heeding, in that it may be that men who were willing to admit to feelings of vulnerability in the face of social sanctions were also willing to admit to distress. These men may be less defensive and concerned about endorsing socially undesirable characteristics than other men, with the implication that they are not more distressed but instead more open and disclosing. Even if we ignore this caution and assume the relationship between internalizing emotions and distress is nonspurious, the correlational nature of the data do not allow us to infer the direction of the causality (or determine whether indeed there is a direct causal link) between worse adjustment and reports of internalizing emotions for men.

The only defense that predicted men's anxiety levels was the use of social preservation defenses, such as affiliation and reaction formation, that related to increased anxiety. It may be that only when men become highly anxious relative to other men do they use defenses that protect their social relationships. Alternatively, both reported anxiety and social preservation defenses may characterize men who have a more communal sense of self than other men, because both serve the function of restoring social relationships perceived to be in jeopardy.

Relationships between reported emotions and defenses. Both a strength and a weakness of this study lies in our decision not to assess emotions and defenses in response to the same situations. We measured the acknowledgment of emotions to specific situations, and we measured self-reports of a general, nonsituationally specific defense style. These independent measurements made it less likely that we could clarify how the acknowledgment of emotions relates to defense use in particular situations, that is, how emotions themselves may be a form of defensiveness. On the other hand, our independent measurements are a more conservative test of the idea that emotional functioning and defensive functioning are related to each other independent of context.

The results did not support our predictions that the use of defenses would be negatively related to reports of internalizing emotions in men and to reports of externalizing emotions in women. For both men and women, acting out and immature defenses (which we defined as those in which distress is not acknowledged and heightened distortion occurs) were related to greater reports of dysphoric emotions in situations of interpersonal stress for both men and women. Also, especially for men, immature defenses were related to reporting appropriate externalizing emotions, such as anger, annoyance, and surprise. Immature defenses, with the exception of reaction formation, seem to bear a linear relationship with reports of negative emotions, and both may be derivatives of the same underlying processes, such as a vulnerable, easily threatened sense of self.

The acknowledgment or experience of dysphoric emotions may

itself be a defense when mature defenses are not in place. In accordance with this idea is the finding that, for women only, use of mature defenses, in which an emotion was recognized in less distorted ways, was related to the lowered acknowledgment of dysphoric feelings (both internalizing and externalizing) in situations in which partners were rejecting. Although these results need to be viewed as tentative, because significant differences were not found between women's and men's correlations, they suggest that, at least for women, mature defenses successfully regulate dysphoric emotions. Alternatively, the experience of less intense dysphoric emotions may lend itself to more mature defense use.

Our data could not address the degree to which the *expression* of feelings serves as a defense against the *experience* of painful feelings. For men, expressing socially acceptable externalizing feelings, such as anger, may be a defense against experiencing internalizing feelings, such as sadness, which may threaten agentic self-construals. Similarly, women may express socially acceptable internalizing feelings, such as sadness, to defend against experiencing externalizing feelings, such as anger, which may threaten communal self-construals. We could not test these ideas, because we did not distinguish between experience and expression and did not include a measure of unconscious experience. Future research could profitably include such measures to sort out the relationships among emotional experiences, emotional expressions, and defenses.

Clinical implications. Our study has interesting and provocative implications for clinical work. Perhaps the clearest clinical implications are that men's and women's self-esteem may be threatened by, and vulnerable to, different types of interpersonal insults and injuries. What one sex may deem threatening, the other sex may not. This finding can help clinicians understand the differential relationship stresses facing women (potential rejection or the termination of a relationship) and men (demands for increased relationship intimacy).

Women's and men's differential use of defenses and reports of feelings may be related to different types of adaptations. Women's expression of internalizing dysphoric feelings, sometimes in response to anger-inducing situations such as rejection, may promote feelings of helplessness, anxiety, and depression in such situations and may also be self-perpetuating. Men's expression of internalizing dysphoric feelings in response to partners' needs may create feelings of helplessness in situations involving demands for intimacy and may promote social relationships in which men fail to take responsibility or in which alienation rather than intimacy is promoted. On the other hand, men's higher use of distancing defenses may promote a sense of agency and control that may be adaptive for self-esteem.

Our data suggest that both clinicians and researchers should not assume that certain defenses are adaptive and others maladaptive, regardless of gender. Although distancing defenses were adaptive for both men and women, the use of internalizing defenses, such as inhibition, were significantly related to anxiety and self-esteem in women, but not in men.

The same caution holds for the relationship between adaptation and emotional expression, which we found to differ for the two sexes. Men, but not women, who reported more internalizing emotions (such as sadness and hurt) also reported more depression, lower self-esteem, and more anxiety. At the very least, these data should make clinicians question whether acknowledging feelings of vulnerability is a fruitful goal for men. Although we have cautioned that these results may be due to a self-presentation bias in men, the relationship between internalizing emotions and distress for men should be a warning signal for clinicians. Whatever the reasons, internalizing emotions expressed by men may be a diagnostic indicator for poor adjustment. These results seem counter to Pennebaker and Beall's (1986) data showing that experimental groups, especially those that include men (Smyth, 1998), who express their feelings about traumatic experiences in writing, show evidence of enhanced functioning compared to control groups who write about nontraumatic issues. Enhanced functioning in experimental groups has been indicated by measures of psychological well-being (e.g., positive affect, adjustment, and general temperament), physical health (e.g., health center visits and upper respiratory illness), physiological functioning (e.g., measures of immune functioning, such as Epstein–Barr antibodies and T-helper lymphoctyes), and general functioning (e.g., grade-point average, reemployment, absenteeism, cognitive functioning, and school behavior). However, analyses of the qualitative aspects of narratives that relate to improvement have not included detailed categorizations of the types of dysphoric emotions expressed, such as internalizing versus externalizing emotions or emotions related to vulnerability versus those related to blaming others. Instead, improved functioning has been shown to be related to decreasing disorganization and more coherence and focus in narratives over time (Pennebaker, 1993; Pennebaker, Mayne, & Francis, 1997); increased use of insight words, such as *understand* and *realize* (Pennebaker, 1993); and, in some samples, the use of positive emotion words (Pennebaker & Francis, 1996). Our data suggest that more detailed analyses of the types of dysphoric emotion words expressed by women and men might be a fruitful avenue for further research.

Our findings also suggest that clinicians should encourage women to use more distancing defenses and denial; fewer internalizing defenses, such as inhibition; and to express more appropriate externalizing emotions, such as anger, in the face of rejection. For both sexes, and consistent with previous literature, using more distancing defenses, attempting to deny distress, and expressing externalizing emotions in the face of rejection by others are associated with better self-esteem. For women in particular, use of internalizing defenses predicts lower self-esteem and higher anxiety. However, there may also be interactions between physical and mental health in relation to emotional expression and defense use that we did not assess. For example, if clinicians encourage women to express more anger, they may indeed increase women's self-esteem but increase their propensity for particular physical diseases, especially cardiovascular reactivity. Future research should continue to explore the complexity of the relationships among gender, emotional expression, defense use, and health, including both mental and physical adaptation.

References

Arendt, H. (1958). *The human condition.* Chicago: University of Chicago Press.

Bakan, D. (1966). *The duality of human existence.* Boston: Beacon Press.

Benjamin, J. (1988). *The bonds of love: Psychoanalysis, feminism, and the problem of domination.* New York: Pantheon.

Bergman, S. J. (1995). Men's psychological development: A relational perspective. In R. F. Levant & W. S. Pollack (Eds.), *A new psychology of men* (pp. 68–90). New York: Basic Books.

Bilsky, L. (1997). Battered women: From self defense to defending the self. *Plilim, 6,* 5–27.

Bion, W. (1962). *Learning from experience.* New York: Basic Books.

Bond, M., Gradner, S. T., Christian, J., & Sigal, J. J. (1983). Empirical study of self rated defense styles. *Archives of General Psychiatry, 40,* 333–338.

Brody, L. (1997). Beyond stereotypes: Gender and emotion. *Journal of Social Issues, 53,* 369–393.

Brody, L. (1999). *Gender, emotion and the family.* Cambridge, MA: Harvard University Press.

Chodorow, N. (1978). *The reproduction of mothering.* Berkeley: University of California Press.

Cooper, S. H. (1998). Changing notions of defense within psychoanalytic theory. *Journal of Personality, 66,* 947–964.

Cramer, P. (1991). *The development of defense mechanisms.* New York: Springer-Verlag.

Cramer, P. (1998a). Coping and defense mechanisms: What's the difference? *Journal of Personality, 66,* 919–946.

Cramer, P. (1998b). Defensiveness and defense mechanisms. *Journal of Personality, 66,* 879–894.

Cramer, P., & Blatt, S. J. (1990). Use of the TAT to measure change in defense mechanisms following intensive psychotherapy. *Journal of Personality Assessment, 54,* 236–251.

Cross, S. E., & Madson, L. (1997). Models of the self: Self construals and gender. *Psychological Bulletin, 122,* 5–37.

Fast, I. (1984). *Gender identity: A differentiation model.* Hillsdale, NJ: Analytic Press.

Ferguson, T., & Crowley, S. (1997). Gender differences in the organization of guilt and shame. *Sex Roles, 37,* 19–44.

Folkman, S., Lazarus, R. S., Pimley, S., & Novacek, J. (1987). Age differences in stress and coping processes. *Psychology and Aging, 2,* 171–184.

Frank, S. J., McLaughlin, A. M., & Crusco, A. (1984). Sex role attributes, symptom distress, and defensive style among college men and women. *Journal of Personality and Social Psychology, 47,* 182–192.

Freud, S. (1959). Inhibitions, symptoms and anxiety. In J. Strachey (Ed.), *The standard edition of the complete psychological works of Sigmund Freud* (Vol. 20, pp. 75–174). London: Hogarth. (Original work published 1926)

Freud, S. (1964). Some psychical consequences of the anatomical distinction between the sexes. In J. Strachey (Ed.), *The Standard edition of the complete psychological works of Sigmund Freud* (Vol. 19, pp. 241–258). London: Hogarth. (Original work published 1925)

Gilligan, C. (1982). *In a different voice: Psychological theory and women's development.* Cambridge, MA: Harvard University Press.

Gross, J. (1998). Antecedent and response-focused emotional regulation: Divergent consequences for experience, expression and physiology. *Journal of Personality and Social Psychology, 74,* 224–237.

Gross, J., & Levenson, R. W. (1993). Emotional suppression: Physiology, self-report, and expressive behavior. *Journal of Personality and Social Psychology, 64,* 970–986.

Helgeson, V. S., & Fritz, H. L. (1999). Unmitigated agency and unmitigated communion: Distinctions from agency and communion. *Journal of Research in Personality, 33,* 131–158.

Horney, K. (1967). *Feminine psychology.* New York: Norton.

Hughes, C. F., Uhlmann, C., & Pennebaker, J. (1994). The body's response to processing emotional trauma: Linking verbal text with autonomic activity. *Journal of Personality, 62,* 565–585.

Kenny, D. A., Kashy, D. A., & Bolger, N. (1998). Data analysis in social psychology. In D. T. Gilbert, S. T. Fiske, & L. Gardner (Eds.), *The handbook of social psychology* (4th ed., Vol. 1, pp. 233–265). Boston: McGraw-Hill.

Kernberg, O. (1980). *Internal world and external reality.* New York: Jason Aronson.

Kernberg, O. (1984). *Severe personality disorders.* New Haven, CT: Yale University Press.

Lee, R. M., & Robbins, S. B. (1998). The relationship between social connectedness and anxiety, self esteem, and social identity. *Journal of Counseling Psychology, 45,* 338–345.

Lewis, H. B. (1971). *Shame and guilt in neurosis.* New York: International Universities Press.

Major, B., Barr, L., Zubek, J., & Babey, S. (1999). Gender and self esteem: A meta-analysis. In W. B. Swann, J. H. Langlois, & L. A. Gilbert (Eds.), *Sexism and stereotypes in modern society: The gender science of Janet Taylor Spence* (pp. 223–253). Washington, DC: American Psychological Association.

Margo, G. M., Greenberg, R. P., Fisher, S., & Dewan, M. (1993). A direct comparison of the defense mechanisms of non-depressed people and depressed psychiatric inpatients. *Comprehensive Psychiatry, 34,* 65–69.

Markus, H., & Kitayama, S. (1991). Culture and the self: Implications for cognition, emotion, and motivation. *Psychological Review, 98,* 224–253.

Modell, A. (1975). A narcissistic defense against affects and the illusion of self-sufficiency. *International Journal of Psychoanalysis, 56,* 275–282.

Modell, A. (1984). *Psychoanalysis in a new context.* New York: International Universities Press.

Muderrisoglu, S. (1999). *Attachment styles in relation to defense.* Unpublished doctoral dissertation, Boston University.

Nolen-Hoeksema, S. (1987). Sex differences in unipolar depression: Evidence and theory. *Psychological Bulletin, 101,* 259–282.

Nolen-Hoeksema, S. (1990). *Sex differences in depression.* Stanford, CA: Stanford University Press.

Nolen-Hoeksema, S. (1998). Ruminative coping with depression. In J. Heckhausen & C. S. Dweck (Eds.), *Motivation and self regulation across the life span* (pp. 237–256). New York: Cambridge University Press.

Nolen-Hoeksema, S., Larson, J., & Grayson, C. (1999). Explaining the gender difference in depressive symptoms. *Journal of Personality and Social Psychology, 77,* 1061–1072.

Nolen-Hoeksema, S., & Rusting, C. L. (1999). Gender differences in well being. In D. Kahneman, E. Diener, & N. Schwarz (Eds.), *Well-being: The foundations of hedonic psychology* (pp. 330–350). New York: Russell Sage Foundation.

Offer, R., Lavie, R., Gothelf, D., & Apter, A. (2000). Defense mechanisms, negative emotions, and psychopathology in adolescent inpatients. *Comprehensive Psychiatry, 41,* 35–41.

Parkes, K. (1990). Coping, negative affectivity, and the work environment: Additive and interactive predictors of mental health. *Journal of Applied Psychology, 75,* 399–409.

Pennebaker, J. (1989). Confession, inhibition and disease. In L. Berkowitz (Ed.), *Advances in experimental social psychology* (Vol. 22, pp. 211–244). New York: Academic Press.

Pennebaker, J. (1993). Putting stress into words: Health, linguistic, and therapeutic implications. *Behaviour Research and Therapy, 31,* 539–548.

Pennebaker, J., & Beall, S. (1986). Confronting a traumatic event: Toward an understanding of inhibition and disease. *Journal of Abnormal Psychology, 95,* 274–281.

Pennebaker, J., & Francis, M. (1996). Cognitive, emotional, and language processes in disclosure. *Cognition & Emotion, 10,* 601–626.

Pennebaker, J., Kiecolt-Glaser, J., & Glaser, R. (1988). Disclosure of traumas and immune infection: Health implications for psychotherapy. *Journal of Consulting and Clinical Psychology, 56,* 239–245.

Pennebaker, J., Mayne, T., & Francis, M. (1997). Linguistic predictors of adaptive bereavement. *Journal of Personality and Social Psychology, 72,* 863–871.

Plutchik, R. (1998). Emotions, diagnoses, and ego defenses: A psychoevolutionary perspective. In W. Flack & J. Laird (Eds.), *Emotions in psychopathology: Theory and research* (pp. 367–379). New York: Oxford University Press.

Pollack, W. S. (1995). No man is an island: Toward a new psychoanalytic psychology of men. In R. F. Levant & W. S. Pollack (Eds.), *A new psychology of men* (pp. 33–67). New York: Basic Books.

Rosenfeld, L. B. (1979). Self-disclosure avoidance: Why I am afraid to tell you who I am. *Communication Monographs, 46,* 63–74.

Schafer, R. (1974). Problems in Freud's psychology of women. *Journal of the American Psychoanalytic Association, 22*, 459–485.

Shedler, J., Mayman, M., & Manis, M. (1993). The illusion of mental health. *American Psychologist, 48*, 1117–1131.

Smyth, J. (1998). Written emotional expression: Effect sizes, outcome types, and moderating variables. *Journal of Consulting and Clinical Psychology, 66*, 174–184.

Sperberg, E. D., & Stabb, S. D. (1998). Depression in women as related to anger and mutuality in relationships. *Psychology of Women Quarterly, 22*, 223–238.

Stapley, J., & Haviland, J. (1989). Beyond depression: Gender differences in normal adolescents' emotional experience. *Sex Roles, 20*, 295–309.

Vaillant, G. (1971). Theoretical hierarchy of adaptive ego mechanisms. *Archives of General Psychiatry, 24*, 107–118.

Vaillant, G. E. (1977). *Adaptation to life.* Boston: Little, Brown.

Waelder, R. (1976). The principle of multiple function. In S. A. Guttman (Ed.), *Psychoanalysis: Observation, theory, application* (pp. 68–83). New York: International Universities Press. (Original work published 1930)

Weinberger, D. A., & Schwartz, G. E. (1990). Distress and restraint as superordinate dimensions of self-reported adjustment: A typological perspective. *Journal of Personality, 58*, 381–417.

Winnicott, D. W. (1965). Ego distortion in terms of true and false self. In *Maturational processes and the facilitating environment* (pp. 142–152). New York: International Universities Press.

Zillmann, D., Weaver, J., Mundorf, N., & Aust, C. (1986). Effects of an opposite-gender companion's affect to horror on distress, delight, and attraction. *Journal of Personality and Social Psychology, 51*, 586–594.

Gender Differences in Morality

June Price Tangney and Ronda L. Dearing

> I cannot evade the notion (though I hesitate to give it expression) that for women the level of what is ethically normal is different from what it is in men. Their superego is never so inexorable, so impersonal, so independent of its emotional origins as we require it to be in men. (Freud, 1925/1961c, p. 257)

One of Freud's most controversial assertions concerns gender differences in moral development—specifically, gender differences in the integrity of the superego. Freud (1924/1961a, 1923/1961b) initially constructed his theory of moral development with the male child in mind. According to Freud, the superego, the seat of one's morality, is the voice of one's conscience and the home of one's ego ideal—the ideal to which one aspires, the ideal that serves as a moral guide for one's behavior.

People are not born as moral beings. In contrast to the basic emotions (e.g., anger, fear, joy), which emerge very early in life, shame and guilt are considered more developmentally advanced. These secondary, or derived emotions emerge later and hinge on two cognitive milestones: (a) a clear recognition of the self as separate from others, and (b) the development of standards against which the self, one's behavior, or both, are evaluated (Fischer & Tangney, 1995; Lewis, Sullivan, Stanger, & Weiss, 1989). In short, children aren't born with the ability to experience shame and guilt, as neither of these cognitive abilities is present at birth. These cognitive milestones emerge in childhood: first as a glimmer of an ability and, later in development, as increasingly complex and elaborated capacities.

In this regard, current developmental research confirms some of Freud's assertions about the development of morality. From Freud's perspective, one's early years are dominated by an amoral id. The superego begins to form only in childhood and is then solidly forged by the resolution of the Oedipal complex. Here is where the gender difference becomes important. The key to the resolution of the Oedipal complex is a dread of castration. In the course of normal psychosexual development, the young male child develops libidinous longings for his mother. She becomes a cherished first object of his awakening sexuality. Unfortunately, the child is immediately faced with a formidable, all-powerful rival: the father. Intense feelings of jealousy and envy envelop the son to the point where he wants to get rid of the father—murder him —and then take his place. This is an extremely uncomfortable and precarious position for a young boy, dwarfed by his towering, powerful, virile adult father. In a defensive attempt to alleviate feelings of anxiety, the child begins to view Dad as a menacing figure who wants to murder *him*—or, worse yet, to castrate him. This notion of castration intensifies his anxiety to the point where the dilemma becomes unbearable.

Then, in a very resourceful move, the child finds a way to resolve this painful, heated conflict. He opts for a "super-repression" of mother-directed sexual feelings and, to bolster this defense further, he identifies intensely with the father. This powerful identification with the father is accompanied by an introjection—a taking in—

of parental authority, which forms the bedrock of the superego. That is the heart of Freud's theory of the development of morality.

Freud's initial theory, however, failed to consider some fundamental anatomical differences between boys and girls: Little girls don't have penises, making the threat of castration moot. In an attempt to resolve this dilemma, Freud (1924/1961a, 1925/1961c) tinkered with his theory, concocting a rather unparsimonious version of female moral development. Freud ultimately concluded (rather than acknowledging a potential weakness in his theory) that there is a fundamental weakness in the superegos of females. According to Freud, because girls' fear of castration is not nearly as profound as it is for boys, their subsequent defensive identification with the threatening father is not as intense or as complete. Lacking intense castration anxiety, the feminine superego is less solidly formed, resulting in an underdeveloped center of morality.

Empirical Findings on Gender Differences in Superego Strength: The Case of Shame and Guilt

What is the empirical support for this Freudian notion of gender differences in the superego? From a Freudian perspective, superegos can be strong or weak—well internalized and independent of external sources, or less fully internalized and more concretely tied to its original sources (the parents or other surrogate authority figures). In an early seminal study, Hall (1964) attempted to evaluate Freud's assertion that men have stronger superegos than women, reporting strong support for the theory. Examining the aggression content of more than 3,000 dreams reported by young adults, Hall reasoned that dreams in which the dreamer is the victim of aggression are a sign of an externalized superego. To be the victim is to place the locus of punishment outside oneself. Consequently, Hall expected to find that women dreamed of being the victim of aggression more often than men. On the other hand, he expected men to dream more frequently of being the victim of some impersonal misfortune. Because impersonal misfortunes do not involve any social interaction, Hall viewed such dreams as signs of an internalized superego.

Indeed, the results of his study confirmed Hall's (1964) hypotheses. As predicted, women were more likely to report dreams in which they were victims of aggression from some external source, and men were more likely than women to dream of misfortunes such as illness, injury, frustration, delay, encountering an obstacle, and so forth, consistent with Freudian theory.

There are, however, at least 20 plausible alternative interpretations of Hall's (1964) results, one obvious one being that women are more likely to portray themselves as victims of aggression simply because of their smaller physical size and lesser strength, and because they are, in fact, less likely to behave aggressively themselves. In fairness, the title of Hall's article was "A Modest Confirmation of Freud's Theory of a Distinction Between the Superego of Men and Women."

Also in fairness, the superego is a difficult construct to measure, as it is an amorphous theoretical structure not open to direct observation. Hall (1964) attempted to study the superego more or less directly—by means of projective methods. An alternative strategy is to focus on what one might consider the *outcomes* of superego operations: moral emotions, moral reasoning, and moral behavior.

Moral affect, in particular, should be closely linked to the superego. Shame and guilt are superego emotions. According to Freud, they are derived directly from the superego. Therefore, any gender difference in the strength or integrity of the superego should be directly observed in gender differences in feelings of shame and guilt. To what degree do men and women differ in their propensity to experience these moral emotions?

To answer this question, we can turn to the broad range of studies we and our colleagues have conducted on shame and guilt in the past 10 years—studies of children, adolescents, college students, and noncollege adults. To assess individual differences in proneness to shame and proneness to guilt, we use our Test of Self-Conscious Affect (TOSCA; Tangney, Wagner, & Gramzow, 1989), a scenario-based paper-and-pencil measure that presents respondents with a range of situations they are likely to encounter in day-to-day life. Each scenario is followed by responses that capture phenomenological aspects of shame, guilt, and other theoretically relevant experiences (e.g., externalization, pride). Respondents are asked to imagine themselves in each situation and then rate their likelihood of reacting in each of the manners indicated. For example, in the adult TOSCA, participants are asked to imagine "You make a big mistake on an important project at work. People were depending on you and your boss criticizes you." People then rate their likelihood of reacting with a shame response ("You would feel like you wanted to hide"), a guilt response ("You would think 'I should have recognized the problem and done a better job'"), and so forth. Across the various scenarios the responses capture affective, cognitive, and motivational features associated with shame and guilt, respectively, as described in the theoretical, phenomenological, and empirical literature.

One common concern with self-report measures is the notion that there is sometimes a lack of correspondence between people's self-report and their actual experiences and behaviors. This may be particularly problematic when assessing domains that are likely to invoke psychological defensiveness. For example, Shedler, Mayman, and Manis (1993) argued that low scores on measures of psychopathology or distress are ambiguous, because some respondents accurately report their psychological health, but others defensively attempt to convey the illusion of mental well-being. One advantage of scenario-based measures of shame and guilt such as the TOSCA is that they are less likely to arouse defensive response biases than other types of self-report measures. Lewis (1971) and others have noted that many individuals routinely repress or deny shame experiences, and others may not even recognize the shame experience as such. Scenario-based measures may help circumvent people's defensiveness, because respondents are asked to rate phenomenological descriptions of shame and guilt experiences with respect to specific situations rather than to acknowledge bluntly their global tendency to experience shame and guilt.

It is worth noting that our TOSCA measures (the TOSCA for adults, the adolescent version of this measure [TOSCA–A; Tangney, Warner, Gavlas, & Gramzow, 1991], and the child version of this measure [TOSCA–C; Tangney, Wagner, Burggraf, Gramzow, & Fletcher, 1990]) are especially well suited to test Freud's assertions because of their scenario-based format. Some measures (e.g., Revised Shame and Guilt Scale, Personal Feelings Questionnaire) ask people how often they experience shame and guilt generally. Results gained from these general frequency measures would be somewhat equivocal, because if women are indeed somehow morally inferior, then they might engage in more frequent immoral acts on a day-to-day basis and, as a result, encounter more frequent opportunities to experience shame and guilt. Our TOSCA measures, on the other hand, present people with a standard set of gender-neutral situations. Thus, it is possible to examine gender differences in the likelihood of shame and guilt reactions with respect to the same set of events. Freud's theory clearly predicts lower levels of superego emotions (shame and guilt) among women than men.

We have adapted this approach to study shame and guilt in children and adolescents as well. For example, the TOSCA–C is similar in format to the adult version. It is scenario based and yields the same subscales, but it is composed of different, age-appropriate items, with simplified language, a different response format, and illustrations.

Table 7.1 shows shame and guilt in samples totaling more than 3,000 participants. The consistency of results across samples is striking. Whether considering elementary school-age children, lower middle-class adolescents, college students, parents and grandparents of fifth-grade students, or adult travelers passing through an airport, female participants consistently report greater shame and guilt than their male counterparts.

In short, there is no evidence that women have defective superegos when considering these quintessential superego emotions. At the same time, it is important to note that these findings do not argue for the moral superiority of females. Recent empirical research indicates that shame and guilt are not equally moral emotions. Across studies of children, adolescents, and adults, shame proneness has consistently emerged as the more maladaptive emotional style, relative to guilt proneness. For example, the tendency to feel shame about the entire self has been repeatedly linked to psychological symptoms such as depression, anxiety, and low self-esteem (Gramzow & Tangney, 1992; Tangney, 1995; Tangney, Burggraf, & Wagner, 1995; Tangney & Dearing, 2002; Tangney, Wagner, & Gramzow, 1992). Moreover, shame proneness has been associated with such "non-moral" characteristics as an impaired capacity for other-oriented empathy (Tangney, 1991, 1994, 1995; Tangney &

Table 7.1

Gender Differences in Proneness to Shame and Proneness to Guilt

Sample	Shame		Guilt	
	M	*SD*	*M*	*SD*
Children (Grade 5)[a]				
Males (*n* = 164)	2.70	0.66	3.75	0.64
Females (*n* = 199)	2.87	0.64*	4.03	0.50***
Children (Grades 4–6)[a]				
Males (*n* = 153)	2.59	0.65	3.64	0.73
Females (*n* = 158)	2.87	0.56***	3.90	0.57***
Adolescents (Grades 7–11)[b]				
Males (*n* = 209)	2.42	0.57	3.43	0.60
Females (*n* = 230)	2.54	0.57*	3.82	0.53***
College students[c]				
Men (*n* = 72)	2.57	0.60	3.37	0.47
Women (*n* = 171)	2.80	0.61**	3.74	0.44***
College students[d]				
Men (*n* = 61)	2.25	0.45	2.88	0.35
Women (*n* = 164)	2.49	0.53***	3.22	0.40***
College students[d]				
Men (*n* = 51)	2.71	0.52	3.76	0.42
Women (*n* = 147)	2.80	0.58	3.94	0.41**
College students[d]				
Men (*n* = 48)	2.62	0.45	3.67	0.41
Women (*n* = 135)	3.02	0.52***	3.95	0.40***
College students[d]				
Men (*n* = 76)	2.66	0.56	3.68	0.45
Women (*n* = 188)	2.93	0.53***	3.97	0.44***
Adults (airport)[d]				
Men (*n* = 105)	2.56	0.51	3.84	0.48
Women (*n* = 88)	2.85	0.63***	4.04	0.34***
Adults (parents)[d]				
Men (*n* = 166)[e]	2.32	0.58	3.80	0.48
Women (*n* = 166)	2.61	0.65***	4.06	0.42***
Adults (grandparents)[d]				
Men (*n* = 73)[e]	2.52	0.58	3.88	0.60
Women (*n* = 73)	2.91	0.62***	4.15	0.46**
Adults (grandparents)[d]				
Men (*n* = 57)[e]	2.48	0.59	3.88	0.50
Women (*n* = 57)	2.92	0.66***	4.20	0.45***

Note. Means reflect the average item rating on a 1–5 point scale.
[a] Test of Self-Conscious Affect (TOSCA), children's version.
[b] TOSCA, adolescent version.
[c] Self-Conscious Affect and Attribution Inventory (SCAAI).
[d] TOSCA (adult version).
[e] Paired *t* tests were conducted for parent and grandparent dyads.
*$p < .05$. **$p < .01$. ***$p < .001$.

Dearing, 2002); high levels of anger and hostility (Tangney, 1995; Tangney, Wagner, Fletcher, & Gramzow, 1992); and self-reported aggressive, destructive strategies for managing anger and interpersonal conflict (Tangney, Wagner, Barlow, Marschall, & Gramzow, 1996). In contrast, in studies of children, adolescents, and adults, proneness to "shame-free" guilt has been unrelated to psychological maladjustment. Rather, guilt proneness has been linked to a range of positive, "moral" interpersonal dimensions, including an enhanced capacity for empathy (Tangney, 1991, 1994, 1995; Tangney & Dearing, 2002); a tendency to accept responsibility for causing others harm (Tangney, 1990, 1992); constructive anger management strategies (Tangney et al., 1996); and self-reported adherence to conventional standards of morality (Tangney, 1994).

Compared to males, females of all ages report a greater propensity to both shame and guilt. In this regard, girls and women are the beneficiaries of the best and the worst of superego emotions.

Women Are Not Less Moral Than Men: Further Empirical Results From the Study of Empathy

How do these findings compare to research on other superego outcomes? In addition to shame and guilt, empathy is another important moral affective process. Empathy is, in essence, the vicarious sharing of another person's emotional experience, requiring a number of interrelated skills or capacities (Feshbach, 1975). First, empathy requires the ability to take another person's perspective —a role-taking capacity. Second, empathy requires the ability to discriminate or to read accurately another person's particular emotional experience. Feshbach (1975) termed this *affective cue discrimination*. Third, empathy requires the ability to experience freely a range of emotions oneself, because empathy involves the sharing of the other's affective experience in one form or another.

There is much evidence on gender differences in empathy, spanning several decades of research. Taken together, the research shows that, if anything, females are more empathic than males (Block, 1976; Eisenberg & Lennon, 1983; Hoffman, 1977; Maccoby

& Jacklin, 1974); that is, where gender differences emerge, they are almost always in a direction favoring females—consistent with the shame and guilt results and in contrast to Freud's notions.

As just one example, Tangney, Marschall, Rosenberg, Barlow, and Wagner (1994) examined gender differences in empathy in several hundred children and adults. Participants were asked to describe recent events in which they had experienced shame and guilt. These narrative accounts of real-life emotion episodes were then coded for markers of other-oriented concern and interpersonal empathy. The results showed gender differences in these empathy variables. Among children, girls were somewhat more likely than boys to take another person's perspective in shame and guilt narratives. Adult women similarly evidenced more perspective taking than men in guilt (but not shame) narratives. With respect to global rating of other-oriented empathy, significant differences were observed in children's shame narratives: Girls were rated as somewhat more empathic than boys.

As in most areas of research, gender differences in empathy were quite modest. In their insightful analysis of the literature, Eisenberg and Lennon (1983) observed that gender differences in empathy tend to be most pronounced in studies in which self-report or other-report (e.g., teacher, peer) measures are used. Few gender differences emerge when more "production" measures are used, such as physiological, facial, or gestural reactions to another person's distress. Graham and Ickes (1997) reached similar conclusions in their more recent review of gender differences in empathy. Both reviews emphasize the potential role of cultural stereotypes that depict females as being more communally oriented and males as being more instrumental and agentic. Eisenberg and Lennon suggested that such stereotypes are most likely to operate in self- and other-report measures, coloring evaluations of the empathic capacity of males and females. Related to this, Graham and Ickes also suggested that motivational factors may contribute to gender differences in some contexts, with females being more motivated to decode accurately and respond empathically, presumably because of gender-role expectations. In any event, although females are often perceived as being more empathic, studies in which "production" measures are used (including most notably Ickes's [1997] empathic accuracy paradigm) show that males do indeed have well developed empathic skills, equivalent in most cases to the empathic skills of their female counterparts. Thus, the empathy literature fails to support the notion of a pronounced gender difference in morality or in the integrity of the superego.

The Bottom Line: Gender Differences in Moral Behavior

Thus far we have focused on moral emotions of one sort or another. However, what about actual moral behavior? It would be hard to argue convincingly that, on balance, males behave more morally than females. When considering behavioral extremes, empirical literatures from criminology and clinical psychology converge: Males commit the majority of crimes in our society (Lipsey & Derzon, 1998), a gender difference that holds at all ages and across all socioeconomic groups. Conduct disorder is much more common among boys than girls, and antisocial personality disorder is much more common among men than women (American Psychiatric Association, 1994).

Even within the normal range, males of all ages are more physically aggressive than females. Meta-analyses of scores of studies of aggressive behavior (Eagly & Steffen, 1986; Hyde, 1984; Maccoby & Jacklin, 1980) have provided converging evidence for this gender difference. Moreover, the greater aggressiveness of males does not appear to reflect that "women have special difficulty expressing their anger effectively and directly" (Lerner, 1977, p. 6). To the contrary, results from a recent cross-sectional developmental study (Tangney, Becker, & Barlow, 2001) challenge the commonly held assumption that women (and girls) have more difficulty acknowledging and expressing their anger than their male counterparts. Rather, Tangney et al. (2001) found a pattern of generally adaptive anger management strategies among females, across the life span. First, women appeared to be more willing than men to acknowledge feeling angry. When asked to imagine themselves in a series of gender-neutral anger-eliciting situations from everyday life (developmentally appropriate situations that most respondents are likely to have encountered in their own experiences), women from adolescence into adulthood indicated that they would experience more anger, as compared to their male peers. Second, females across the life span appear to be more inclined than males to adopt constructive, proactive behaviors once angered. Across ages 8–80, females rated themselves as more likely than males to attempt some sort of rational, nonhostile discussion with the perpetrators of anger-eliciting situations. Also, consistent with several decades of research on aggression (Eagly & Steffen, 1986; Frodi, Macaulay, & Thome, 1977), females in Tangney et al.'s (2001) study were less inclined toward other-directed aggressive responses than were male participants. Finally, little evidence supports the popular notion that females are generally more inclined to suppress or turn anger inward in a maladaptive manner. In fact, results showed that, across the life span, females manage their anger more constructively than males.

It is important to emphasize again, however, that the magnitude of the observed gender differences was small (Tangney et al., 2001). Although females within each age group showed somewhat more adaptive responses to anger than their male counterparts, the differences were modest and, on balance, women and men, boys and girls, were more similar than they were different in their reported characteristic anger management strategies. For example, although male participants showed a somewhat greater inclination toward aggressive behavior than females, these male participants nonetheless endorsed such proactive constructive responses as rational discussion and corrective action to a much greater extent than they did the maladaptive aggressive responses. In fact, the overall pattern of means portrays an encouraging picture of how individuals of both genders manage everyday episodes of anger. These results are consistent with the broader literature on gender differences in aggression—the difference is consistent, but quite modest. In their comprehensive meta-analyses, both Hyde (1984) and Eagly and Steffen (1986) reported a mean weighted effect size of less than 0.3 SD among adults. Hyde considered age of respondents, and her meta-analysis showed somewhat greater effect sizes in preschool and middle childhood, but even here the effect sizes were relatively modest. The gender differences refute Freud's notion of a weak feminine superego, but they do not argue for the notion of "man as beast," either.

Finally, turning to more positive behavioral markers of superego strength, there is no evidence that men are more altruistic or pro-social than women. In fact, women are more heavily represented in the helping professions and are more likely to volunteer for worthy causes. They are the primary caretakers of the poor, the sick, and the needy in society.

Each of these areas—the moral emotions of shame and guilt; interpersonal empathy; crime and sociopathy; aggression; and al-truistic, helping behavior—represent conceptual outcomes of su-perego development. In each area, where gender differences emerge, the findings favor women. This consistent pattern of re-sults across such diverse domains is certainly difficult to reconcile with the notion that "The male sex seems to have taken the lead in all these moral acquisitions; and they seem to have then been transmitted to women by cross-inheritance" (Freud, 1923/1961b, p. 37). Women seem to have pretty healthy superegos. They do not seem to be terribly disadvantaged by their anatomy in this regard.

Gender Differences in the Character of the Superego: An Ethic of Care Versus an Ethic of Justice?

Thus far we have discussed gender differences in the strength or integrity of the superego. Do women appear to have an inferior, underdeveloped *level* of morality? The empirical evidence strongly argues that they do not. Shifting from a quantitative to a qualitative view, a second set of questions concern the *nature* of one's moral sense, or superego. Specifically, do men and women evaluate moral issues from the same perspective, using similar principles? The psychological literature on moral reasoning is most relevant to this question.

Researchers interested in moral reasoning focus on how people *think* rather than how they *feel* or *behave* in the face of moral dilem-mas. Most notable is Kohlberg's (1969) cognitive–developmental theory of moral reasoning. Kohlberg proposed that human thought about moral issues progresses in stages, paralleling Piaget's (1952) more general theory of cognitive development. At the lowest levels of moral reasoning the focus is on concrete ideas of right and wrong (e.g., "that's the rule") and consequences for the self (e.g., "getting in trouble"). At successively higher levels of moral reasoning the arguments become more complex and less egocentric, incorporating notions of community, justice, and reciprocity (e.g., "fairness for the common good"). Colby, Kohlberg, and colleagues (Colby & Kohlberg, 1987; Colby et al., 1987) used a series of moral "dilemmas" to assess individual differences in level of moral reasoning. For example, there's the classic dilemma faced by Heinz, who must decide whether to steal a prohibitively expensive drug to save his dying wife. The issue is not *what* people decide (i.e., steal vs. not steal) but *how* they decide. At lower levels of moral reasoning a person might emphasize that stealing is against the rules or that Heinz might get caught and go to jail. At higher levels of moral reasoning a person might also argue against stealing but draw on notions of fairness (someone else equally deserving would be deprived of the drug) or the need for order and justice in society.

Reminiscent of Freud's jaded view of female morality, psychologists for many years believed that men reasoned at a higher moral developmental level than women on Kohlberg's Moral Judgment Interview. However, Walker (1984) conducted a comprehensive review of the empirical research on gender differences in moral reasoning and concluded that there is actually little evidence for such gender differences in level of moral reasoning (see also Baumrind, 1986, and Walker, 1986a, 1986b). Instead, psychologists have increasingly focused on gender differences in the nature or substantive content of moral reasoning.

In this regard, Gilligan's (1982) landmark book *In a Different Voice* makes a compelling argument for two different, but equally legitimate bases, for evaluating moral issues. Traditional views (e.g., Kohlberg's) tend to emphasize an ethic of justice, focusing on rights and rules and emphasizing notions of fairness, equality, and reciprocity. In contrast, an ethic of care emphasizes selflessness, interdependence, and responsibility in the context of relationships. Gilligan suggested that women are more inclined to reason about moral issues from an ethic-of-care perspective, whereas men are inclined to reason from a justice perspective. As Tavris (1992) stated, "Women feel the 'moral imperative' to *care* for others; men, to protect the *rights* of others" (p. 80).

Considerable empirical evidence now supports Gilligan's (1982) assertion that women are inclined to rely more heavily than men on an ethic of care in their reasoning about moral dilemmas. Numerous studies in which several distinct methods for assessing an ethic of care have been used have shown a gender difference favoring women (Eisenberg, Fabes, & Shea, 1989; Gilligan & Attanucci, 1988; Lyons, 1988; Pratt, Golding, Hunter, & Sampson, 1988; Skoe & Gooden, 1993; Skoe, Pratt, Matthews, & Curror, 1996; Soechting, Skoe, & Marcia, 1994; Stiller & Forrest, 1990; Wark & Krebs, 1996; White, 1994; White & Manolis, 1997). The few studies that have examined care versus justice reasoning among children have shown a parallel effect for girls (Johnston, 1988; Skoe et al., 1999, Canadian sample), although there are the occasional null results (Axelrod, 1998; Ford & Lowery, 1986; Nunner-Winkler, 1994; Skoe et al., 1999, Norwegian sample). However, it is notable that no studies have shown a significant gender difference in ethic-of-care reasoning favoring men.

The notion that men and women may differ in the ways in which they evaluate moral dilemmas raises the question of possible gender differences in the types of events that cause moral emotions such as shame and guilt. Do men and women differ in the kinds of failures and transgressions about which they feel bad?

Tangney et al.'s (1994) study of children's and adults' autobiographical narratives of shame, guilt, and pride experiences examined the types of situations that elicited these moral emotions (Tangney et al., 1994). There were surprisingly few (albeit interpretable) gender differences in the content of emotion-eliciting situations. Among adults, men were somewhat more likely than women to cite accomplishments at work as a pride-eliciting event, whereas women were somewhat more likely to mention accomplishments at school; among children, boys were somewhat more likely than girls to mention poor performance as a shame-eliciting event. What is notable is how few differences were observed. Men and women did not differ in their likelihood of mentioning justice-related situations such as lying, cheating, stealing, or breaking the law as shame- or guilt-eliciting events. Neither did they differ in citing relationship-relevant events such as infidelity, hurting or neglecting others, or relationship rifts.

Summary and Conclusion

In this chapter we examined gender differences in morality from a Freudian perspective. We summarized evidence from several literatures refuting Freud's notion that women have a weaker, less internalized sense of morality than men because of defects in the formation of the superego. Freud suggested that because girls experience less castration anxiety during the Oedipal phase, the feminine superego is less solidly formed, resulting in an underdeveloped center of morality. Empirical studies, however, indicate that females experience more, not less, shame and guilt in response to failures and transgressions. Moreover, research shows that females are more empathic than males, whereas males engage in more aggressive, antisocial behavior. In short, women do not appear to have a quantitatively inferior, underdeveloped level of morality. If anything, the data favor the feminine superego—albeit with generally modest effect sizes.

We also considered the possibility of gender differences in the qualitative nature of superego. Do men and women process moral issues from the same perspective, using similar principles? Like Freud, many psychologists working from a Kohlbergian perspective have assumed a higher level of moral reasoning among men. Empirical evidence, however, does not support this assumption. We discussed more recent theory and research suggesting that women tend to reason from an ethic-of-care perspective, whereas men are inclined to reason from a justice perspective.

Future work on gender differences in morality will likely focus less on a quantitative dimension (are men or women more moral?) and more on qualitative dimensions (how do men and women grapple with issues of morality?). In the meantime, psychological research has clearly refuted Freud's notion that women have inferior superegos. We have no doubt that there are some situations, some contexts, in which a penis is important—but moral development is not one of them.

References

American Psychiatric Association. (1994). *Diagnostic and statistical manual of mental disorders* (4th ed.). Washington, DC: Author.

Axelrod, E. D. (1998). The relationship between moral orientation, gender, and context when reporting honor code violations in business school. *Dissertation Abstracts International, 58* (10), 5686B. (UMI No. AA69811375)

Baumrind, D. (1986). Sex differences in the development of moral reasoning: Response to Walker's (1984) conclusion that there are none. *Child Development, 57*, 511–521.

Block, J. H. (1976). Assessing sex differences: Issues, problems, and pitfalls. *Merrill–Palmer Quarterly, 22*, 283–308.

Colby, A., & Kohlberg, L. (1987). *The measurement of moral judgement: Theoretical foundations and research validation* (Vol. 1). Cambridge, England: Cambridge University Press.

Colby, A., Kohlberg, L., Speicher, B., Hewer, A., Candee, D., Gibbs, J., et al. (1987). *The measurement of moral judgement* (Vol. 2). Cambridge, England: Cambridge University Press.

Eagly, A. H., & Steffen, V. J. (1986). Gender and aggressive behavior: A meta-analytic review of the social psychological literature. *Psychological Bulletin, 100*, 309–330.

Eisenberg, N., Fabes, R., & Shea, C. (1989). Gender differences in empathy and prosocial moral reasoning: Empirical investigations. In M. M. Brabeck (Ed.), *Who cares?: Theory, research, and educational implications of the ethic of care* (pp. 127–143). New York: Praeger.

Eisenberg, N., & Lennon, R. (1983). Sex differences in empathy and related capacities. *Psychological Bulletin, 94*, 100–131.

Feshbach, N. D. (1975). Empathy in children: Some theoretical and empirical considerations. *The Counseling Psychologist, 5*, 25–30.

Fischer, K. W., & Tangney, J. P. (1995). Self-conscious emotions and the affect revolution: Framework and overview. In J. P. Tangney & K. W. Fischer (Eds.), *Self-conscious emotions: Shame, guilt, embarrassment, and pride* (pp. 3–22). New York: Guilford.

Ford, M. R., & Lowery, C. R. (1986). Gender differences in moral reasoning: A comparison of the use of justice and care orientations. *Journal of Personality and Social Psychology, 50*, 777–783.

Freud, S. (1961a). The economic problem of masochism. In J. Strachey (Ed. and Trans.), *The standard edition of the complete psychological works of Sigmund Freud* (Vol. 19, pp. 159–170). London: Hogarth. (Original work published 1924)

Freud, S. (1961b). The id and the ego. In J. Strachey (Ed. and Trans.), *The standard edition of the complete psychological works of Sigmund Freud* (Vol. 19, pp. 12–66). London: Hogarth. (Original work published 1923)

Freud, S. (1961c). Some psychical consequences of the anatomical distinction between the sexes. In J. Strachey (Ed. and Trans.), *The standard edition of the complete psychological works of Sigmund Freud* (Vol. 19, pp. 248–258). London: Hogarth. (Original work published 1925)

Frodi, A., Macaulay, J., & Thome, P. R. (1977). Are women always less aggressive than men? A review of the experimental literature. *Psychological Bulletin, 84,* 634–660.

Gilligan, C. (1982). *In a different voice: Psychological theory and women's development.* Cambridge, MA: Harvard University Press.

Gilligan, C., & Attanucci, J. (1988). Two moral orientations: Gender differences and similarities. *Merril-Palmer Quarterly, 34,* 223–237.

Graham, T., & Ickes, W. (1997). When women's intuition isn't greater than men's. In W. Ickes (Ed.), *Empathic accuracy* (pp. 117–143). New York: Guilford.

Gramzow, R., & Tangney, J. P. (1992). Proneness to shame and the narcissistic personality. *Personality and Social Psychology Bulletin, 18,* 369–376.

Hall, C. (1964). A modest confirmation of Freud's theory of a distinction between the superego of men and women. *Journal of Abnormal and Social Psychology, 69,* 440–442.

Hoffman, M. L. (1977). Sex differences in empathy and related behaviors. *Psychological Bulletin, 54,* 712–722.

Hyde, J. S. (1984). How large are gender differences in aggression? A developmental meta-analysis. *Developmental Psychology, 20,* 722–736.

Ickes, W. (Ed.). (1997). *Empathic Accuracy.* New York: Guilford.

Johnston, D. K. (1988). Adolescents' solutions to dilemmas in fables: Two moral orientations—Two problem solving strategies. In C. Gilligan, J. V. Ward, & J. M. Taylor (Eds.), *Mapping the moral domain* (pp. 49–71). Cambridge, MA: Harvard University Press.

Kohlberg, L. (1969). Stage and sequence: The cognitive developmental approach to socialization. In D. A. Goslin (Ed.), *Handbook of socialization theory and research* (pp. 347–480). Chicago: Rand McNally.

Lerner, H. (1977, Winter). The taboos against female anger. *Menninger Perspective, 8,* 5–11.

Lewis, H. B. (1971). *Shame and guilt in neurosis.* New York: International Universities Press.

Lewis, M., Sullivan, M. W., Stanger, C., & Weiss, M. (1989). Self-development and self-conscious emotions. *Child Development, 60,* 146–156.

Lipsey, M. W., & Derzon, J. H. (1998). Predictors of violent and serious delinquency in adolescence and early adulthood. In R. Loeber & D. P. Farrington (Eds.), *Serious and violent juvenile offenders: Risk factors and successful interventions* (pp. 86–105). Thousand Oaks, CA: Sage.

Lyons, N. P. (1988). Two perspectives: On self, relationships, and morality. In C. Gilligan, J. V. Ward, & J. M. Taylor (Eds.), *Mapping the moral domain* (pp. 21–48). Cambridge, MA: Harvard University Press.

Maccoby, E. E., & Jacklin, C. N. (1974). *The psychology of sex differences.* Stanford, CA: Stanford University Press.

Maccoby, E. E., & Jacklin, C. N. (1980). Sex differences in aggression: A rejoinder and reprise. *Child Development, 51*, 964–980.

Nunner-Winkler, G. (1994). Two moralities? A critical discussion of an ethic of care and responsibility versus an ethic of rights and justice. In W. Puka (Ed.), Caring voices and women's moral frames: Gilligan's view. Moral development: A compendium (Vol. 6, pp. 260–273). New York: Garland.

Piaget, J. (1952). *The origins of intelligence in children.* New York: International Universities Press.

Pratt, M. W., Golding, G., Hunter, W., & Sampson, R. (1988). Sex differences in adult moral orientations. *Journal of Personality, 56*, 373–391.

Shedler, J., Mayman, M., & Manis, M. (1993). The *illusion* of mental health. *American Psychologist, 48*, 1117–1131.

Skoe, E. E., & Gooden, A. (1993). Ethic of care and real-life moral dilemma content in male and female early adolescents. *Journal of Early Adolescence, 13*, 154–167.

Skoe, E. E., Hansen, K. L., Morch, W., Bakke, I., Hoffmann, T., Larsen, B., & Aasheim, M. (1999). Care-based moral reasoning in Norwegian and Canadian early adolescents: A cross-national comparison. *Journal of Early Adolescence, 19*, 280–291.

Skoe, E. E., Pratt, M. W., Matthews, M., & Curror, S. E. (1996). The ethic of care: Stability over time, gender differences, and correlates in mid- to late adulthood. *Psychology and Aging, 11*, 280–292.

Soechting, I., Skoe, E. E., & Marcia, J. E. (1994). Care-oriented moral reasoning and prosocial behavior: A question of gender or sex role orientation. *Sex Roles, 31*, 131–147.

Stiller, N. J., & Forrest, L. (1990). An extension of Gilligan and Lyons's investigation of morality: Gender differences in college students. *Journal of College Student Development, 31*, 54–63.

Tangney, J. P. (1990). Assessing individual differences in proneness to shame and guilt: Development of the self-conscious affect and attribution inventory. *Journal of Personality and Social Psychology, 59*, 102–111.

Tangney, J. P. (1991). Moral affect: The good, the bad, and the ugly. *Journal of Personality and Social Psychology, 61*, 598–607.

Tangney, J. P. (1992). Situational determinants of shame and guilt in young adulthood. *Personality and Social Psychology Bulletin, 18*, 199–206.

Tangney, J. P. (1994). The mixed legacy of the super-ego: Adaptive and maladaptive aspects of shame and guilt. In J. M. Masling & R. F. Bornstein (Eds.), *Empirical perspectives on object relations theory* (pp. 1–28). Washington, DC: American Psychological Association.

Tangney, J. P. (1995). Recent advances in the empirical study of shame and guilt. *American Behavioral Scientist, 38*, 1132–1145.

Tangney, J. P., Becker, B., & Barlow, D. H. (2001). *Gender differences in constructive vs. destructive responses to anger across the lifespan.* Manuscript submitted for publication.

Tangney, J. P., Burggraf, S. A., & Wagner, P. E. (1995). Shame-proneness, guilt-proneness, and psychological symptoms. In J. P. Tangney & K. W. Fischer (Eds.), *Self-conscious emotions: Shame, guilt, embarrassment, and pride* (pp. 343–367). New York: Guilford.

Tangney, J. P., & Dearing, R. (2002). *Shame and guilt.* New York: Guilford Press.

Tangney, J. P., Marschall, D. E., Rosenberg, K., Barlow, D. H., & Wagner, P. E. (1994). *Children's and adults' autobiographical accounts of shame, guilt and pride experiences: An analysis of situational determinants and interpersonal concerns.* Manuscript submitted for publication.

Tangney, J. P., Wagner, P. E., Barlow, D. H., Marschall, D. E., & Gramzow, R. (1996). The relation of shame and guilt to constructive vs. destructive responses to anger across the lifespan. *Journal of Personality and Social Psychology, 70,* 797–809.

Tangney, J. P., Wagner, P. E., Burggraf, S. A., Gramzow, R., & Fletcher, C. (1990). *The Test of Self-Conscious Affect for Children (TOSCA–C).* Unpublished instrument, George Mason University, Fairfax, VA.

Tangney, J. P., Wagner, P. E., Fletcher, C., & Gramzow, R. (1992). Shamed into anger? The relation of shame and guilt to anger and self-reported aggression. *Journal of Personality and Social Psychology, 62,* 669–675.

Tangney, J. P., Wagner, P. E., Gavlas, J., & Gramzow, R. (1991). *The Test of Self-Conscious Affects for Adolescents (TOSCA–A).* George Mason University, Fairfax, VA.

Tangney, J. P., Wagner, P., & Gramzow, R. (1989). *The Test of Self-Conscious Affect (TOSCA).* Unpublished instrument, George Mason University, Fairfax, VA.

Tangney, J. P., Wagner, P. E., & Gramzow, R. (1992). Proneness to shame, proneness to guilt, and psychopathology. *Journal of Abnormal Psychology, 103,* 469–478.

Tavris, C. (1992). *The mismeasure of woman.* New York: Simon & Schuster.

Walker, L. (1984). Sex differences in the development of moral reasoning: A critical review. *Child Development, 55,* 677–691.

Walker, L. J. (1986a). Experiential and cognitive sources of moral development in adulthood. *Human Development, 29,* 113–124.

Walker, L. (1986b). Sex differences in the development of moral reasoning: A rejoinder to Baumrind. *Child Development, 57,* 522–527.

Wark, G. R., & Krebs, D. L. (1996). Gender and dilemma differences in real-life moral judgment. *Developmental Psychology, 32,* 220–230.

White, J. (1994). Individual characteristics and social knowledge in ethical reasoning. *Psychological Reports, 75,* 627–649.

White, J., & Manolis, C. (1997). Individual differences in ethical reasoning among law students. *Social Behavior and Personality, 25,* 19–48.

Author Index

Numbers in italics refer to listings in reference sections.

271

Subject Index

Ability
  concept of, 15–16
Achieved identity
  and identification defense, 119
  in college students, 113–114
Achievement motivation
  development of, 15–21
  in kindergartners, 17–18
  mediation of
    cognition in, 40
  in psychodynamic theories, 12
  psychosocial issues in, 12
  socialization of, 21–27
  temperament and, 21–22
Achievement tasks
  child cognitions and, 32–34
  helplessness and, 7
  parental control and, 32–33
  outcomes and self worth and, 32–34, 37
  parent behaviors and, 32–33
  performance goal in, 33–34
  security *vs.* insecurity and, 39–40
Acting out-defenses
  emotion and, 226, 227
Adaptation
  defense mechanisms in, 81–82
  distancing defense in, 244
  emotions and defenses in
    gender specificity of, 243–244
  projection and, 118
Adaptive Regression score
  in creativity
    gender differences and, 65–66
  definition of, 62
  gender differences in, 63
  in reading achievement, 64–65
  relationship to creativity and problem-solving, 63

Adjustment
  defenses and emotions and, 215–217
  and defense style, 225
  distancing defenses and, 239–240
  emotions and, 230
    in rejection and demand for intimacy, 226, 227, 230
  externalizing emotions and defenses and, 217
  mediation of
    defenses in, 235–245
    emotions in, 235–245
  in men
    in cross-gender defenses and emotional styles, 241–242
Affect
  in dependency, 38–39
  and divergent thinking, 58
  evaluation of, 59
  generation of
    association in, 59
  identification and control of
    in bulimia, 139–140
  negative
    defense use in, 97–102, 104
  in play
    divergent thinking and, 70–71
    studies of
      summary of, 72
  in primary process thinking, 54, 60
  in transformation of personal data to universal image, 60
Affect in Play Scale
  affect content on *vs.* on Rorschach, 72
  cognition in, 68
  and creativity, 69–72

About the Editors

Robert F. Bornstein, PhD, is a professor of psychology at Gettysburg College. He received his PhD in clinical psychology from the State University of New York at Buffalo in 1986. Dr. Bornstein wrote *The Dependent Personality* (1993), coauthored (with Mary Languirand) *When Someone You Love Needs Nursing Home Care* (2001), coedited (with Thane Pittman) *Perception Without Awareness: Cognitive, Clinical, and Social Perspectives* (1992), and coedited (with Joseph Masling) six previous volumes of the *Empirical Studies of Psychoanalytic Theories* book series. Dr. Bornstein's research has been funded by grants from the National Institutes of Mental Health and the National Science Foundation, and he received the Society for Personality Assessment's 1995 and 1999 Walter Klopfer Awards for Distinguished Contributions to the Personality Assessment Literature.

Joseph M. Masling, PhD, is an emeritus professor of psychology at the State University of New York at Buffalo. He has written numerous articles on interpersonal and situational variables influencing projective tests and has published widely on the empirical study of psychoanalytic concepts. Dr. Masling edited the first three volumes of the *Empirical Studies of Psychoanalytic Theories* book series (1983, 1986, 1990); coedited (with Robert F. Bornstein) the next five volumes, including *Psychoanalytic Perspectives on Developmental Psychology* (1996), *Empirical Studies of the Therapeutic Hour* (1998), and *Empirical Perspectives on the Psychoanalytic Unconscious* (1998); and coedited (with Paul R. Duberstein) the ninth volume in the series, *Psychodynamic Perspectives on Sickness and Health* (2000). Dr. Masling received the Society for Personality Assessment's 1997 Bruno Klopfer Award for Lifetime Achievement in Personality Assessment.